# CHILDREN AND THE GEOGRAPHY OF VIOLENCE

Violence sabotages development, both children's development and the development of the communities and neighbourhoods they rely on. There is abundant evidence of the deep and lasting harm that can be done. Violence breaks bodies and minds and exerts an insidious influence at every level. The effects are immediate but can also linger, damaging health, trust and capability, travelling through generations. This book argues that it is impossible to understand the violence in young children's lives or to respond to it adequately without considering how embedded it is within their physical surroundings. The relations of power that are the context for violence within households, within communities and beyond are often expressed through control over space and the material conditions of life.

This book links the abstract concept of structural violence to the stark reality of personal harm, drawing on evidence from a range of disciplines and from countries throughout the global south. It explores the dynamics of cramped, insecure housing, poor water and sanitation, neglected neighbourhoods, forced evictions, cities that segregate the rich and the poor, landscapes of conflict and disaster, and discusses their implications for young children. An alternative approach to child protection is proposed, anchored in the actions of organized communities negotiating to challenge inequities, mend their environments and achieve security. There is a fundamental synergy between building community and protecting children. These are not separate agendas. A place that works for children works better for everyone else as well.

This book will be essential reading for all those interested in young children in a global context, whether as child protection professionals, or with a more general interest in children's rights issues or in cross-cultural approaches to child development. It will also be of great interest to students and researchers of development studies, conflict studies, family studies, child development, public health and urban planning.

**Sheridan Bartlett** works primarily on issues of urban poverty as they affect children in low-income countries, bridging the gap between the work of child-focused agencies and the broader development agenda.

"This remarkable, authoritative volume makes a unique contribution to our understanding of the causes, consequences and most effective means of addressing the numerous forms of violence endured by children across the globe. Arguing that children's surroundings can be a crucial determinant, Sheridan Bartlett makes a forceful case for expanding child protection beyond the immediate and personal to embrace the spatial and material conditions that structure children's lives. Bartlett's razor sharp observation is substantiated by compelling research evidence and concrete examples; I highly recommend this book, with its fresh perspective, to all who seek to get to grips with and bring an end to one of the world's gravest social problems."

*Jo Boyden, Professor of International Development, University of Oxford*

"Sheridan Bartlett offers a trenchant analysis of the complex network of physical and sociocultural features that constitute the ecology of childhood violence. Her book unpacks this network, with critical insights for policy and practice, organizing and extending what we know about how environments transact with people and institutions to endanger children."

*Gary William Evans, College of Human Ecology, Cornell University, Ithaca, New York*

"Mainstream development rarely considers violence against children and its catastrophic impacts. This book makes a compelling case for bringing children's protection into development practice, and especially for supporting the organized communities that can best meet children's needs, alongside their efforts for equity and better living conditions."

*David Satterthwaite, International Institute for Environment and Development, London*

"Ranging expertly across child development, protection, poverty, urbanization and community development, Sheridan Bartlett makes a compelling case for considering the physical dimensions of violence. This book forever changes our understanding of violence by opening up its framing beyond the personal and by masterfully embedding it in a larger socio-spatial ecology."

*Sudeshna Chatterjee, CEO, Action For Children's Environments, New Delhi*

# CHILDREN AND THE GEOGRAPHY OF VIOLENCE

## Why Space and Place Matter

*Sheridan Bartlett*

 Routledge
Taylor & Francis Group

LONDON AND NEW YORK

First published 2018
by Routledge
2 Park Square, Milton Park, Abingdon, Oxon OX14 4RN

and by Routledge
711 Third Avenue, New York, NY 10017

*Routledge is an imprint of the Taylor & Francis Group, an informa business*

*British Library Cataloguing-in-Publication Data*
A catalogue record for this book is available from the British Library

*Library of Congress Cataloging-in-Publication Data*
A catalog record for this book has been requested

ISBN: 978-1-138-04085-4 (hbk)
ISBN: 978-1-138-04087-8 (pbk)
ISBN: 978-1-315-17472-3 (ebk)

Typeset in Bembo
by Taylor & Francis Books

# CONTENTS

# ACKNOWLEDGEMENTS

This book grows out of a perennial inclination to try out what comes along, and a dependence on the people I come across to help me find my feet. After time as a teacher, a rural coop bookkeeper, a community day-care director and a house builder, I was drawn to graduate work on housing and families in poverty in the rural USA, and this led by chance to work halfway around the world. As a researcher, consultant and privileged observer, I've been involved in experiences as varied as post-tsunami construction in Sri Lanka, early childhood policy in Zanzibar, psychosocial assessment in Tajikistan, conflict in Nepal, toilets in India, all as they affect young children. Add to this time in many other countries in people's homes, schools, day care centres, local government offices, with grass-roots groups, humanitarian workers, national ministry officials. People are eager to talk about their lives and work. My curiosity has been generously rewarded, and my lack of specialization has come to seem as much an advantage as a limitation. This book makes an argument that builds on all of these encounters.

Research from the global south still gives scant attention to the garden-variety problems of everyday home and neighbourhood life as they affect children. We know surprisingly little about the impact of housing, common space, traffic, toilets, waste, transportation, migration, eviction, flooding, drought, displacement, especially for very young children. So I've needed the wealth of other people's experience and wisdom to add to my own reading and observations. Some joker once described a net as a set of holes tied together with string. That's a good description for this book. There are unquestionably more holes than fabric here, but with the strands of knowledge available to me, formal and informal, it has been possible to create a net that captures something of the day-to-day reality of young children's experience of violence in the multiple settings that they occupy.

More helpful than I might have imagined has been my role over many years co-editing a practice-oriented urban journal with my friend and mentor David Satterthwaite. *Environment and Urbanization* has provided me an education and a valued partnership with David, but also with researchers and practitioners from all over the global south as they work to frame and reflect on their experiences.

Sheela Patel has been an important part of this education. She's answered endless questions over many years, never failing to teach me something new about the strategies of the urban poor, and always extending a warm home base in India.

There are many other people I'd like to acknowledge and thank – more than is reasonable here, so I'll limit it to those I've depended on most. Selim Iltus, first of all, got this particular ball rolling by commissioning a "think piece" on violence and the material environment, knowing how much I'd enjoy the project. He was also a beloved colleague and co-conspirator on other projects, and I miss him. Long before this, though, Roger Hart steered me away from building houses to thinking about what they meant to the parents and children that occupied them, and he opened many doors. Three women in Vermont, my most patient teachers, then gave me many hours of their time every week for over a year, continually complicating and refining my assumptions about life in poverty and in the environments of poverty.

I owe many thanks to Caroline Arnold, who made one interesting research project available after another, sending me off to more places than I can quickly count, always confident that I'd rustle up something useful. To Beth Povinelli, whose work puts my brain through a wringer, and who always leaves me feeling weirdly inspired. To Gary Evans who has been willing so many times over the years to apply his rigorous quantitative perspective to my very different work, and always with generosity. To Anu Nallari, whose research has been a gold mine for me, and who is a faithful, tenacious collaborator. To Gabriella Olofsson, who somehow almost always managed to talk her organization into funding the projects I was dying to do, including the work with Selim and Anu in Cooks Nagar.

Thanks also to Pashupati Sapkota, whose companionship and good nature I so valued over long mountain walks and in remote villages, and whose curiosity and empathy made him one of the world's most naturally talented researchers. And to Basanti Sunar, who somehow managed to jump from clerical work to become Pashupati's successor, and who, from under a small town hotel bed, was thrilled by fusillades of rebel gunfire because now she could understand how terrifying that experience was for children.

Thanks to Cindi Katz for stiffening my spine and cheering me on; to Somsook Boonyabancha who explains her vision with such clarity and conviction; to Tom Kerr for his knowledgeable reading and editing; to Christopher Potter for more of the same. Thanks to Ramya Subrahmanian for her kind and knowledgeable help; to Jo Boyden for her encouragement and for always knowing exactly what is missing; and to Kirrilly Pells and Mike Wessels for walking me so kindly through unfamiliar territory. Thanks also to Irene Karanja and Jack Makau, so willing to share their experiences and their time. They are just two of the many people connected with Slum Dwellers International whose brains I have picked.

Thanks to what must by now be hundreds of people who have warmly welcomed me into their homes, their camp shelters, their schools, their streets, their vehicles, their offices, and so patiently and knowledgeably explained the world to me.

And most of all thanks to my family for always being willing to encourage, read, discuss, organize, push – to Ed, Mary, Thomas, Hillary, Zach.

# 1

# CHARTING THE TERRITORY

Violence sabotages development, both children's development and community development. This is not just a convenient semantic device. The two – children and community – are intimately linked. You cannot protect one without attention to the other. Children need vital, stable families and communities in order to flourish, and places that are good for children tend to be better for everyone else as well. Violence disrupts all of this. It erodes trust and instils dread. Some children withdraw, others act out aggressively. The same thing happens in the community – streets empty out, fear and aggression take over. Healthy development can stop in its tracks.

On a visit to South Africa in the early 2000s, I spent time in the Pretoria office of an organization that works on children's rights. The child protection staff there talked about responding to the sexual harassment of young girls who were frightened to move around their neighbourhoods. As young as 10 and 11, they were routinely intimidated on their way to school, to the shops, to community toilets. It was not just harassment either. Rape was becoming unbearably commonplace. In a focus group to discuss the problem, the girls explained that the streetlights in their neighbourhood didn't work. This made them more vulnerable and much more fearful. I assumed naively that the child rights organization was working with the municipality and the local community to fix the lights. But community organizing was not part of the organization's mandate, nor was public maintenance. Instead they continued to hold focus groups with the girls, encouraging them to talk about their fears, advising them not to go out after dark.

That, in a nutshell, is what this book is about. Violence is not just the aggressive act. It is also the absence of streetlights, the assumptions that make their absence unremarkable, the burden placed back at the girls' feet. And it is not just girls and streetlights. It's about young children and their homes, their streets, their toilets and shops, schools and play spaces, emergency camps and displacement centres. It's about the multiple arrangements and assumptions that allow space for aggression and about the distortions inherent in the role of the aggressors. I will argue in this book for responses to the violence in children's lives that start by taking this entire assemblage into account.

This situation in Pretoria is more commonplace than might be imagined. There are girls all over the world, and many boys too, who still dread walking to the toilets or to the shops – in slums, in villages, in peri-urban areas, in refugee camps. Nor is it just about getting from here to there. A look at the news on any given day reveals a catalogue of barbarity from the most personal to the most abstract, from wife-beating to large-scale ethnic cleansing. Violence appears in so many forms, and the words used to describe it – rampant, escalating, endemic – conjure up an intractable plague. The world, it seems, is becoming an ever nastier, more frightening place.

Some take a more optimistic view. Psychologist Steven Pinker claims that violence has declined over human history and even within recent times. He acknowledges the horrors that are a routine part of the daily news, but argues that our very awareness of the problem shows a growing rejection of violence as a default reality. Brutalities that were taken for granted in earlier times are now exposed and debated. Torture is mostly frowned on. Capital punishment is losing ground. Not that long ago even in socially progressive countries, what happened in the privacy of home was dismissed as no one else's business, but in most countries, we are paying more attention now. Violence is more widely viewed as a public health issue, not an uncontrollable plague but a phenomenon that is responsive to treatment and prevention (Pinker, 2011).

Much of the concern about violence revolves around the implications for children. Many people believe that young children forget the disturbing things they experience and see. Some still feel that beatings are acceptable, maybe even a necessary part of proper discipline. But the weight began to shift a while ago. One expression of this changing awareness is the sheer quantity of research on how violence affects children. There is widespread recognition now that lasting harm can be done. We know that a 1-year-old's exposure to repeated abuse may be forgotten in narrative terms, but it is remembered in the unconscious, in the wiring of that child's brain and possibly even at a chromosomal level.

In recent years the UN system has risen to the challenge posed by violence with high-level reports and calls to action on violence against children, violence and health, violence in schools, conflict-related sexual violence, armed conflict and children. This trend has culminated in an ambitious 2015 commitment by world leaders, part of the Sustainable Development Goals, to end all forms of violence against children by 2030. To take the lead on this astonishing commitment, a Global Partnership to End Violence against Children was launched, anchored in legislation, child protection services and a firm public health orientation.

In some quarters, however, there is far more scepticism about whether violence can actually be tackled and solved this way. A bold public health campaign makes sense for measles. Applied to violence, it runs the risk of depoliticizing a stubborn structural phenomenon, offering superficial coping strategies at best. Framing the problem as a structural predicament suggests responses that might aim less at "ending all violence" and more at managing its impacts and contesting its structural causes.

Regardless of how structural our orientation is when it comes to responses, there is general agreement that the endangered child inhabits a larger system. In recent decades, there has been a move away from a narrow fixation on the acts of individual perpetrators – in academic understandings of the issue, if not in the practical interventions proposed. We recognize the social ecology of violence. We agree that abusive parents may have been abused themselves, that gang violence is a response to exclusion and frustration, that ethnic cleansing has a history and an economy, and that to a large extent, money buys safety.

This book expands on this more ecological perspective by considering the physical environment as integral to the issue. It explores how the material and spatial dimensions of life are related to violence as it affects children and those around them. I argue that it is impossible to fathom the problem or to protect endangered children without also considering how deeply embedded violence is within the production and control of their material environment. This is where the abstract notion of structural violence touches down and takes on tangible form. Framing the problem of violence as a narrow personal protection issue steers the discussion away from the arrangements that underpin it. If attempts to respond and protect are not anchored in the links between the personal and the structural, they run the risk of being thin and partial. This is not to challenge the value of child protection, but more to note the limits of its less substantial manifestations.

We need parameters for this discussion. Violence, first of all, needs to be defined. It sounds simple, but raises a lot of questions. How extreme must an aggressive act be to qualify as violence? How personal? How intentional? Must there be immediate suffering as an outcome? Is fear part of the concern? Is violence an act or can it be inherent in a condition?

The World Health Organization defines violence as "the intentional use of physical force or power, threatened or actual, against oneself, another person, or against a group or community, that either results in or has a high likelihood of resulting in, injury, death, psychological harm, maldevelopment or deprivation" (WHO, 2002). This definition goes well beyond the personal, beyond immediate harm, beyond physical suffering. Threat is part of violence, and with it comes fear. Deprivation can be an outcome along with injury, death and psychological hurt. This definition, widely accepted, provides a flexible frame for a concern with the physical environment.

What about neglect? How completely does the notion of violence (as inflicted) overlap with suffering (as experienced)? Is there a distinction between beating a child and tying her to a bedpost all day while her mother stitches in a garment factory? What about the practice by which two small girls in Nepal share a bowl of rice while their brother gets one to himself? The WHO definition expands on more conventional understandings of violence and, importantly, it also includes these quieter acts of neglect by those with the power to decide.

Do we also include here the policies and omissions of the state? Anthropologist Elizabeth Povinelli, writing of the official neglect of Australia's indigenous people, calls into question the distinction between "making die" and "letting die" (2011). The WHO's broad definition of violence should logically cover the purposeful actions and non-actions of officialdom. The use of force to accomplish an eviction is certainly an act of violence, often accompanied by injury and the destruction of household possessions, sometimes even by death. But evictions that do not involve bullhorns and bulldozers can still mean the forced displacement of communities and all the varieties of suffering that follow. It's a small distance from those displacements to an official refusal to acknowledge a squatter settlement or to allow its residents access to piped water or waste removal or the vote – or functional streetlights. The power *not* to act is surely equivalent to the active use of force when equal harm results. Very quickly, then, we arrive at a point where "violence" and "structural violence" begin to overlap.

Povinelli retells Ursula Le Guin's fable of the child in the broom closet. In the city of Omelas, everyone is happy, their needs fulfilled. But their contentment depends on the imprisonment of a small child in a dark closet in some basement in the city. The child is fed occasionally, beaten occasionally, but mostly left in the dark, afraid, sitting in her own excrement. The citizens of Omelas know about this. They come to peer at the child and are shocked by what they see. Some leave the city, unable to accommodate to the price of their happiness. But most come to accept it. They explain the situation to their children in terms they feel they can understand.

One way to talk about children and violence is to look at the behaviour of the people who beat the captive child. In the context of this discussion of the material world, the broom closet is particularly interesting – the way its darkness and isolation intensify the child's suffering; perhaps also the way that imprisonment in that tiny space, in the dark, in her own excrement, renders the child less than human, an other who becomes an acceptable target for abuse.

But it is not really useful to think about this child's misery only in terms of those who torment her. There are all the other happy citizens who let it happen. Structural violence – the poverty, exclusion and suffering inherent in the accepted order of things – is not just a metaphor even in our more complex real world. Gandhi said that poverty is the worst form of violence. The humiliations intrinsic to this state, to the "letting die" that is part of the accepted order, translate inevitably into more explicit forms of violence, public and private. Might the child in the broom closet ever turn on her tormenters? If she had a companion, a small dog maybe, would she soothe it or scratch its eyes out?

This allegory of the child in the closet may seem an extreme way to represent the spectrum of ills categorized here as violence. Another helpful frame is Cindi Katz's depiction of the child as waste. Katz describes the mechanisms of dispossession by which children are rendered disposable, whether as labourers, combatants or simply the stunted products of a failure to invest in the systems that should nourish them. Children who are beaten, overworked, ill fed, unschooled all represent "a willed wasting of lives", a more or less violent alternative to the obligation to nurture (Katz, 2011). Waste and waste management are endemic to any political economy and too often involve the bodies and minds of the dispossessed.

There is also the "slow violence" described by Rob Nixon, the gradual, quiet, dispersed environmental destruction that results from climate change, from deforestation, from toxics and contamination (2011). On the face of it, this kind of violence affects everyone, and yet it inevitably tends to settle in the embattled communities of the poor, and especially in the vulnerable bodies and minds of their children.

In this book, I draw a porous boundary around acts that cause suffering to young children, neglect as well as abuse, emotional harm as well physical force. I give more rather than less attention to the explicit, the active, the personal – but with the constant reminder that ambient violence also takes a heavy toll and can be experienced in personal ways; and with an insistence that we not overlook the routine misery for children that results from the deprivation, frustration and humiliation of their families and neighbours. In considering responses to violence and neglect we need to be alert to policies and practices that censure the ways families live their lives and cope with their children while neatly ignoring the conditions that structure those lives and actions. If we accept Pinker's claim that violence is diminishing, we are perhaps also pushed to consider a parallel proposition – that as personal violence becomes less acceptable, the frame simply becomes larger and the issue more diffuse and impersonal. We may no longer condone spanking, but the chain of responsibility that leads to children crossing seas on inflatable rafts or dying of malnutrition in the ever-drier Sahel should be as difficult to ignore.

A definition of the physical environment is less complicated by shades of meaning, but it is burdened by a lower level of recognition. It is oddly difficult to persuade people – developmental psychologists among them – of the significance of the material world as it relates to young children. The "environments" of childhood are most often taken to mean the social relationships that are critical to children's development. In the world of practice also, children's physical surroundings can be so taken for granted that their profound impact is often overlooked.

What I am talking about here is the materiality of life – where our bodies take shelter, what they lie on, where they clean themselves, how they are heated or cooled, the means by which they move from place to place, the distances they are required to move, the boundaries, real or symbolic, that define where they may or may not go, what they can or cannot get access to. Crowding and privacy, roofs and pavements, trees and tables, excrement and smoky air, comfort, convenience and chaos, are all fundamental to our existence, our sense of ourselves and our own worth, our levels of energy and exhaustion, our capacity to enjoy or endure, to engage, cooperate, love and learn. "The cues from place", says psychiatrist Mindy Fullilove, "dive under conscious thought and awaken our sinews and bones, where days of our lives have been recorded" (Fullilove, 2005, p. 10). A concern with the physical environment is not a footnote to a larger concern with violence. It is a more encompassing way of considering the problem, taking into account its more general ecology and the range of ways violence can be experienced.

In the equation that includes children, violence, space and place, connections radiate in many directions. Material conditions can contribute to the likelihood of violence, and often this relationship is mediated by stress. Cramped housing, for instance, can push a parent to erupt at a small child who is always underfoot. Violence is often linked to the lack of a place or to being out of place, or to not knowing one's place – think of the violence so routinely experienced by children living on the street in cities around the world. Causality also moves in the other direction, and violence can be experienced through its effect on surroundings. When neighbourhoods are dogged by crime and insecurity, children's mobility and opportunities shrink dramatically. War, eviction and displacement can mean a grave deterioration in living conditions, and the chronic everyday hardships that follow may far outweigh the initial violence in the toll they take. Spatial and material restrictions can also be the route through which violence is inflicted, whether it means tying that child to a bedpost, excluding "untouchables" from village water points, or redlining residential neighbourhoods. Material conditions can themselves constitute violence, whether for the lead-poisoned children of Flint, Michigan, or the millions forced from their homes by flooding in Bangladesh. This violence can all be conceived in terms of cause and effect, whatever the direction, but it is more productive simply to see material conditions as the ground of our existence, inescapably bound up in the everydayness of violence, in its invisible forms, in its causes and effects, problems and solutions.

Framing the issue this broadly may seem unproductive. When the intention is to address a practical problem, why expand the definition of the problem rather than refining it? This expansion can in fact widen and deepen the opportunities for practical action. By going beyond a narrow view of violence and of child protection, we can consider more complex responses that come closer to shifting the intricate constellation of circumstances in play. The relations of power that govern the world, whether within households or neighbourhoods or the wider society, also define where violence occurs. Recognizing the nexus of power, violence and the control of space and place is a starting point in responding to the ecology of violence.

If violence and the physical environment are broadly framed in this book, the discussion narrows around the where and the who. My concern is primarily with the global south, and with communities in poverty in the global south, because this by virtue of my work life is what I am more familiar with and best equipped to explore. It is also where the evidence and the discussion are thinner, where the challenges are more intense and where solutions are most sorely needed. For the same reasons, this account gives more liberal attention to young children, whose everyday lives and experience have been less closely documented in the global south, and who, because of their stage of development and relative powerlessness in the world, may be especially at risk from the varieties of violent experience. These are not tight boundaries. Twelve-year-olds in homeless shelters in New York are of interest here too, even if I focus more on 3-year-olds in Mumbai slums. Given the focus on younger children, this book admittedly neglects an important aspect of the children and violence discussion, that of young people as perpetrators of violence and all the pathways through which this identity emerges. I do touch briefly on bullying, on the attraction of violence, on some of the experiences of older children, especially as they then affect their younger siblings. But these experiences are somewhat more peripheral in this account.

It is always easier to point to problems than to find effective solutions. There is no panacea for violence, but plenty of reasons to suppose that decent, equitable material conditions provide an indispensable foundation for reducing at least some of its manifestations. There is a moral imperative not to pretend otherwise. Poor sanitation provides a clear parallel and a simple case in point. When young children suffer high rates of death and diarrhoea in settlements without clean water and sanitation, the response, when there is one, is often to address the hygiene practices of their mothers rather than the lack of piped water and toilets that makes good hygiene almost impossible to achieve. Clean hands can help prevent diarrhoea, but keeping the hands of an active 2-year-old clean is a feat even in well-provisioned uncontaminated neighbourhoods. By what offensive logic do middle-class families get running water, while those without water get lessons in hygiene?

The intention here is not to disrespect the work of either hygiene counsellors or child protection professionals. If miseries were dealt with only through a focus on root causes, there would be much more distress in the world. Child protection systems are not irrelevant any more than handwashing is irrelevant. But in the absence of the larger, more politically attuned response, both run the risk of pushing responsibility off onto vulnerable children and households, a way of assenting to business as usual.

The construct of resilience is key here. A central interest of child protection – or of handwashing – is enlisting "protective factors", be they support groups or soap and water, in order to render children more resilient to difficult life circumstances. But the concept of resilience is subject to misunderstanding and can distract attention from the things that make children vulnerable in the first place, placing the emphasis instead on arming them for their dangerous world. We need to question why some children have so much greater a need to be so armed than others, and what the costs of resilience actually are. Resilience should not be a substitute for equity and social justice.

In discussions of children's rights, a distinction is often made between the rights of Provision, Protection and Participation – the three Ps. They have the right, in other words, to be provided with what they need in order to thrive, to be protected from what will harm them, and to have their opinions and capacities respected. The argument I make here is that provision should be intrinsic to protection. While they do not entirely overlap, a clean separation is simplistic. If children are protected by virtue of being adequately provided for, the need for resilience may be far less pressing. And as far as participation is concerned, let us not confuse children's agency with an obligation to somehow cope. We are often rightly reminded that children are not just victims but resourceful agents in their own lives. But this should not become an endorsement of that "willed wasting of lives". We cannot let children's resilience be used against them.

In considering the physical environment, and discussing how protection can be achieved through provision, those Pretoria girls and the absence of streetlights make a good example. Functioning streetlights would not solve the problem of sexual violence in these neighbourhoods. They might alleviate the girls' fears and reduce the chance of rape in particular alleyways. But streetlights on their own are more a band-aid than a silver bullet. The process that accompanies the repair of those streetlights is of more interest here. Attention from a municipal maintenance team would imply, for a start, the acceptance of a social contract. It would express responsibility on the part of the city for those particular neighbourhoods and citizens. When the neglect of a community is a function of structural inequity, then addressing that neglect is more than trivial.

It is still more significant when these improvements involve community efforts. In the Pretoria case, if some neighbours decided to take on the streetlight problem rather than simply letting the girls cope, it could catalyse something much larger. It would mean, first of all, taking the girls seriously, acknowledging that this should not be their problem alone. It would require negotiation with other people, an agreement to make this issue a priority. A case would have to be made, local authorities pulled in, funds secured. Attention might be brought to the lack of policing in the area, to the alcohol outlets that are open at all hours. By the time a group of people had come together with enough energy and organization to address the streetlights, a more expansive process would have been set in place. Neighbours who may have assumed that public streets are no place for young girls would now have invested their time, and might have a vested interest in protecting all their children and in improving their surroundings more generally. The streetlights could become a rallying point for negotiations and partnerships that could lead to other things – perhaps even a concern with what is happening to those other children at home. This is a catalytic process, and a far more substantial one than a focus group to remind young girls to be careful. There is potential here for the formation of social capital, for the growth of collective efficacy. The implications go deep, even for the youngest children.

The goal of this book, then, is an expanded paradigm for child protection, one anchored in the transformative potential of community-driven development, undertaken in negotiation and collaboration with the local state. My personal experience of this potential is as an observer over twenty years of the creative struggles of networks and federations and associations of the poor, pooling their frustrations, their experience and their knowledge to work, ideally in collaboration with government, to challenge those larger structural forces and to create a life of dignity.

The morality inherent in this collaborative mending of the world is different in some important ways from the morality of child protection. If that protection comes only from outside, necessary as that may be at times, it cannot be expected to root itself deeply in daily practice. If it is in everyday life that children encounter most of the array of miseries that we catalogue together as violence, it is also here that the mending should happen. It important to acknowledge the moral visions that are already embedded in everyday life, and to engage with existing efforts to address the inequities and exclusions that accompany so many of these miseries. Susan Smith refers to this as a situational ethic of care – "an ethic that is already rooted in the fact that everyday life is full of ideas and practices which lean towards what is good, fair and care-full" (2009, p. 208). The question becomes not so much how to protect children but rather how to create a world that keeps them safe and allows them to thrive as a matter of course. There is a fundamental synergy between building community and protecting children. These are not separate agendas. A place that works well for children works better for everyone else as well.

This book focuses on three scales of experience – home, neighbourhood and the loss of home and neighbourhood, the latter in the context of the many push-and-pull factors that provoke this loss, including eviction, migration, conflict, disaster and resettlement. At all three scales, I describe the forms that violence can take in the context of the material and spatial practicalities there that frame children's experience. The final two chapters consider responses to violence, first reviewing the practices and approaches that are most common within the global child protection enterprise, and then discussing how this paradigm might be expanded, through attention to the material improvements that can anchor a community's development and aspirations.

## References

Fullilove, Mindy Thompson (2005) *Root shock: How tearing up city neighborhoods hurts America, and what we can do about it*, New York: Ballantine Books

Katz, Cindi (2011) Accumulation, excess, childhood: Toward a countertopography of risk and waste, *Documents d'Anàlisi Geogràfica* 57(1), 47–60

Nixon, Rob (2011) *Slow violence and the environmentalism of the poor*, Cambridge, MA: Harvard University Press

Pinker, Steven (2011) *The better angels of our nature: Why violence has declined*, New York: Penguin

Povinelli, Elizabeth (2011) *Economies of abandonment: Social belonging and endurance in late liberalism*, Durham and London: Duke University

Smith, Susan J (2009) Everyday morality: Where radical geography meets normative theory, *Antipode* 41(1), 206–209

WHO (2002) *World report on violence and health*, Geneva: WHO

# 2

# BACKGROUND

Before I move on to the patchwork of evidence that links violence and the material world at the different scales of home, neighbourhood and beyond, some background may be useful on certain themes and connections that emerge repeatedly throughout the book. This chapter starts with an overview, however rough, of the global extent of the violence experienced by children – mostly to give a sense of how very commonplace the experience is. It goes on to consider the connections between violence and the deprivations associated with poverty and inequality. The concept of stress is basic here, since it mediates the links in so many situations. It then reviews very briefly what we know about the impact of violence for children's well-being and development, and how both stress and the concept of resilience come into play here. Finally, it provides some introduction to the contribution of the physical environment to young children's development, especially as it pertains to violence.

## The prevalence of violence against children

How common is the violence that children experience? One revealing answer comes from the longitudinal Young Lives study, which has followed 12,000 children in Ethiopia, Peru, India and Vietnam over fifteen years, aiming to shed light on the circumstances affecting children in poverty. When this study was initially designed, it gave no explicit attention to violence as a primary theme. But when the analysis of the early rounds of data showed that violence was a routine and troubling feature of life for almost every child in their samples, the research team had to expand the focus.

Estimating the extent and the depth of the violence experienced by children around the world is a frustrating exercise for those who attempt it. Official records on the abuse and neglect of children are unsatisfactory, because they show the very tip of the iceberg. Medical records are relevant only for those who are taken for treatment. Police records are even sparser; only a percentage of those who seek medical treatment go on to report an incident to the police. Sexual abuse is more commonly reported, but not when family members are the perpetrators, and this is most often the case. Vital statistics on mortality may be useful in determining the numbers of deaths resulting from abuse or neglect, but in many places the information on death certificates may be too limited to accurately reflect the cause of death.

Self-report measures by children or those who care for them are generally accepted as the most reliable source of information. These show rates of violence dramatically higher than anything revealed by official accounts – seventy-five times higher in the case of physical violence, thirty times higher for sexual abuse (UNICEF, 2014). But even the population-based surveys drawing on self-reports can have limited utility as a basis for comparison because of their lack of uniformity in definitions and methods.

The most recent, most comprehensive effort to date to estimate the global burden of violence against children synthesizes data on the combined physical, emotional and sexual violence experienced by 2–17-year-olds over the previous year in almost 100 countries, drawing from reliable and representative surveys that used standard self-report measures (Hillis et al., 2016). This synthesis looks at direct victimization wherever it occurred – at home, at school, in institutions and in the community – and whether inflicted by parents, teachers, neighbours, peers or others. The review uses conservative measures. For physical violence, for instance, it excludes spanking, slapping and shaking, restricting the analysis to more severe forms (kicking, choking, smothering, burning, scalding, branding or repeated beating with an object).

This review finds that over half of all children between the ages of 2 and 17 experienced violence in the previous year – somewhat more than half in Northern America, Asia and Africa, and less than that in Europe and Latin America. Given that these figures are considered reasonably representative of the countries that were not included, this means that about a billion children had experienced serious episodes of violence over the previous year. When more moderate forms of physical violence are also included, the overall percentage of affected children rises to 76 per cent. Rates exceed 60 per cent in Northern America and Latin America, 70 per cent in Europe, and 80 per cent in Asia and Africa. The review was not able to break down the experience of violence by age or type, except to note that violent discipline at home dominates the experience of children under 14, and that fighting, bullying and other experiences beyond home are more common for those older than 14. The authors consider the main limitation of the report to be an underestimation of the scale of the problem, given the strictness of the criteria for the inclusion of data.

This review leaves out children under 2, for whom there is generally scant information, but who are estimated to be at especially high risk of death and injury from violence and abuse (Landers, da Silva e Paula and Kilbane, 2013). It also leaves out neglect, which is understudied and difficult to measure, but which is generally accepted to be at least as widespread as harsh treatment, and which is a particular concern for young children, potentially as harmful as the experience of physical violence. What numbers there are on neglect come almost exclusively from high-income countries, but even there, inconsistencies abound. A meta-review of self-report surveys (focusing on people's memories of neglect) found prevalence rates that ranged dramatically from 1 to 80 per cent depending on how neglect was characterized and how questions were asked. In the USA, the average prevalence across widely diverse studies was about 16 per cent for physical neglect and 18 per cent for emotional neglect – if averages count for anything in the context of this much variation (Stoltenborgh, Bakermans-Kranenburg and van IJzendoorn, 2013).

Also excluded from this review, and equally harmful for children, is the witnessing of violence. The most common variant for young children especially is watching the abuse of their mothers at home. The cumulative evidence, based on a compilation of available studies and surveys, indicates that 30 per cent of "ever-partnered" women over 15 have experienced physical or sexual violence, with some variation by region and country (WHO, 2013). UNICEF estimates that more than a quarter of a billion children endure the experience of witnessing this abuse every year. This is disturbing and destructive for children in its own right, but in addition it often goes hand in hand with their own abuse. Evidence from numerous culturally distinct countries points to an overlap of violence towards children and violence towards their mothers that ranges from 30 to 70 per cent (UNICEF, 2014).

The form of violence most commonly documented for children is harsh discipline at home, and the most detailed and comprehensive information on this front comes from UNICEF's Multiple Indicator Cluster Survey (MICS), which collects comparable information on a sample of women and children from over 10,000 households in more than 100 countries. The majority of these countries include in this survey an optional module on the modes of child discipline used over the previous month. A 2014 report, drawing on data from this module, indicates that most children between ages 2 and 14 are routinely subjected to either physically or psychologically harsh forms of discipline, more or less extreme. Rates are slightly higher for younger children and for boys. About seven out of ten children on average experience routine psychological aggression (defined to include screaming, verbal abuse, terror and humiliation), and six out of ten physical aggression (ranging from shaking and slapping to beating children repeatedly and as hard as possible with some implement). These often occur together. About 17 per cent are reported to be routinely subjected to more extreme forms of violent discipline – but this figure, drawn as it is from parent responses, is quite likely to downplay the situation. Less than 20 per cent of children experience only non-violent forms of discipline (explanation, distraction, removal of privileges) (UNICEF, 2014).

Population-based surveys on sexual abuse suggest that it is less common than other forms of physical violence. A meta-analysis based on adolescent self-reports points to rates that range from 4 to 25 per cent of children, with variation by region and with higher rates for girls than for boys (Stoltenborgh et al., 2011). But figures are generally considered to greatly underrepresent the scale of the problem.

Research has shown that up to 80 per cent of victims do not disclose their abuse until they are adults, while presumably others remain silent even then (UNICEF, 2014). Boys even more than girls are reluctant to reveal their abuse. And even when families know about the event, they are often unwilling to disclose it, especially if a relative is responsible. Hospital-based studies report disproportionate numbers of very young children among those treated for abuse, but at least in part this is because of the greater likelihood of serious physical damage to young children (Lalor, 2008). Figures from the global north suggest that the peak age of vulnerability for sexual abuse is between ages 7 and 13, but that about 20 per cent of cases involve even younger children (Finkelhor, 1999). Sexual abuse away from home is more likely to involve older children, and often it can take the form of transactional sex, especially in situations of serious hardship.

However much these estimates vary and however much they underrepresent the scale of the problems, what comes through clearly is the fact that the experience of violence is not unusual for children. Some of those who face it may be exposed to only isolated episodes. But for most, the experience is more routine and in most cases it includes more than one form of violence. Most young people who are victims of sexual abuse, for instance, also report physical and emotional abuse; and children who are abused are also more commonly neglected. High levels of violence in a neighbourhood are often accompanied by higher rates of abuse at home – and as just noted, children whose mothers are abused are more likely to be abused themselves.

## Violence and structural violence

Violence of every kind and at every scale has been related to levels of poverty and inequality. The numbers indicate that family violence is most common among low-income people; that community violence occurs most often in poor neighbourhoods, that countries with lower per capita incomes and higher levels of disparity have more episodes of violent conflict, higher homicide rates, higher levels of youth violence and school bullying.

The Children's Defense Fund in the United States, which describes poverty as the single best predictor of child abuse and neglect, notes that fluctuations in maltreatment rates closely track changes in national poverty levels. The CDF's 2005 figures showed, for instance, that children in families with incomes of USD 15,000 or less a year were twenty-two times more likely to be abused or neglected than those with incomes above USD 30,000 (Children's Defense Fund, 2005). The first thing to keep in mind here is how much of this difference is actually related to neglect, which, among these low-income families, was estimated to be over three times as common as physical abuse. Even if we ignore the neglect, though, there are still far higher rates of abuse among those living in poverty.

Child abuse is clearly not exclusive to people in poverty. But there is, and has been for many years, strong, consistent evidence of the higher prevalence of child abuse and neglect among low-income groups in both high- and low-income countries. Where there are formal systems for reporting child abuse, a labelling bias often comes into play. In the United States, for example, there is evidence that children from low-income families coming into emergency rooms are more likely to be considered victims of abuse, while those from affluent families are often assumed to have had an "accident". But even research based on self-report measures from parents has found rates of violence to be higher among the poorest households (Gelles, 1992).

These kinds of figures can contribute to naive assumptions about the dysfunctional, abusive, aggressive nature of people in poverty. Structural violence is a useful concept here, a way to put these simplistic equations into perspective. Originally coined in 1969 by Johan Galtung, the term has been succinctly explained by Dr Paul Farmer as "one way of describing social arrangements that put individuals and populations in harm's way ... The arrangements are *structural* because they are embedded in the political and economic organization of our social world; they are *violent* because they cause injury to people" (Farmer et al., 2006).

But how does structural violence – arguably a metaphor of sorts – relate to the immediate violence directed at a person, whether in the context of mugging or mass murder? The deprivations associated with structural violence are violent in their own right and part of a larger continuum of harm. But they also comprise a fertile ground for the more immediate, more personal, more direct forms of violence.

A case study from Santiago, Chile, looking at three distinct neighbourhoods, clarifies some of the ways that violence is produced and inequitably distributed as a function of those larger structural forces. In 1973, Chile, at that point a fairly equitable country, experienced a military coup, and was subsequently reorganized along neoliberal lines, a trend that was only reinforced after the return to democracy. This meant widespread public disinvestment, the privatization of services, banning of trade unions, deregulation, the loss of public space and the increasing concentration among the wealthiest of the benefits of an expanding economy. A familiar pattern in many places, this was accompanied by the growing exclusion of the poorest residents, economically, spatially and in terms of education and other services. High levels of unemployment followed, especially among poorly educated young people from families that couldn't afford private schooling. This was accompanied, as it so often is, by burgeoning gang activity and a growing reliance on the drug trade.

In the lowest income neighbourhood tracked in this study, the power struggles associated with the bottom rung of drug trafficking networks generated considerable violence and fear, and local residents became reluctant to use their increasingly unsafe neighbourhood space. Women and children especially stayed confined in their cramped apartments in poorly served and increasingly ghetto-like public housing, where they had been resettled when their old neighbourhoods were cleared for development. There at home there was considerable family conflict around the illicit activities and addiction of some family members. In these stressful circumstances, child abuse and domestic violence became increasingly common, feeding off the violence out in the community.

Residents in the more affluent neighbourhoods were also affected by the generally high levels of violence in the city, but in their case this tended far more often to take the form of robbery, more often outside their home districts in unpoliced poorer neighbourhoods. The murder rate changed very little between 2005 and 2010 in the two more affluent neighbourhoods, but there was a striking increase in homicides in the poorest neighbourhood, where the rate was about three times higher than in the middle-income neighbourhood (Rodriguez et al., 2014).

Poverty and exclusion are detrimental in themselves for children and families. But there are generally mediating factors that explain their association with violence and harsh treatment. These are related to higher levels of stress and lower levels of support, whether in terms of services and resources or the presence of social capital, which can be sorely eroded in situations of scarcity, inequity and insecurity. The same connections hold true at home and at the neighbourhood level. It is not just poverty *per se* that fuels stress and frustration and precipitates higher rates of violence and insecurity, but also inequalities and relative deprivation. The inherently taxing nature of exclusion and low social status has been documented for many years, most notably in the work of Richard Wilkinson and Kate Pickett, whose book *The Spirit Level* drew general attention to the fact that poor performance on almost every social measure of well-being – whether life expectancy or mental illness or rates of violence or educational achievement – is closely tied to how unequal and discriminatory a society is (Wilkinson and Pickett, 2009).

## The role of stress

Stress plays a fundamental mediating role in this relationship. This is a tricky term, and often loosely used. We are all "stressed" – in need of more sleep, more time, more appreciation, more income. The word is commonly used to express both the stressful experience and our stressed response to it. Stress, that is, causes us to feel stress. If the term is scrutinized, one can start to wonder whether it is not too loose to mean anything very concrete. Since the concept of stress is critical to this discussion of violence, it is worth briefly unpacking the physiological mechanisms as they are understood by psychologists and biochemists.

Stress comes into play when the stability of the human system is threatened, whether by an infection, a fall down the stairs, an earthquake or upsetting news. The body shifts its priorities and activates certain responses, sidelining others. Stress hormones are released – epinephrine, cortisol, norepinephrine in particular – blood pressure and heart rate surge, breath quickens, muscles tighten, senses sharpen. These responses are adaptive. The body galvanizes its resources to cope with the immediate threat, and the responses become inactive when the stressful situation is resolved. But when stress-provoking events are chronic, the system is continually or repeatedly vigilant and aroused.

What is adaptive and protective in the short run can result over the longer term in considerable wear and tear. An effective response to a predator is less useful as a reaction to an eviction notice or to a blaring radio next door. And even when the heightened vigilance might be appropriate – for instance in bracing for harassment or worse on the way to the community toilet – this takes its toll day after day. The "allostatic load", or cumulative wear and tear that results from prolonged exposure to these stress hormones, actually increases vulnerability and affects both physical and mental health (McEwen, 1998). Consider, for example, the impact of racial or ethnic discrimination. In the six months after the 9/11 attack in the United States, hospital records showed that pregnant women in California with Arabic names were significantly more likely to give birth to preterm and low birthweight infants than in the previous six months. This was not the case for other women (Lauderdale, 2006).

Research on telomeres, the protective tips on chromosomes, points to a mechanism that appears to underpin the impact of accumulated stress over time. Biochemist Elizabeth Blackburn and psychiatrist Elissa Epel together found that the stress hormone cortisol is responsible for eroding the length of these telomores, hastening the onset of otherwise age-related degenerative diseases. Telomeres, they say, "powerfully quantify life's insults" (Blackburn and Epel, 2012, p. 3). Although their work is still greeted with scepticism in many quarters, it has gained wide recognition and has led to calls for policy responses to the stressful quality of social disparities.

A considerable body of research has for many years now related stress to such environmental conditions as noise, crowding, dilapidation and high temperatures. The classic contribution of Gary Evans and Sheldon Cohen in 1987 emphasized not only the stressful potential of such environmental features, but also the way their effects accumulate and even multiply (Evans and Cohen, 1987). Difficult living conditions can amplify other social stressors. An angry frustrated man who cannot find work may find it much harder to stay calm in his crowded shack when children are fighting, the neighbour is complaining about noise and there is no water left for him to wash with. Coping with these multiple demands depletes resources, leaving people feeling less able to cope, and to exert control over the circumstances in their lives. In the context of low- and middle-income countries, the available research has focused primarily on crowding as a source of stress. However, it is clear that billions of people in the world live in conditions that present multiple sources of stress, as will be described in the chapters that follow.

The connection between stress and violence is dynamic and reciprocal. Violence, whether experienced or witnessed, can excite a stress response. But the release of stress hormones that leads to physical and mental arousal also stimulates aggression and impairs self-control. In the 1990s, Richard Gelles and his colleagues, looking at the association between stress, poverty and the maltreatment of children, found a direct connection between the accumulation of stressful life events and severe violence (Gelles, 1992). Noting that more affluent families use their resources to lessen the burden of stressful events, they suggested that the capacity to manage stress is key. A sense of control over one's life is fundamental to psychological health. Yet one facet of poverty is the relative lack of control that inevitably accompanies it.

## The impact of violence for children

What does it cost a young child to experience violence, fear and neglect? Beyond the physical harm, a wide range of emotional and psychological consequences have been documented over the years, including shame, guilt, fear, anxiety, depression, anger and aggression. It's not just the immediate feelings and behaviour that are a concern. Violence, especially in combination with poverty, can sabotage a child's development across all domains. The processes that lead to these outcomes do not play out the same way for every child. They are shaped by numerous factors, including the age of the child, the type of violence and its intensity and frequency, and the accumulation of both protective factors and risks that can minimize or exacerbate the damage (Foster and Brooks-Gunn, 2009).

According to Seth Pollack, a clinical psychologist, "There are many ways in which an abusive family environment might influence a child's associative learning processes … Physically abusive parents tend to be some combination of impulsive, emotionally volatile, and inconsistent in their parenting, and less verbal in discussing/explaining emotional states with their children" (Pollack, 2016, p. 5). This affects the way children understand and respond to the world. Their social experience shapes their feelings, their thoughts and their behaviour. They become more alert to threats and signs of anger, and may give most of their attention to negative cues, often perceiving hostility in other people where it does not in fact exist. Children who are abusively treated often have problems learning how to regulate their own emotions and behaviour and they can act out aggressively, reflecting what they are familiar with. They often have difficulty processing social information and lack the skills to conduct positive relationships, which can leave them without satisfying friendships. Their perseveration on sad or fearful thoughts can leave them at higher risk of depression and anxiety, and their vigilance may also mean they are unable to attend to the kinds of positive experiences and stimuli that might brighten their mood and foster their cognitive growth. Learning requires such executive functions as impulse control, working memory, organization and the capacity to plan and initiate tasks. These may be disrupted by the threat of violence, and school outcomes can suffer.

These challenges can lead, as Pollack says, to "a cascade of developmental challenges", leaving children compromised socially, emotionally and cognitively and unable to develop effective strategies for coping with their often demanding environments. Their responses may reflect a reasonable adaptation to a hostile environment in the short term – vigilance makes sense when a drunken father comes in the door – but in the long term they impose distinct penalties, as maladaptive behaviour hardens into pathology. Longer-term outcomes can include school drop-out, substance abuse, eating disorders, delinquency and aggression. Research is increasingly pointing to longer-term health impacts as well. Witnessing violence towards other people can have very similar effects (Walker et al., 2011), as can exposure to larger-scale violence outside the home. Being around ethnic and political violence, for instance, seems to dispose children towards aggression as a way to deal with social conflicts (Dubow, Huesmann and Boxer, 2009). Children who have experienced violence are more likely to become violent people themselves, continuing the cycle (Sabri et al., 2013).

Older children, with their more extended worlds, may encounter more violence, but violence can have the most serious implications for the youngest children. First of all, they are more likely to be injured or to die as a result of abuse. The psychological impacts can also be more extreme. Joy Osofsky pointed years ago to the mistaken impression that very young children are less affected by violence because they don't understand what they are experiencing or observing. In fact, she said, their very lack of understanding leaves them at a disadvantage. They can't ask questions as easily or understand responses, and they have fewer ways of organizing their experience or managing their feelings. They may become irritable, unable to sleep, fearful of being alone or exploring new things, and their development can start to lag or even to regress (Osofsky, 1999).

Neglect can also take a serious toll, both emotional or physical, although the processes are somewhat different. Where abused children can be hypervigilant to threats, neglected children may have a harder time differentiating between emotional cues. A lack of basic care has obvious implications for health and well-being. But the absence of interaction and stimulation is also significant for psychosocial development. Occasional inattention is not a problem and can even encourage children's independence. But habitual under-stimulation can lead to developmental delays. Extreme levels of psychosocial deprivation, like those experienced in some institutional settings or in the case of very depressed and withdrawn mothers, can disrupt the development of a child's brain and result in a range of emotional, cognitive and behavioural disorders (National Scientific Council on the Developing Child, 2012).

It is hard to unravel the effects of violence or neglect from those of more general stress, and there is probably no need to. Violence is certainly among the more potent sources of stress, and for children as well as adults, it increases the allostatic load. The neurobiological responses that are adaptive in the very short term can impose critical costs and become pathological if they become a more chronic state of affairs (McEwen, 1998; Mead, Beauchaine and Shannon, 2010). The message is clear, say Blackburn and Epel. "Failure to alleviate severe stress caused by prolonged threats such as war, financial hardship, abuse and emotional neglect, particularly in children, will result in exponentially higher costs further down the line – personal, economic and otherwise" (p. 169).

These disheartening outcomes, whether the result of neglect, abuse or exposure to violence, are not inevitable. For example, although about a third of abused children have been found to become abusive adults (as opposed to 5 per cent of the general population) the majority are not abusive towards other people (Margolin and Gordis, 2000). Why are some children robust and flexible in the face of hardship while others suffer more severe effects? Protective factors can have a marked effect, countering to some extent the risks that a child is facing. Children can be buffered, for instance, from harmful long-term consequences of violence if there are also warm, stable, supportive relationships in their lives. Having a mother or an older brother or even a neighbour who is sensitive and responsive can lessen the harmful effects of chronic stress in childhood. The interplay of risk and protective factors is interactive more than additive. A higher cumulative exposure to risk, for instance, may leave a child less able to benefit from later protective experiences (Wachs and Rahman, 2013).

There has been considerable emphasis over recent years on children's "resilience", whether in the face of violence or other adversities, as noted in the previous chapter. The concept is intuitively attractive, implying as it does a focus on strengths rather than deficits, and pointing to the potential for preventive action through the identification and support of protective factors.

But there are questions about the uncritical use of this appealing concept in thinking about children's responses to hardship. The notion can be exploited. Luthar and Cicchetti point to the very common tendency to see resilience as an individual attribute that allows children to adapt more positively to adversity. But resilience, they explain, is not a personality trait. It describes a broader interactive supportive process (Luthar and Cicchetti, 2000). This may be a difficult distinction for policy makers to take on board, and an enthusiastic embrace of a more simple-minded version of this concept can mean shifting attention away from the risks and towards children's presumed capacity to be robust in the face of hardship. If some people can be resilient when things are hard, then why not raise the expectations for all? It is a short step from this to letting authorities off the hook. This perspective suggests that the problem must be in the victim, not in the circumstances, and it can end up justifying an official reluctance to invest in improving unjust and inequitable circumstances.

There is the concern, too, that resilience can come at a cost, as illustrated by a study in rural Georgia in the United States. Economically deprived children, identified by their teachers at age 10 or 11 as competent, self-controlled and focused on success – in other words, resilient in the face of hardship – were found at age 19 to display much greater signs of physical distress than their less "resilient" peers (Brody et al., 2013). What we consider to be resilience in the face of adversity might be experienced by the body as just another stressor, elevating the allostatic load.

A variation on this theme from a distinctly different discipline is the evolution in the understanding of resilience in the context of work on climate change adaptation. Here the concept of resilience has been applied to the capacity of both physical and social entities (drainage systems and communities) to "bounce back" after a challenging event. In a response that is related to the misgivings around the psychological understanding of resilience, observers in the field are increasingly seeing the emphasis on resilience in this context as a confirmation of a status quo that perhaps contributed in the first place to the vulnerability. If a community without storm drains manages to repair the damage from floods that fill their huts with a foot of mud most years, do we consider those residents resilient? Is "bouncing back" adequate here? Shovels and a dry stretch of road to sleep on are good. Storm drains are better. Better still would be local land management policies that make affordable land available beyond the city's flood plains. In the climate change adaptation domain, we are increasingly urged to think in terms of "bouncing forward" – embracing a goal of transformation rather than of resilience, and using the climate event as an opportunity to rectify the structural injustices and inequities that have contributed to vulnerability – rather than being involved in "an acceleration of the status quo" (Ziervogel et al., 2017).

Children in harmful situations, however, cannot always wait for structural change. Jo Boyden and her colleagues suggest relinquishing the metaphor of resilience in favour of a more practical consideration of specific factors that actually moderate the experience of hardship for children (Boyden and Cooper, 2009). Children can be buffered from harmful long-term consequences by, for instance, warm, stable, supportive mothers. Parenting classes might be helpful on this front – they are certainly the solution that the child protection enterprise most frequently offers in most countries around the world. But what about the grab bag of stressors that make it difficult for mothers to be reliably sensitive and responsive in the first place? Moderating hardship is never as powerful as removing or attenuating the risk exposure in the first place. The chapters that follow consider how the physical environment comes into play here. First, though, I consider briefly how this material environment actually affects children's development, and how in a theoretical sense it might combine with exposure to harsh treatment and to neglect to penalize children.

## How the physical environment contributes to risk and protection

Children do not develop in a vacuum. They grow and change within a complex matrix of interacting processes, biological and environmental. Urie Bronfenbrenner's classic model places the child at the centre of a nested hierarchy of influences that include everything from the child's genotype to the larger political economy (1979). Her father's beliefs about discipline, her mother's unpleasant employer, her brother's teasing, the friendly dog who comes by for scraps, her neighbour's kindness, the open hours at the local clinic, the interest rates at the credit union, the political party in power, all play their parts. But even in the context of this ecological perspective, surprisingly little attention is given to the material and spatial sides of life, either in developmental psychology or in the policies that it informs. The physical environment is viewed at best as the stage set where the social drama plays out.

This is intriguing. We are all so inevitably embedded in a concrete physical world. We shape it and endow it with meaning. We are also shaped, excited, confined, sustained by the places we occupy. Consider a small child and her home – the spatial frame for the next chapter. It is far from being just the setting for play with her brother or for time on her mother's lap. The house is a presence in its own right with its own smells, familiar corners, memories, rules and limits, all part of this child's sense of herself and of the world. She tries to climb up on the table, puts her grubby hand in the water pail, picks the flowers, gets too close to the fire, runs towards the street, and people respond. One might dismiss this as self-evident. A child's interactions are necessarily with and through the objects and spaces around her. But this is exactly the point. These objects and spaces provide the child with opportunities to gain competence and understanding. And the way they are arranged, made available or not available, their threat to the child's safety, the boundaries imposed, their importance to other people, also structure and mediate the social interactions that ensue. The more challenging the environment is, the more it colours the interaction between children and the other people in their lives.

Parents set limits to protect children. But they also make use of the material world as they socialize their children. Cultural rules for behaviour are often expressed around the use of space and of material objects. Denis Wood and Robert Beck illustrated this in painstaking detail in the 1990s, identifying with the help of Wood's sons over 200 rules for the use of the objects and space in one small family room, which together constituted an operating manual for social behaviour and a way of life. Consideration, respect, protection, appreciation. Make sure your feet are clean. Don't spill on the carpet. Don't open the door to strangers. No fighting on the couch. Don't use the lampshade as a space helmet. Don't touch the special box, just look at it (Wood and Beck, 1994).

Wood's work is just one expression of a rich body of research and discussion on the significance of space, place and the object world. Yet this work remains outside the mainstream of academic and professional thinking about children. Nor has mainstream given much attention to the global south. An international peer-reviewed outline of research on children's development and the physical environ-ment concluded that there is in fact very little work documenting this aspect of children's lives in the global south. This is a concern, the authors point out, given the extraordinarily wide range of spatial and material realities that this majority world represents (Ferguson et al., 2013).

This general lack of attention extends to the discourse around children's rights. The Convention on the Rights of the Child has served as a framework for attention to children internationally, yet few of its provisions make reference to children's material living conditions. It calls briefly for attention to housing, clean drinking water and environmental pollution and it recognizes the importance of basic *knowledge* about sanitation, if not provision (Articles 24, 27). Article 25 establishes the right to "a standard of living adequate for the child's physical, mental, spiritual, moral and social development", but it does not tease out what this standard of living might entail. This lack of specificity stands in marked contrast to the Con-vention's much more detailed recognition of children's civil rights, for instance with regard to involvement with the justice system or separation from parents or a voice in the issues that concern them.

Yet some of the most common violations of children's rights globally relate to their living environments. The ground breaking Bristol study (2003) on global child poverty found that over a third of the children in the world lived in squalid housing (defined as having a mud floor or more than five people per room); a third had no access to any toilet facilities, and over 20 per cent depended on drinking water from unsafe open sources. By contrast, fewer than 15 per cent suffered severe deprivation in the areas of food, health care or education (Gordon et al., 2003). Globally, under-5 mortality has dropped by more than half since the 1990s. But the leading causes of death remain the same: after complications around birth, the biggest killers of young children are still pneumonia and diarrhoea. Both are highly preventable and unquestionably tied to children's living conditions – to the quality of sanitation and water provision and to the indoor air pollution so closely related to the unventilated burning of solid fuels (Hanf et al., 2014).

A stark indication of the impact of living conditions is the well-being of children in urban slums. Although their household incomes are on average higher than those of their rural peers, their outcomes tend to be as bad or worse – a function of higher densities, lack of basic infrastructure, higher levels of contamination. In Bangladesh in 2010, a comparative analysis of country-wide household survey data found more extreme child deprivation in urban slums on average than in *any* single rural district in the country, despite the higher incomes in the slums. Under-5 mortality was 44 per cent higher in slums, access to acceptable sanitation was 83 per cent worse, drop-out rates from primary school were seven times worse, child labour was three times more common, and there were far higher rates of violence (UNICEF Bangladesh, 2010).

Although the connections with mortality and morbidity have been the most widely researched, the impact of the physical environment goes well beyond children's health. There are documented impacts for their cognitive development, much less extensively researched in the global south, but nonetheless clear in some areas. Exposure to lead, for example, affects both mental and motor functioning, and an estimated 40 per cent of children in low- and middle-income countries have elevated lead levels (Walker et al., 2007). Other toxins, including those in pesticides and polluted air, along with the quality of water and sanitation provision, can also affect children's cognition and long-term mental development. And then there are the numerous factors that influence not just cognition, but also children's more general psychosocial development. Levels of crowding, of noise, of chaos, of dilapidation, residential mobility, housing security, space for play, access to green space, proximity to traffic, for example, all have demonstrated effects for children, short and long term.

The impact of environmental factors tends to be relatively modest for children living in reasonably good surroundings. It is far more extreme for children in conditions of deprivation. A very small apartment, for instance, may be an inconvenience for families whose children can go out to a pleasant yard, or who have a safe, welcoming neighbourhood to play in. For children who have no alternative space, that same small apartment can be a prison. There is far too little evidence from the global south on most of these fronts to be able to draw hard conclusions about the impacts of a far greater spectrum of material conditions than exist in the north. This is especially true when it comes to children's social and emotional development. But what evidence there is points to the significant impact of features of the physical environment, both at home and beyond, which can both mitigate and amplify the social pressures in children's lives. This is especially the case for children in poverty who are far more likely to be affected, and indeed sabotaged, by their material conditions. Environmental determinism may be passé. But it is a considerably more persuasive dogma in the context of material deprivation.

There are three dimensions of the relationship between children and their physical surroundings that are of particular interest in this discussion of violence: the emotional security that the material world can provide for a child; the opportunities it provides for play and learning; and the level of stress that environmental conditions can impose on children and those around them.

## Emotional security and place

It is well established that children need secure, nurturing, responsive relationships over a sustained period of time with at least one important person in their lives and ideally more than one. The quality of the attachment that develops as part of this relationship has been recognized for years as fundamental to a child's social and emotional development, a defining touchstone that affects how subsequent relationships are approached. When children have had secure attachments early in life, there is a foundation for trust and confidence. Without this security, they can be anxious and conflicted in their dealings with people (Bowlby, 1969). Recall that this is one of the risks associated with the experience of violence and abuse.

The importance of children's attachment to place is seldom discussed, but it is familiar to any parent. Our childhood memories, too, remind us of the powerful significance of places. Louise Chawla, an environmental psychologist, argues that, while predictable, secure human relationships are paramount, a stable comforting physical base is also fundamental to a child's security and sense of self, and can be especially important when relationships with other people are not that dependable (Chawla, 1992). Familiar routines are anchored in this home base and are a source of comfort and refuge. When the relationship to familiar surroundings is disrupted, however modest the home, however deficient the neighbourhood, this can be acutely unsettling. This is especially true for young children. A study of the effects of housing mobility, for example, showed that preschoolers had significantly higher rates of behaviour problems after moving than was true for older children (Fowler et al., 2014). Residential instability wreaks havoc on children's social relationships and often leads to very difficult experiences with school. This kind of disruption can put a child in jeopardy, leaving him with a persistent sense of loss and uprootedness.

Violence can upend this relationship to place in a number of ways. Repeated abuse can turn homes into places of fear rather than refuge. When neighbourhoods are violent, children don't get the chance to explore them and to know them on their own terms, which deprives them of a sense of security and belonging in a larger world. Forced evictions and displacement can ravage a child's confidence in that world even if family relationships remain intact. When the threat of violence is a default reality, children's connection to the places they are attached to becomes ambivalent at best.

## Opportunity and interaction in an expanding world

"Healthy place attachments", Chawla says, "balance the inward hold of an intimate familiar center with the outward attractions of an expanding world" (1992). Those "outward attractions" are the second piece of this relationship with the material world. Children's interaction with that "expanding world", mostly through play, is basic to the development of their own expanding minds and bodies. This relationship was described by Jean Piaget, who saw children's play within the material environment as an attempt to build mental models for how the world works (Piaget, 1952). Much of children's time and energy, especially in the early years, is spent exploring and manipulating the objects and places around them, driven as they are by curiosity and the desire for competence. Play is not just random activity. It is fundamental to becoming a capable human being. It provides children with the chance to try things out, to solve problems, to overcome challenges, to make sense out of what they observe. Young children don't learn primarily by memorizing facts or reciting the alphabet. They learn with every part of themselves and this happens most productively through play.

Lev Vygotsky expanded on Piaget's focus on the material world as a medium of development, emphasizing the critical role of other people. What children know is not just a function of their relationship with the object world (although Piaget would not have simplified it to this extent either). It is shaped by an understanding of cultural meanings and it often happens through interaction with more knowledgeable others (Vygotsky, 1978). Piaget might have seen a child washing a stone in a pail of water as part of a process of learning about density, volume, cause and effect. For Vygotsky, the frame for this same event might widen to include the conscious mimicking of an older sister washing potatoes or dishes, and the implicit exploration of social roles and cultural meaning. It might be supported by the comments of that sister, flagging the event as socially meaningful and perhaps providing a real potato to wash and slice.

Within either frame, the experience is richer and more consequential for the presence of the pail, the water and the stone. It doesn't happen without them. Children need a place to play, things to play with, and this interaction with the world depends on the diversity of the available opportunities and the stimulation they provide. The concept of "affordances" is helpful here. Affordances are the range of activities that a particular place or object allows for. A stool, for instance, is not just a place to sit. It is also something to climb on, jump off, crawl under, turn over. A puddle is something to wade through, a place to splash, a reflective surface that can be broken by a dropped pebble. All these activities provide a child with a sense of her own capacity to act on the world and make something happen, a step in the direction of competence and mastery. The more responsive affordances there are in a child's environment, the more likely she is to have the selection of challenges and opportunities that fit her particular needs at a particular time. A 1-year-old will walk up and down the same three steps over and over again with intense concentration until that experience is fully conquered and absorbed, and then she will want to move on to something else.

As children grow older, their opportunities need to expand. Their socialization hinges on the range of physical settings available to them as part of their daily lives. A marketplace, a football field, a temple, a workshop where a neighbour mends bicycles, a water point where women do laundry, all imply particular routines and activities and expose children to different rules of engagement. The diversity of children's surroundings is important, but so is their access to this diversity. In situations of violence, mobility and the range of possibilities can become very limited. Children may instead spend hours a day indoors, isolated from other children and from the life of their neighbourhoods. The presence of violence in their environment, whether at home or further afield, can also limit their motivation and curiosity, and their heightened vigilance affects the quality of attention that they are able to bring to what *is* available.

## The environment as a source of stress for children

The local environment can offer refuge and stimulation; it can also be a potent source of stress. This is especially the case for those in poverty. This has already been discussed in this chapter and will continue to come up in the context of specific situations in the rest of the book. At the risk of being repetitive, it seems important here to clarify again that the physical environment can contribute very specifically to stress for young children and their family members, influencing both the likelihood of violence and their capacity for coping with it.

Environmental psychologist Gary Evans has spent his career expanding our understanding of the links between poverty and stress for children. Stress, he explains, may predispose adults towards more punitive, less responsive behaviour towards children. But it can also have immediate and profound effects on a developing child, causing significant changes in the chemistry of the brain and body, which have implications for health and development over the long term. Concrete evidence for the relationship of children's living conditions to these stress-related changes comes from some studies on substandard housing. One of these, a cross-sectional study by Evans and a colleague, found that 8–10-year-old children living in poor-quality, crowded housing showed higher levels of stress hormones (epinephrine, norepinephrine and cortisol in urine samples) than their peers in better housing. This was after controlling for income and other potentially confounding factors (Evans and Marcynyszyn, 2004). Another study, which followed children over their first four years, found that those in lower quality housing (based on measures of safety, crowding and cleanliness) had higher levels of salivary cortisol, starting at about seven months (Blair et al., 2011).

Coley and colleagues find correlations between poor housing quality and longer-term emotional and behavioural problems for children, as well as lower skills in math and reading. According to these researchers, "rather than being a source of security and escape from life's pressures, a home with quality deficiencies may add to other stresses experienced by poor families, leading to a cumulative negative impact on well-being" (Coley et al., 2013, p. 1787).

Housing is not the only source of stress. As Evans and colleagues explain, "The physical form is well documented; poor children are exposed to substandard environmental conditions including toxins, hazardous waste, ambient air and water pollution, noise, crowding, poor housing, poorly maintained school buildings, residential turnover, traffic congestion, poor neighborhood sanitation and maintenance, and crime" (Evans, Brooks-Gunn and Klebanov, 2011, p. 24). These factors, they add, can be associated with and accompanied by higher levels of family turmoil and lower levels of routine and organization in their daily lives.

Children's well-being is often discussed in terms of risk factors and protective factors, and the importance of cumulative risk is well established in understanding their responses to adversity. The likelihood of poor developmental outcomes increases in more than linear fashion with a greater number of risk factors (Evans and English, 2002). Being born into poverty means a greater accumulation of exposure to risk, resulting in higher levels of the chronic and toxic stress that leads to physical and cognitive deficits and that undermines children's capacity to thrive in the face of hardship. Children living in the stressful environments of poverty are not only more likely to be exposed to violent treatment; they may also be less well equipped to cope with the demands that violence makes on their overtaxed systems. They are placed in effect in double jeopardy. We lack the evidence from the global south to state with conviction that the same equations prevail everywhere. Local expectations and cultural norms for the use of space may certainly moderate the degree of stress experienced. But what limited evidence there is, both quasi-experimental and anecdotal, suggests that negative responses to adverse conditions hold true across cultures. Thresholds may vary, but so too does the depth and range of the adversities experienced.

## References

Blackburn, Elizabeth H and Elissa S Epel (2012) Telomeres and adversity: Too toxic to ignore, *Nature* 490, 169–171

Blair, C, C C Raver, D Granger, R MillsKoonce, L Hibel and Family Life Project Key Investigators (2011), Allostasis and allostatic load in the context of poverty in early childhood, *Development and Psychopathology* 23, 845–857

Bowlby, J (1969) *Attachment and Loss*, Vol. 1: *Attachment*. New York: Basic Books

Boyden, J and E Cooper (2009) Questioning the power of resilience: are children up to the task of disrupting the transmission of poverty?, in J Addison, D Hulme, and R Kanbur (eds) *Poverty dynamics: Measurement and understanding from an interdisciplinary perspective*, Oxford: Oxford University Press

Brody, Gene, Tianyi Yu, Edith Chen, Gregory E Miller, Steven M Kogan and Steven R H Beach (2013) Rural African Americans' socioeconomic status-related risk and competence in preadolescence and psychological adjustment and allostatic load at age 19, *Psychological Science* 24(7), 1285–1293

Bronfenbrenner, Urie (1979) *The ecology of human development: Experiments by nature and design*, Cambridge, MA: Harvard University Press

Chawla, L (1992) Childhood place attachments, in I Altman and S Low (eds) *Place attachment*, New York: Plenum

Children's Defense Fund (2005) Child welfare: Poverty and families in crisis, in *The State of America's Children 2005*. Available at http://cdf.childrensdefense.org/site/DocServer/ Greenbook_2005.pdf?docID=1741

Coley, Rebekah Levine, Tama Leventhal, Alicia Doyle Lynch and Melissa Kull (2013) Relations between housing characteristics and the well-being of low-income children and adolescents, *Developmental Psychology* 49(9), 1775–1789

Dubow, Eric F, L Rowell Huesmann and Paul Boxer (2009) A social-cognitive-ecological framework for understanding the impact of exposure to persistent ethnic–political violence on children's psychosocial adjustment, *Clinical Child and Family Psychology Review* 12, 113–126

Evans, Gary W and Sheldon Cohen (1987) Environmental stress, in D Stokols and I Altman (eds) *Handbook of environmental psychology*, Vol. 1, New York: Wiley, 571–610

Evans, Gary W and K English (2002) The environment of poverty: Multiple stressor exposure, psychophysiological stress, and socioemotional adjustment, *Child Development* 73(4), 1238–1248

Evans, Gary W and LA Marcynyszyn (2004) Environmental justice, cumulative environmental risk, and health among low- and middle-income children in upstate New York, *American Journal of Public Health* 94(11), 1942–1944

Evans, Gary W, Jeanne Brooks-Gunn and Pamela Kato Klebanov (2011) Stressing out the poor: Chronic physiological stress and the income-achievement gap, *Pathways* Winter, 16–21

Farmer, P E, B Nizeye, S Stulac and S Keshavjee (2006) Structural violence and clinical medicine, *PLoS Med* 3(10), e449, doi:10.1371/journal.pmed.0030449

Ferguson, Kim, Rochelle C Cassells, Jack W MacAllister and Gary W Evans (2013) The physical environment and child development: An international review, *International Journal of Psychology* 48(4), 437–468

Finkelhor, David (1999) Child sexual abuse: Challenges facing child protection and mental health professionals, in Elisabeth Hullman and Werner Hilweg (eds) *Childhood and trauma: Separation, abuse and war*, Aldershot: Ashgate

Foster, Holly and Jeanne Brooks-Gunn (2009) Toward a stress process model of children's exposure to physical family and community violence, *Clinical Child and Family Psychology Review* 12, 71–94

Fowler P J, D B Henry, M Schoeny, J Taylor and D Chavira (2014) Developmental timing of housing mobility: Longitudinal effects on externalizing behaviors among at-risk youth, *Journal of the American Academy of Child and Adolescent Psychiatry* 53(2), 199–208

Gelles, Richard (1992) Poverty and violence towards children, *American Behavioral Scientist* 35(3), 258–274

Gordon, David, Shaileen Nandy, Christine Pantazis, Simon Pemberton and Peter Townshend (2003) *Child poverty in the developing world*, Bristol: The Policy Press

Hanf et al. (2014) Global determinants of mortality in under 5s: 10 year worldwide longitudinal study, *BMJ* 347, f6427

Hillis, S, J Mercy, A Amobi and H Kress (2016) Global prevalence of past-year violence against children: A systematic review of minimum estimates, *Pediatrics* 137(3), 1–13

Lalor, K (2008) Child sexual abuse and HIV transmission in sub-Saharan Africa, *Child Abuse Review* 17(2), 94–107

Landers, C, C Da Silva e Paula and T Kilbane (2013) Preventing violence against young children, in P R Britto, P L Engle, and C M Super (eds) *Handbook of early childhood development research and its impact on global policy*, Oxford: Oxford University Press, pp. 242–260

Lauderdale, Diane (2006) Birth outcomes for Arabic-named women in California before and after September 11, *Demography* 43(1), 185–201

Luthar, Suniya and Dante Cicchetti (2000) The construct of resilience: Implications for interventions and social policies, *Developmental Psychopathology* 12(4), 857–885

Margolin, Gayla and Elana B Gordis (2000) The effects of family and community violence on children, *Annual Review of Psychology* 51, 445–479

McEwen, Bruce (1998) Stress, adaptation, and disease: Allostasis and allostatic load, *Annals of the New York Academy of Sciences* 840, 33–44

Mead, Hilary K, Theodore P Beauchaine and Katherine E Shannon (2010) Neurobiological adaptations to violence across development, *Developmental Psychopathology* 22(1), 1

National Scientific Council on the Developing Child (2012) *The science of neglect: The persistent absence of responsive care disrupts the developing brain*, working paper 12. Available at http://developingchild.harvard.edu/resources/the-science-of-neglect-the-persistent-absence-of- responsive-care-disrupts-the-developing-brain/

Osofsky, Joy (1999) The impact of violence on children, *The Future of Children* 9(3), 33–49

Piaget, J (1952) *The origins of intelligence in children*, New York: International Universities Press

Pollack, Seth (2016) Multilevel developmental approaches to understanding the effects of child maltreatment: Recent advances and future challenges, *Developmental Psychopathology* 27 (4 Pt 2), 1387–1397

Rodriguez, Alfredo *et al.* (2014) Visible and invisible violence and inequality in neoliberal Santiago, *Environment and Urbanization* 26(2), 359–373

Sabri, B, J S Hong, J C Campbell and H Cho (2013). Understanding children and adolescents' victimizations at multiple levels: An ecological review of the literature, *Journal of Social Service Research* 39(3), 322–334

Stoltenborgh, M, M H van IJzendoorn, E M Euser and M J Bakermans-Kranenburg (2011) A global perspective on child sexual abuse: Meta-analysis of prevalence around the world, *Child Maltreatment* 16, 79–101

Stoltenborgh, Marije, Marian J BakermansKranenburg and Marinus H van IJzendoorn (2013) The neglect of child neglect: A metaanalytic review of the prevalence of neglect, *Social Psychiatry and Psychiatric Epidemiology* 48(3), 345–355

UNICEF Bangladesh (2010) *Understanding urban inequalities in Bangladesh: A prerequisite for achieving Vision 2021*, Dhaka: UNICEF

UNICEF (2014) *Hidden in plain sight: A statistical analysis of violence against children*, New York: UNICEF

Vygotsky, L S (1978) *Mind in society: The development of higher psychological processes*, M Cole, V John-Steiner, S Scribner and E Souberman (eds) Cambridge, MA: Harvard University Press, pp.79–91

Wachs, Theodore and Atif Rahman (2013) The nature and impact of risk and protective influences on children's development in low-income countries, in P R Britto, P L Engle, and C M Super (eds) *Handbook of early childhood development research and its impact on global policy*, Oxford: Oxford University Press, pp. 85–122

Walker, Susan P, Theodore Wachs, Julie Meeks Gardner, Betsy Lozoff, Gail Wasserman, Ernesto Pollitt and Julie A Carter (2007) Child development: Risk factors for adverse outcomes in developing countries, *The Lancet* 369(9556), 145–157

Walker, Susan P, Susan M Chang, Marcos Vera-Hernández and Sally Grantham-McGregor (2011) Early childhood stimulation benefits adult competence and reduces violent behavior, *Pediatrics* 127(5), doi:10.1542/peds.2010–2231

WHO (2013) *Global and regional estimates of violence against women: Prevalence and health effects of intimate partner violence and non-partner sexual violence*, Geneva: World Health Organization, WHO/RHR/HRP/13.06

Wilkinson, Richard G and Kate Pickett (2009) *The spirit level: Why more equal societies almost always do better*, London: Allen Lane

Wood, Denis and Robert Beck (1994) *Home rules*, Baltimore and London: Johns Hopkins University Press

Ziervogel, Gina, Mark Pelling *et al.* (2017) Inserting rights and justice into urban resilience: A focus on everyday risk, *Environment and Urbanization* 29(1)

# 3

# HOME

In a harsh world, home is often assumed to be the safest place for children. But pressures within households can be extreme, young children are a captive audience, and the very privacy of those four walls can encourage behaviour that might not be sanctioned elsewhere. Home is where children, especially younger children, most commonly face violence, whether they experience it themselves or watch it happening to other people – most often their mothers. The more hidden quality of trouble at home adds to its burden for children. It strikes at a basic sense of security and is more personal and harder to avoid. In Nepal, even in the context of civil war, with abduction, injury and death as daily possibilities, children made it clear to my Nepali research assistant that their own drunken fathers were much more frightening than the shadowy Maoist combatants in nearby forests.

How common is the experience of violence? As I noted in the last chapter, this is a difficult question. It is not like establishing the prevalence of road traffic accidents or malaria (although that also has its challenges). Data collection is uneven; definitions can differ and there is an understandable reluctance to report acts of abuse, especially sexual abuse. Figures vary considerably depending on who is being asked. Rates reported by children who have experienced harsh treatment, whether at the time or in later years, are many times higher than those reported by parents or other informants. But our imprecise knowledge about prevalence is not really the issue here. My interest is in exploring what precipitates the violent event, how it is experienced and how it relates to the home itself.

## The experience of violence at home

Data from UNICEF's regular MICS household surveys, which draw on parent reports, indicate that the great majority of children in the world are routinely disciplined at home through the use of physical force or verbal intimidation, more or less extreme. Harsh discipline is considered, in fact, to be the most common form of violence that children experience (excluding neglect) (UNICEF, 2014). This fact, and the corresponding level of attention given to this concern in the global child protection enterprise, calls for some initial discussion.

Discipline and child abuse are of course not really the same thing, although the overlap can be considerable. Even the most abusive parents often think of their behaviour in terms of teaching children or protecting them from harm. The line between discipline and abuse is not drawn in the same place even by people in the same country dealing with the same legal constraints and social norms. And indeed the range of behaviours involved covers a wide spectrum. According to their parents, about seven out of every ten children are routinely subjected to psychological assaults – and this can include everything from insults and shouts to extreme humiliation and terror. Six out of ten children are physically disciplined on a routine basis. Some of them are slapped or shaken, but for two of the six, the punishment is extreme – they may be kicked, burned, choked and battered. More often than not, children experience a combination of more or less violent methods.

There are ongoing debates around corporal punishment especially, with tensions between firm rights-based standards that reject it completely, and a more fluid acceptance of local values. The normative framework of children's rights is far from congenial to all. Michael Wessells, a child protection practitioner and researcher, points to the strong backlash from many frustrated parents. In Sierra Leone, for instance, when community members were asked to identify the various harms that children could experience, they included child rights in their list – along with heavy labour, teenage pregnancy, a lack of schooling and other evils. The rights-based demonization of corporal punishment had from their perspective undermined their parental capacity to control children and instil good values, and could potentially lead to more harmful alternatives, like denying children food instead (Wessells, 2015). This disagreement is at the core of much of the child protection enterprise worldwide. Parenting programmes, the most ubiquitous protection intervention, are designed, among other things, to shift local norms and to persuade parents of the sound rationale for modifying their harsher practices.

An interesting question in the MICS survey is whether parents believe corporal punishment is a necessary part of child rearing. Only a minority of mothers, as it turns out, three out of ten on average, agree that it is a necessity, and fathers' attitudes are very similar. In some countries the figure is higher, but there are only three countries where more than half the mothers think that corporal punishment is necessary. The gap between these figures and the number of parents who actually report using physical punishment is anywhere from 10 to 60 per cent (UNICEF, 2014). This discrepancy between belief and practice is intriguing. People often say what they feel is expected in surveys, and that could be a factor here. The question, coming at the end of the survey module, implies a value judgement in a way that the other questions do not, and that might cause parents to pull back and reconsider their response. But it is also worth bearing this discrepancy in mind when we consider the extent to which harsh treatment may stem from factors other than parental conviction and a sense of duty. This is at least in part where the role of stress comes in.

What these surveys signally fail to uncover is the intention behind the disciplinary event, and the meaning that children give to it. These numbers do not represent a single phenomenon. The harsh treatment of children is a complex stew of discipline, custom, control, worry, exasperation and sadism. When the purpose is to inflict pain and fear, children feel the difference. Trevor Noah, in his account of growing up poor in South Africa, explains: "In all the times I received beatings from my mom, I was never scared of her. I didn't like it, certainly … I didn't necessarily agree with her thinking but I understood it was discipline and it was being done for a purpose. The first time Abel [stepfather] hit me, I felt something I had never felt before. I felt terror" (Noah, 2016, p. 262). Without knowing how a child experiences treatment at the hands of an adult, our understanding of the harm done is seriously incomplete.

Trevor Noah didn't like it when his mother beat him, but he wasn't frightened of her or especially undone by the experience. Possibly he found it no worse than many of the other tedious aspects of being parented. But in an impoverished rural area in Somaliland, there were cases where, according to some parents, "beating and scolding upset children so profoundly that they became suicidal, and some reportedly killed themselves by hanging or jumping into the water catchments" (Wessells et al., 2013, p. 17). This is a response of an entirely different order, and it is not clear how we can reasonably see these experiences as equivalent, even if the scoldings or beatings were of similar intensity.

Another important metric that is not explored by the MICS survey is the degree to which parents consider corporal punishment to be harmful. The fact that most see beating as unnecessary says nothing about whether they view it as detrimental. In Wessell's ethnographic study in Sierra Leone, and in related studies in several other countries in Africa, when community members were asked to list the most significant harms to children, physical abuse barely made it onto the radar. The far more important issues as perceived by parents were the lack of education, sexual abuse, early pregnancy, drug and alcohol use (Kostelny, Wessells and Ondoro, 2014; Kostelny et al., 2013; Wessells and Kostelny, 2012). This does not mean that parents everywhere would share this perspective, but it is another insight into how variable views can be on the subject. Some parents rely on physical discipline. Some are conflicted about it. Some don't see it as a weighty issue one way or another. Some wonder how else in a violent world children might learn that they won't break when struck, and that they can have confidence in their own hardy bodies. Firm rights–base standards make excellent sense if they can prevent the agony of the suicidal children in Somaliland or deny the sadists a justification for their brutality. They remain a more understandably contested domain when they challenge locally accepted norms around responsible parenting.

Sexual abuse is generally considered a more serious concern by almost all parents, but is also surrounded by far greater secrecy. The available reports – which point to sexual abuse for between about 5 and 30 per cent of children – are thought to be significant underestimates because of the general reluctance to discuss the problem (UNICEF, 2014). What figures are available tend not to distinguish between sexual abuse at home and away from home. The general consensus is that, especially for younger children, home is most often the site of this abuse, with the perpetrator most often a male household member, although neighbours and relatives are also frequently involved. The targeting of younger children has been noted particularly in some places where HIV is prevalent, sometimes as a way to avoid infection, in other cases in the belief that sex with a small child may even be curative (Lalor, 2008). But our understanding of the situation within homes remains limited.

Neglect as noted is the most understudied and least measured form of child maltreatment, despite having a potential impact as severe as that of violent abuse. This is not unexpected, given levels of poverty in many countries and the difficulty of determining culpability in situations of deprivation. Neglect is generally defined as the failure to meet children's physical or psychological needs by those responsible for them who have the means to do so – but the "means to do so" aspect can be tricky, as will be discussed in this chapter.

Violence between siblings is the means by which young children are considered most likely to experience aggression (at least in the United States, the only place where relevant research appears to be available). Yet even here it is a little studied and seldom reported form of family violence (Krienert and Walsh, 2011). It is more common and more likely to be chronic than violence among peers outside the family, especially for younger children. Its significance, however, is often downplayed and it tends to be treated as a normal part of growing up. Acts that might be viewed as serious assaults if they were inflicted by an adult are seldom taken seriously when they occur between children. And yet sibling violence can be frightening and unremitting. The very normality that is assumed around it can make it more difficult for a victimized child to avoid, and the effects, like other forms of violence, can be damaging and long-lasting.

Domestic or intimate partner violence is a critically important feature of children's experience of violence in their homes. One young girl in Bogotá describes her mother's experience: "He abused her a lot. He hit her a lot, a lot, a lot, a lot. And that's how it was … I never forget that, never, never, never … He hit her with everything … We saw a lot of that and it affected me a lot … it still affects me" (Ritterbusch, 2012, p. 74). There is considerable evidence, as noted in the last chapter, that simply witnessing family violence can be as damaging for children as experiencing it personally. A multi-country study found that among the most consistent risk factors for suicide attempts on the part of women in low-income countries was having had a mother who experienced domestic violence (DeVries et al., 2011).

Intimate partner violence is increasingly recognized as a serious social issue. Forty years ago, even in a country as progressive as Sweden, attention had to be drawn to the scale of the problem and to the fact that violence in the privacy of the home should not be politely ignored. But despite the growing mass of evidence from country after country, and despite rights conventions and national laws, women in high numbers continue to endure violence from their partners. In some countries, progress is even being rolled back – in 2017, the Russian parliament voted to decriminalize domestic violence.

Despite the growing attention to the problem, remarkable numbers of people still acknowledge that they find spousal abuse acceptable. A standard question in routine global demographic and health surveys is whether men are justified in beating their wives under certain circumstances. Surprisingly, women are more likely to justify wife-beating than men are, and adolescents are just as likely to condone it as older men and women. In a sample of over 100 countries, almost all of them low and middle-income, 44 per cent of adolescent girls felt that wife-beating was acceptable in some circumstances. In some countries over 90 per cent of those questioned justified spousal abuse (UNICEF, 2014).

When women are being beaten, children are also more likely to be a target. It is not always the father in these cases who abuses the children – the experience of violence can also push women over the edge. Nor does the abuse of children necessarily end if their parents are separated. There is also the potential harm directly to the developing foetus when violence is directed at pregnant women, a not uncommon situation that can mean higher risks of miscarriage, complications, pre-term delivery, perinatal death and low birth weight. Infants' health may also be affected. Women who are the victims of abuse themselves are less likely to be able to provide good care and more likely to be depressed, more likely to neglect children.

There is an interesting conflation of acceptance and secrecy in the case of violence towards both women and children. In Peru, for example, children in the Young Lives sample staunchly defended the harsh treatment they were subjected to as being "not violence" but an appropriate strategy on the part of parents, who had the responsibility to rear them properly. At the same time, they spoke of their reluctance to disclose these beatings to their friends and neighbours. They didn't want to embarrass their parents, or to call down further punishment on themselves. This combination of secrecy and acceptance can be a lethal package – and the acceptance in particular helps to reproduce violence as a solution from generation to generation. Yet the very disquiet around violence in the home probably provides an entry point for alternatives (Guerrero and Rojas, 2016).

Although abuse occurs within all social strata, the evidence points to higher rates for low-income women, as for children. There are some specific questions for this chapter: how much does housing mediate these higher rates of abuse for women and children in poverty, and to what extent does abuse, in turn, complicate the business of being adequately housed? With regard to neglect as well, we look at the degree to which is intensified and made difficult to avoid by the material circumstances of the home and its surroundings.

## The physical ecology of abuse and neglect

Over recent decades, the understanding of child abuse has for the most part moved away from a clinical view of adult deviance and towards a recognition of the context in which both child and perpetrator are embedded. This ecological model of child maltreatment was articulated in 1977 by James Garbarino, who suggested that the problem was more productively approached by considering all the things that can encourage a "climate for child abuse" – from immediate household pressures and an absence of social support in the community, to larger conditions like crop failures, unemployment or cultural attitudes about the right way to rear children. Multiple adversities can combine to create a threshold at which abuse or neglect are more likely to occur – unemployment along with drug abuse and social isolation, for instance, would be more likely to precipitate abuse than any of these factors alone. For families in poverty, these kinds of risk factors more often co-exist and reinforce one another (Garbarino, 1977). There is plentiful evidence from the global north, and some from the south, relating parents' poverty, their stress and their sense of control in life to the risk of physical child abuse and neglect. Mothers who are exhausted, frustrated or depressed are more likely to compromise in their desire to do their best for their children, and may even become abusive. As researchers from Scotland point out, it is not just what a child does but how the parent is feeling. According to one mother, "This is terrible but when I'm stressed, you know what I mean … you snap easier. And that's not my son's fault" (Brownlie and Anderson, 2006).

Given the more general lack of attention to the physical environment in children's lives, it is perhaps not unexpected that even within these ecological approaches to child abuse and neglect, it is unusual to find attention to housing. Leroy Pelton, a professor of social work and a tireless advocate for the homeless over many decades, was perhaps the first to point explicitly to this link. He proposed in the 1990s that in many situations it was the material hardships related to poverty rather than poverty itself that explained the connection to abuse. Physical conditions, he insisted, are critical mediating factors (Pelton, 1994). There are two pathways, as Pelton explained it, that can lead from poverty to child maltreatment. One has to do with the child harm that can result directly from the health and safety hazards of inadequate housing. The other pathway relates to the parental stress that results from material hardships, leading to the anger that can result in abuse, or the depression that contributes to neglect. Later research by Pelton continued to support the contention that difficult material conditions contribute to the higher rates of "what is construed as child abuse and neglect" among people in poverty – "construed" because of how hard it is to justify in many cases the allegations of neglect especially. Pelton's later work contains a careful analysis of the social justice implications for the field of child protection, and will be returned to in a later section (2015). (In a horrifying and ironic coda, Pelton was found dead of multiple stab wounds in his Nevada apartment in 2016.)

Since Pelton's early work in the 1990s, Gary Evans (who was discussed in the last chapter) and his colleagues have provided compelling evidence of the cumulative strain that bad housing can impose on family relationships (Evans and English, 2002; Evans, Brooks-Gunn and Klebanov, 2011). People in poverty, it goes without saying, are most likely to experience these conditions and are most constrained in the capacity to deal effectively with them.

Living conditions are fundamentally related to the way caregivers deal with children.

Difficult conditions drain energy and emotional resources, whether through crowding, dilapidation, high noise levels, unsuitable space, insecurity or a sheer lack of the basic amenities needed for day-to-day survival. These stressors are not conducive to responsive, supportive, flexible behaviour with young children. Overcrowded housing or a lack of safe play space or an inability to pay the rent may not be sufficient in themselves to result in abuse or neglect, but they contribute to a situation within which harm is more likely to occur. Sometimes housing is a precipitating factor; sometimes it just adds to the burdens. When people feel they cannot control their circumstances, they may also be more likely to believe that harsher and more coercive discipline is necessary with children.

I'll first discuss the connections between neglect and living conditions, and then the ways that housing quality and organisation contribute to the abusive treatment of children and women. Then I'll turn to housing security and its often reciprocal relationship with domestic abuse. After a look at how chaotic neighbourhoods can affect children's home lives, the chapter closes with a final section on children in residential care. Because there is so little research from the global south that adequately explores the dynamics within homes, this chapter leans more heavily towards the global north than is true for most of the book. Several examples here come from my own research in rural Vermont in the 1990s with young mothers who had moved in and out of homelessness or near homelessness for years.

## Neglect and material conditions

The absence of data on the prevalence of neglect in most of the world is not surprising. It is simply too difficult to separate culpable neglect from the difficulties and impossible choices that often face parents in poverty. As Leroy Pelton pointed out, "Because the diligence of care necessary to protect a child in a dangerous environment is greater than in a safer environment, poor parents are more susceptible to a judgment of neglect" (2015, p. 34).

The difficulties for many households can include a lack of sanitation, a long distance to water points, long lines once there and punishing loads to carry back. There can be bedding to put away and take out each day, poor protection from the elements, finicky cooking arrangements, no refrigeration, no waste collection services. These trying conditions most often occur in clusters. Overburdened mothers can be forced to leave children unsupervised and to cut corners in every aspect of childcare. Women in many settings speak of their gruelling workloads and the fatigue that undermines their capacity to cope adequately with their children's needs. In the Dominican Republic, for instance, mothers were well aware of the importance of protecting their children from diarrhoea but said that frequently they were just too exhausted to boil water (Mclennan, 2000). They didn't need hygiene classes. They needed clean water.

I refer repeatedly to mothers here, and will continue to. This is not because I don't recognize fathers, grandparents, sisters, neighbours and all they do. It's because mothers still do most of the childcare in most places, and because the word "caregiver" seems a bit clinical. I'll assume that readers are mentally flexible enough to include these other "caregivers" in their understanding where that seems appropriate.

The heavy burdens faced by mothers are not exclusive to households in third world slums. Liz, one of the young mothers I worked with in Vermont, was repeatedly scolded by social workers because of the reeking piles of urine-soaked bedding and unwashed clothing stacked in plastic bags around her apartment. She had four small sons, no day care, no car, no washing machine, no place outdoors to hang wet laundry. The nearest laundromat was two miles away and there was no public transportation in this small town. Because taxis were expensive and it was so difficult to supervise four small children in the laundromat, she made the trip as seldom as possible. The two younger children went unclothed most of the time, and for that reason were seldom taken outdoors.

It is not only a matter of time and money pressures. When mothers lack the control over conditions to be able to cope with children adequately, they often become more fatalistic and less appropriately vigilant. In a Kathmandu slum where I spent time, shallow open drains crisscrossed the settlement, carrying all kinds of foul waste to the river nearby. It was almost impossible for small children to play in the area without coming into contact with the contents of these drains. Despite their awareness of the health dangers, busy mothers often turned a blind eye to small children playing in the contaminated muck. When a ball bounced into a drain, for instance, children just jumped in after it, and mothers, weary of shouting or hauling them out by the arms or fetching and washing the ball themselves, just pretended not to notice. The alternative was leaving children unattended in their small shacks, isolated from friends, while the women washed clothing or dishes outdoors.

Women do manage for the most part, but at a considerable cost in terms of effort and anxiety. A mother in Bangalore described the effort it took to cope with her small children when she went to squat in the high weeds, in the absence of a nearby toilet:

> I take both of them with me when I need to go ... or they need to go, as I'm scared to leave them alone here ... it is very difficult; when I squat I have to hold both their hands ... or when I am with one of them the other one wanders away and I have to shout at them to come back ... the tracks are right there so I am scared they might go there ... or to the khada – god knows what is there, bad people, snakes everything!
>
> (Nallari, 2014, p. 328)

The risks are significant – and not only snakes or bad people or railroad tracks or contaminated surroundings. The housing problems that contribute to de facto neglect are also frequently the cause of young children's injuries, 95 per cent of which occur in low- and middle-income countries, and 90 per cent of which are related to the lack of supervision (WHO and UNICEF, 2008). Faulty wiring, unprotected cooking arrangements, unsafe heating, an absence of proper storage for kerosene, insecticides and the like, all increase the need for vigilance. In a settlement occupied by displaced people in Puntland, fires sometimes erupted, spreading rapidly through the flimsy huts constructed from scraps of material. They frequently killed children who were unable to escape because they had been tied to a pole to prevent them from wandering when their mothers were out. It was also common for babies to be seriously burned when they crawled into open cooking fires (Wessells et al., 2013).

In a resettlement community I visited in South Africa, some young children had been poisoned by drinking paraffin, which they thought was water. Households had been running dry because city water tankers failed to arrive when scheduled in the distant part of the city the community had been moved to. Accidental paraffin poisonings are not uncommon. Paraffin is often the most convenient fuel available for lighting, cooking and heating in poor settlements and safe storage can be difficult to provide in one-room shacks. In the context of sub-par housing and provision, it can be hard to avoid sometimes lethal neglect.

Even housing layout can be a factor. In public housing in the Bronx in New York City, where tiny kitchens were separated visually from other rooms, mothers were unable to monitor small children as they played – but nor could they safely allow them underfoot in the kitchen (Iltus, 1994). Far from the Bronx, in Tamil Nadu, India, after the 2004 tsunami, I worked with women whose homes had been destroyed, to see how the one-size-fits-all replacement housing plans might be improved without a substantial increase in cost. Most women pointed out how difficult it would be to monitor small children in one-room houses without a window in the kitchen area or enough space indoors for play. The shock of the tsunami made them especially anxious about their children. Most women expected that they would just have to do their cooking outdoors.

The fear of children drowning goes beyond floods and tsunamis. In Bangladesh, 17,000 children drown each year, and in several Asian countries, drowning is the leading cause of death for children between 1 and 4. The vast majority of these mostly rural deaths occur in the course of everyday life, mostly very close to home, when children escape the supervision of their busy mothers (Linnan et al., 2012).

Mothers coping with material constraints may find it difficult to be as vigilant as they would like, but also to manage the emotional responsiveness that is so crucial to young children. This is why severe neglect may be as damaging to children's outcomes over time as physical abuse. It can interfere with cognitive and social development and even result in substantial impairment. The situation can be complicated by depression or mental illness, which may contribute to mothers being withdrawn or inconsistently present, placing children at risk for a range of developmental delays, behavioural issues and later problems.

Evidence globally of the high burden of mental health problems shows poor women in low-income countries at highest risk (Patel and Kleinman, 2003). This evidence indicates that common mental disorders are linked less to income levels than to the unpredictability, anxiety, insecurity and hopelessness that can accompany poverty and the lack of basic necessities. These factors are so clearly intensified by difficult and insecure housing conditions.

A critical component of neglect is the difficulty finding adequate care for young children while parents work. Tens of millions of young children under 5 are left alone every day, or with other small children. In Botswana, Mexico and Vietnam, interviews with working caregivers (a sample of over 500 who attended government health clinics) revealed that in over a third of their families, young children were left unattended while parents went to work. This was never the solution of choice. One Mexican woman explained that she had recently left her violent husband and had to support herself and her 3-year-old son. She had no one she could turn to for child care. "If I took him to work, la señora would tell me: 'I don't want you working here with your son.' ... I would be heartbroken when I saw that my son stayed there crying ... It was something very sad that I wish it doesn't happen to anybody" (Ruiz-Casares and Heymann, 2009, p. 316).

Another study in the very violent city of Ciudad Juarez, Mexico, where many women work in the *maquiladora* assembly plants, found that three mothers out of ten left their children shut up alone at home for at least three hours a day in the absence of childcare options. Their work hours changed weekly, making childcare especially difficult to arrange. Mothers pieced together care as best they could, but found it impossible in the end not to leave even small children alone for at least some of the time. The outcomes for children are distressing, according to a local child advocacy and research group – "namely delay and regression in development, in sphincter control and in psychomotor and language skills, with boys and girls barely five years old displaying symptoms of anxiety and stress" (Ramírez Hernández, 2012, p. 16).

Few countries, rich or poor, make childcare a priority. In India alone, an estimated 20 million children under 6 with parents in the informal work force have no access to childcare, and this is a country that actually has a system in place, just not one that is good enough. UNICEF reports that globally 17 per cent of children under 5 are left alone at home or under the care of a child under 10 (UNICEF, 2012), and that there are only seventeen countries where high-quality affordable care is available to at least half the preschool population (UNICEF, 2015). This is extraordinarily pound-foolish. Decent childcare is a starting point in tackling poverty. Especially in urban areas, changes in family structure and women's work patterns make it critical to the survival strategies of households. There are also all the important consequences for children – their physical safety, the proven cognitive gains and the entry point that childcare services provide for health and nutrition supports.

Because of the dearth of reasonable childcare options, many parents who move to the city for work leave young children behind with grandparents, many of them frail and hard-pressed to make this arrangement work. It is not surprising that in China, the drowning rate for children left with grandparents is three times higher than for children living with their parents (Linnan et al., 2012).

In Kyrgizstan, in the villages I visited, there were more small children living with grandparents than with their parents, most of whom had left for work in Bishkek.

One old woman, caring alone for two children, was in poor health and spent most of her time in bed. Her 6-year-old granddaughter took care of almost everything, fetching water with her small brother, carrying wood, lighting fires. Sometimes, said the old lady, as her grandchildren patted her cheek and urged her to eat, she would pretend to be dead so that the children could get used to the idea.

The World Health Organization acknowledges that parents (or grandparents) without the resources to ensure their children's needs, whether to adequate shelter or other basics, cannot reasonably be considered guilty of neglect. But WHO does not take the extra step of placing explicit responsibility at the feet of government or other actors. And where formal systems *are* in place to respond to neglect, parents may be penalized by their poverty rather than supported to deal with it. The National Coalition for Child Protection Reform in the United States highlights the risks even in a high-income country:

> Imagine that you are an impoverished single mother with a four-year-old daughter and an infant son. The infant is ill with a fever and you need to get him medicine. But you have no car, it's very cold, pouring rain, and it will take at least an hour to get to and from the pharmacy. You don't know most of your neighbors and those you know you have good reason not to trust. What do you do? Go without the medicine? That's "medical neglect." The child savers can take away your children for medical neglect. Bundle up the feverish infant in the only, threadbare coat he's got and take him out in the cold and rain? That's "physical neglect." The child savers can take away your children for physical neglect. Leave the four-year-old to care for the infant and try desperately to get back home as soon as you can? That's "lack of supervision." The child savers can take away your children for lack of supervision. And in every one of those cases, the child savers would say, with a straight face, that they didn't take your children "because of poverty alone".
>
> *(NCCPR, 2011)*

Another of their examples illustrates the way housing problems increase a family's vulnerability to accusations of neglect:

> In Houston, a family living in unsafe housing moves to the only "gated community" it can afford after the father loses his job: a 12 x 25 foot storage unit. The father builds a loft area and shelves. The unit has electricity, heat and air conditioning. The family lives there, and the children do well, for three years. Then someone calls Child Protective Services. CPS removes the children on the spot – without lifting a finger to help to find the family housing.
>
> *(NCCPR, 2011)*

Halfway around the world in one of the remoter provinces in Afghanistan, there is wide acceptance of wife-beating and harsh discipline with children, all in the context of more general conflict that seems never to end. But consider also what a local doctor described to me – the endless winters and the cramped houses shared by animals and large extended families, where it is impossible to stay warm. The miserable outdoor latrines are virtually unusable, and children are pushed outside to defecate in the filthy packed snow right by the door. The mountain roads are impassable and people cannot grow enough food to last them through the winter. Hunger is a constant. Opium poppies grow far better than food crops in the rocky soil, and to placate hungry children it is not unusual for mothers to blow opium smoke into their mouths. Is this neglect? Abuse? And can it possibly be separated from the grinding poverty that results in this unbearable solution to children's hunger pains?

## Housing quality and abuse

Although the quality of housing can most intuitively be related to neglect, there are also close connections to the likelihood of abuse. The association of crowding with violence towards children is the most solidly researched aspect of this relationship – it has been noted for some time and in a range of settings in both the global north and the south. A study in the USA by Susan Zuravin in the 1980s concluded that residential density was far more than simply a proxy for social class or income. When these other variables were controlled for, higher density (measured as 1.51 persons per room) was still significantly associated with reported incidents of child abuse and neglect (Zuravin, 1986). One can only speculate what this might mean in places where that ratio is closer to five persons per room, a level of household crowding that applies to a third of children globally. But is this not a question of what people are used to? Density may be an objective measure, but it is widely accepted that culture mediates what we perceive as crowding. In fact, though, there is research (from Gary Evans again) demonstrating that high residential density is physiologically stressful in the same ways for people regardless of culture and regardless of their sense of whether a given situation is in fact "crowded" (Evans, Lepore and Allen, 2000).

Confined household space limits the activities that are possible for children and often means they are underfoot at inconvenient times. Behaviour that might be acceptable under other conditions can become intolerable when space is tight and can mean higher levels of irritation on the part of adults. Crowded living may also mean that adults have no place to withdraw to for a break when they need to control their irritation. Crowded conditions increase the need for discipline, and when stress levels are high, this can take punitive forms. Crowding may contribute to the likelihood of abuse, but also to the subsequent level of fear and anxiety for the children involved.

In my Vermont research, one of the families lived in a tiny cramped dilapidated apartment, only a marginal improvement over the homeless shelter. The few small rooms were too tight to turn around in, the front porch was rotted through, and right beyond it was a busy road. Clarissa, the young mother, described how hard she found it to deal with her two children there. "You get a sense that you are trapped. There's no place for kids to run, not much space for them to play in. I get very edgy. I get grouchy and snappish. I don't really want to deal with them. I just want them to leave me alone. I feel so trapped …" (Bartlett, 1998, p. 411).

An important issue here is the extent to which a developing child can respond to her need for play and exploration without adding substantially to adult stress. A parent's frustrations with a small child often stem from her interaction with the physical environment – knocking things over, making too much noise, running where it is not appropriate. The most common reason that mothers gave for "smacking" a small child in Scotland was that they had done or were about to do something dangerous. The harder it is to arrange a house to minimize danger, the more opportunities there are for smacking. Bad wiring, unprotected stairways, exposed hot water pipes, wobbly side tables, a lack of safe storage space all conspire to maximize the smacks. This is the flip side of neglect. Many mothers, depending on their mood and their energy level, may swing back and forth from ignoring to erupting.

The concept of "environmental chaos" is useful here. This is a summary term that refers to crowding, dilapidation, high noise levels, people coming and going and a lack of structure and control in daily life, and it has been found across cultures to be linked to fatigue and to less sustained, less predictable, less well-regulated interactions between children and adults (Wachs, 2010). Children become less responsive to social cues, more prone to problem behaviour and adults are more likely to use harsh discipline. Given that younger children are more likely to be those underfoot at home, it stands to reason that they are most frequently the victims. Older children are better able to put distance between themselves and an angry adult.

Many of the same pressures seem to fuel violence towards women as well. Crowding, housing problems, frequent family moves, a lack of home conveniences, features of rental housing and of public housing, have all been related in the United States to both women's and children's exposure to violence. Some of these factors, it is hypothesized, affect the quality and frequency of interaction between households, an important protective factor in family life. Research from the global south is more limited, although some work points to connections between crowding and violence.

There is also the implicit violence in the often sub-standard housing solutions that are made available to people in poverty. Tess Lea describes, in the context of indigenous communities in Australia, state housing so shoddy in quality as to send a not-so-hidden message about the value of the inhabitants. When the housing then falls into disrepair, householders are pathologized as the culprits (Lea and Pholeros, 2010). The stigma for families, so quickly communicated to children, carries its own burden of harm.

## Service provision

Poor provision for basic amenities complicates workloads and contributes to time burdens and stress in a range of ways. But it can also provoke abuse in situations where men feel their needs are not being adequately met. Long distances to fetch water, inefficient stoves, a lack of fuel and of provision for electricity, can all conspire to mean that clothes are not clean and food is not cooked in time. Common reasons for justifying wife-beating are that children are neglected or food is burned, and women all too often, as mentioned, consider this an adequate justification for their abuse. The Young Lives research has also pointed out that children in poorer homes are more likely to be overworked because of poor provision, and to risk punishment when they fail to perform these kinds of tasks satisfactorily. Work at home can also make them late for school, which means that children risk beatings from their teachers (Guerrero and Rojas, 2016; Morrow and Singh, 2016; Pankhurst, Negussie and Mulugeta, 2016; Vu, 2016).

There are implications for very small children too. Poor provision for sanitation and clean water contributes to malnutrition and repeated illness. (Malnutrition does not result just from the lack of calories. A contaminated environment means that calories go towards fighting infection rather than supporting growth.) This can make children more irritable and demanding, eroding parents' patience. A bizarre and fascinating explanation in this context is parasite stress theory, which relates the high prevalence of infectious disease and parasite loads to more general social trends including higher violence against children, and especially young children. Randy Thornhill and Corey Fincher postulate that the lower levels of health and ability in children who are infested with parasites, or whose mothers have been infested while they are in utero, make them more likely to become victims of violence than healthy children. Like other "parental animals", they explain, human parents "exhibit discriminative parental solicitude" (Thornhill and Fincher, 2011, p. 3473). Using population data from the United States, these researchers demonstrate that parasite levels (and the physical conditions that support them) are more strongly predictive of child abuse than either income levels or wealth disparities.

## Spatial organisation

It is not just a matter of the pressures that material conditions impose. The way space is organised and controlled can become a compelling part of how children are managed. This kind of control can be practical and constructive when it keeps children safe or protects privacy. But boundaries can also be punitive and damaging. The spatial rules imposed within any home are a potent means for defining and shaping family relationships, not all of them amiable. A British social worker described the value of making home visits: "It gives you a lot of ideas about how the family operates and who's in control. Sometimes, it's not what they say, it's what's about and how it's organised ..." (Jeyasingham, 2016, p. 7).

Clarissa, the young mother who chafed so at her children's demands in her cramped apartment, used boundaries as a way to cope with her frustration, in the process inflicting considerable confusion and emotional pain on her 5-year-old son. The connections between their housing and their family interactions were complicated and dynamic. There were two bedrooms in this apartment, neither one much larger than a big closet. She, the older man she lived with (not the father) and her 2-year-old daughter were crammed into one of these bedrooms. The edgy active boy had the other bedroom. This was repeatedly presented to him as a valuable privilege – he was the only one in the family with a room to himself. In the United States, the ability to give children their own rooms is an aspirational goal for many families in poverty. But the privilege in this case was more of a nightmare. Every time the boy became active or restless, raised his voice, fought with his sister, made demands or just took up too much space, he was sent to his room and told to close the door. He spent most of his time imprisoned alone in this dark, boring, lonely cave, cut off from interaction, denied the warmth and affection that his younger sister received. When he asked to come out, his mother would remind him how lucky he was to have his own room and most often would tell him to close the door again. All of this was communicated in a calm pleasant voice. Clarissa had attended parenting classes and had learned that it was better to explain than to scream or to beat. The boy's resentment of his sister was extreme – and when he acted on it, he quickly found himself incarcerated again. It stands to reason that aggression between siblings could have territorial overtones, especially in the context of limited space or resources, or when boundaries are used in this way to privilege one child over another.

There was another possibility here too, although Clarissa didn't mention it. Could she have been protecting her son? It's not an unreasonable guess. Her partner, unemployed and around the house most of the time, clearly disliked the boy. The less the child was around, the less chance there was of provoking this irritable man.

Spatial restrictions can be a legitimate expression of parental care. Healthy attachment between parent and child has a strong spatial dimension. Anthropologist Margaret Mead classified children of different ages in spatial terms – she talked about lap children, knee children, yard children and community children. Very young children instinctively seek contact and proximity, and are reluctant initially to go too far away from their mothers, who ideally respond to this need in a warm, protective way. But growing children also need to explore and experiment with independence. As they move from being knee children to being yard children (those who are fortunate enough to have a yard), they need more space. Most children still want to maintain some level of voice or visual contact with the person caring for them – and most parents are more relaxed if this contact is possible. Typically, small children come and go – venturing away, checking back in, going off again. When there is no yard or its equivalent, but just a heavily trafficked street or no easy access to the outdoors at all, it can thwart a child's natural tendency to explore and her mother's (or father's) natural tendency to become confident with a gradually increasing distance. Spatial restrictions can interfere with the flexible evolution of that attachment relationship between parent and child. Ideally this would stretch to accommodate the child's increasing range – like a rubber band connecting them. Instead these spatial restrictions seem to stimulate a kind of anxious inflexibility on both sides.

Liz, the young mother with four small boys who took part in my Vermont research, lived for a year in a low-income unit that opened directly onto a dead-end street. She was very anxious, though, about letting her boys out to play, worried that they might be hit by a car, no matter how slowly the traffic moved here. She had no way to take the children to a safer place to play, so she kept her younger boys indoors all the time and watched the others through a window, shouting at them constantly to be careful. Her 3-year-old, a headstrong, impulsive child, watched his older brothers through the window and resented being trapped indoors with a toddler. He made many attempts to break free, wrenching loose the bolts on doors, smashing through a window with his head, even climbing out a second-storey window onto the roof one day, and Liz responded with ever harsher punishment and control. She and the child were locked in a cycle of frustration and abuse (Bartlett, 1997).

More affluent households, even living in tight quarters, are better able to make up for confinement with outings to parks and playgrounds. For families in poverty, transportation is more of a challenge, parks are fewer and farther apart, neighbourhoods may be more daunting in a lot of ways. There is not much research exploring this link, especially in the south, but it does not take much imagination to understand how a small child's natural drive for play and exploration might result in conflict and abuse when children and caregivers are trapped together in a small apartment or a one-room shack – either that or a neglect born of exhaustion that could have serious results.

## Privacy

Not much formal evidence relates material conditions to the sexual abuse of children – but what there is focuses primarily on issues of privacy. Rachel Marcus, in her review of the connections between poverty and the sexual violation of children, notes the problems with shared sleeping space in overcrowded homes. Children in Botswana, for instance, said that this exposed them early to sexual activity and the likelihood of abuse. Marcus also points to the fact that poor families often depend on the good will of relatives or neighbouring landlords for shelter. When they are the abusers, a not uncommon reality, parents may be inclined to overlook the problem to ensure they keep a roof over their heads (Marcus, 2013). Research from Mombasa, describing the frequency with which small girls were raped or abused, also noted the reluctance of parents to disclose the situation when it involved a family member or a friend, especially when any dependency was involved. Instead, sleeping arrangements might be changed, or the child in question might be sent away to relatives to reduce the chance of repeated abuse (Kostelny et al., 2013).

In Kampala, Uganda, many Congolese refugees who could not afford more than one room for the family found children's exposure to sexual activity the most distressing aspect of the situation. "The father with the mother are here and the children are here, in between there is a curtain … There is no way an ear can be closed, you can close the eyes but cannot close the ears" (Horn et al., 2013, p. 45). They had concerns about awakening sexual feelings in children, and often older boys, deeply uncomfortable with the situation and especially with sleeping in such close quarters with their sisters, would simply move out – sometimes establishing a sexual relationship with an older woman on her own in order to have a place to stay.

Formal research on this topic is not plentiful, but the subject can come up more or less obliquely in the course of informal discussion. In a Mumbai slum resettlement project, for instance, the plans called for one-room units of 150 square feet for a family, and women spoke about the importance of adding room dividers to allow couples some privacy and to help protect children from unwanted attention. And after the 2004 tsunami in both Sri Lanka and India, it was a concern when replacement housing plans were being debated by the women I spent time with. Most of the planners and engineers working on the rebuilding efforts assumed that one-room replacement housing made sense since "this is what people are used to". In fact, though, both women and children made it clear that privacy was a serious problem, even if one-room dwellings *were* what they were accustomed to. Everywhere I went, some women sooner or later would raise the issue of the sexually fraught nature of one-room living. They wanted to use the rebuilding programme as a chance to tackle this problem (a fine example of the "bouncing forward" I mentioned in the last chapter). Young girls also talked about how uncomfortable it was to have no private place to dress and wash, and nowhere to hang their laundered menstrual cloths where they would be hidden from public view. This lack of privacy may or may not actually contribute to incidents of sexual harassment and abuse – but in the minds of young girls in country after country, the chance to wash, dress and use a latrine without this being a public event is a high priority. This will be discussed more in the chapter on neighbourhoods.

Although privacy can be deeply valued, especially by women and girls, it is definitely a double-edged sword. Feminist geographer Rachel Pain pointed out in 1997 that "an accurate map of urban rape would highlight far more bedrooms than alleyways and parks" (p. 233). Home can provide the kind of privacy and isolation that allows abuse to take place. Mo Hume points out in the context of urban El Salvador that even symbolic privacy can provide impunity for the abuser. It was hardly possible to conceal domestic abuse in the communities where she worked – walls were thin and houses close together. Yet men's violence towards their wives was treated as a strictly private affair (Hume, 2004).

Paula Meth brings another perspective to this conundrum. She argues that prevailing assumptions about privacy and abuse do not sufficiently question the material realities of the domestic space within which violence presumably occurs. She speaks of women in informal settlements in South Africa for whom the threat of violence is closely tied to the very flimsiness of their housing. Living in shacks made of cardboard, plastic tarpaulins and metal sheeting, they are unable to secure a door, to lock windows, or indeed to prevent their very walls from being ripped down. For women in Meth's study, questions about home were often more emotional and painful than questions about physical and sexual violence (Meth,

2003). Sturdy housing *can* provide the privacy (or the semblance of privacy) that allows for abuse, but on the other hand it can also offer protection, not only from male partners, but from burglary and rape by others. The point here is that the relationship between material conditions and violence is not simple or predictable, amenable to cookie cutter solutions. Many factors weigh in, but the material aspects cannot be dismissed.

## Housing security

It is not simply a matter of housing quality. Affordability and security are also fundamental to family stability. When resources are tight, a secure place to live is generally the most intractable problem for a family to deal with. A large body of research in the United States has pointed to the connections between this problem and the abuse of both children and women. Legal and social work professionals indicate across the board that they consider housing security to be a primary concern in these situations. Insecure housing can be a precipitating problem, but it also amplifies other problems, exacerbating the stress felt by parents. Unfortunately, almost no research exists on these links in the countries where housing insecurity is most common.

An increase in child abuse was a disturbing aspect of the trend of foreclosures in the United States after the 2008 housing bubble burst, with a spike in hospital admissions for abuse-related injuries. In 2011, for every 1 per cent increase in foreclosure rates over the prior twelve months in specific metropolitan areas, the rate of child abuse admissions was reported to have risen by up to 6.8 per cent. By contrast, and this is telling, no relationship was detected between unemployment rates and child abuse admission rates (Brunk, 2011).

It doesn't require the loss of a home. Even moving from one house to another can trigger the stress and become a risk factor for abuse. A robust relationship has been found between the occurrence of childhood abuse and the number of moves a household has experienced, even after controlling for other variables (Dong et al., 2005). In Thailand, research has also pointed to much higher rates of physical and emotional abuse for children in migrant families than in other demographically similar families (Jirapramukpitak et al., 2011). It is generally postulated that the parental stress associated with moving and the social isolation resulting from it are the reasons for increased rates of abuse.

My Vermont research made it clear how easily punitive treatment might also follow from having to live doubled up with friends or relatives. One mother, staying for some months with her mother-in-law in a small apartment, found it wore down her patience with her daughters, although they were not difficult children, "... here I'm always after the kids. Noise, how they treat stuff. I mean they can't break anything. I can understand. It's her home. But it's really hard for us. It's just not our home and I hate it!" This same family had moved twenty-four times in the nine years since the elder daughter was born – an average of once every four or five months, including time in homeless shelters or with relatives.

This 9-year-old was a remarkably bright, competent child – she taught herself to read at the age of 4, liked school and made friends easily in spite of the frequent moves. She was, perhaps, the classically "resilient" child that parents and policy makers dream of. But even for her, the moves began to take their toll. She was anxious about being left behind, despondent about the repeated loss of friends, and her mother worried that she would stop trying so hard at school. Another participant in this study remarked that teachers just stop paying attention to you if you're one of those children who never stay around for long.

## How domestic violence contributes to housing insecurity

The link between housing and violence is not uni-directional. Violence is also a pathway into housing problems, and is frequently what precipitates homelessness for women and children. As one child protection social worker described a situation, "… she's 26 years old years old, she has two children and she's pregnant. This woman didn't do anything to her children, she had a home, she was chased out of this home by an abusive relationship" (Shdaimah, 2009, p. 215).

In the United States, over half of all homeless women were found to be fleeing domestic violence (Guo, Slesnik and Feng, 2016). In Australia, despite legal provisions that can require the perpetrator to leave the violent home, it remains far more likely that the woman, in need of refuge, will be the one to leave (Meyer, 2016). A British study revealed that about 60 per cent of women who had left home did so because they were afraid that they or their children would be killed (Humphreys and Thiara, 2002). Rates could be as high in other parts of the world, but the research is primarily from high-income countries.

Janet Bowstead in the United Kingdom has focused in detail on women's use of space as a strategy to cope with domestic violence. She mapped the movement of over 500 women and their children, forced out of their homes by fear of violence. They took refuge in homeless shelters in different parts of the country as the first step in the long effort to find new housing; many women made multiple moves to a series of temporary homes. Sixty per cent had children with them, mostly under 5 years of age (Bowstead, 2012). More recently, Bowstead drew on administrative, survey and interview data to identify cases of internal migration in the country that fit this category of escaping abuse, which has remained invisible in most national surveys. Women typically stay as local as they can while attempting to avoid detection, but often cross administrative boundaries to access adequate support services (Bowstead, 2015).

Not all women fleeing violence become homeless, but they may be forced to move in with friends, to pay far more than they can afford, to skimp on other necessities, or to live in housing that is physically unsafe or illegal. Moving into a shelter may also be possible, but many women are reluctant because of crowding, inadequate security, potential abuse by other residents and rules that require residents to spend the day outside the shelter. There is also the fear that if they go to a shelter, their children might be taken away from them. This is not an unrealistic concern. Guo reports that among families seeking emergency shelter, in 62 per cent of cases, their children were placed in foster care (Guo, Slesnik and Feng, 2016).

Difficulty in finding alternative housing can leave mothers and children trapped by ongoing violence. Many women who try to leave home are forced back to their abusers because of economic needs, the most pressing of which is the cost of housing. When children are part of the situation, the economic difficulties of escaping violent relationships are even more daunting.

Women are often judged both for leaving and for failing to leave abusive partners, but the structural forces that shape these decisions are more often the issue than women's personal traits or shortcomings. A woman may move in with an abusive boyfriend because she has lost a housing subsidy, or invite him to move in with her because she cannot afford a mortgage payment. One women begged a judge not to incarcerate her abusive husband after a series of violent attacks, because she would have been unable to pay her bills without his contribution (Velonis et al., 2015).

Women are also more likely to experience eviction when they are victims of abuse, because of physical damage to a rental unit or because the police have been called in. Women who have been victims of abuse are also more likely to have subsequent housing problems; they are less likely to qualify for subsidized housing if they are residents of shelters for abused women or if they are known to have been victims of abuse. Women in Texas, for example, were told "'not to bother applying' for public housing because the local housing authority did not want people with 'that kind of history' living in public housing"(NNEDV–NLCHP, 2007, p. 113).

The impacts for children can be far-reaching. Time in shelters or constantly on the move can compound the risks presented by exposure to violence, contributing to the likelihood of behavioural problems, anxiety, depression, disrupted school attendance and poor academic performance. Children under 6 are especially vulnerable (Guo et al., 2016). Homelessness increases children's chances of becoming victims of violence and puts them at high risk of health problems – in the United States they were reported to have four times as many respiratory problems and five times as many episodes of diarrhoea. Mothers, preoccupied by their situation, find it much harder to provide the kind of care their children need.

People who experience abuse as children are also more likely to end up homeless later in their lives as a result of the impaired social relationships, behavioural problems and low levels of social support that are among the consequences of abuse. In one Ottawa sample of homeless individuals, 42 per cent of the men and 76 per cent of the women had been abused as children (Farrell et al., 2000).

Most of this body of research is from Canada and the USA. One exception is a study from Kenya on the "forced migration" of many pregnant women in the context of domestic violence. Women in rural Kenya are unlikely to initiate a move away from home because of their almost total dependence on the husband and his family. But it is not uncommon for men to force women out when they are considered to have transgressed, whether because they are HIV positive or guilty of actions considered inappropriate for a woman, such as pursuing an education, applying for a job, or refusing sex. Being "sent packing" or "chased away" is often the culmination of other kinds of violence and is considered a severe and deeply shaming form of punishment, which can result for women in the loss of accommodation, food security and support for children, as well as social status. Most often women are forced to return to their parents' home, although this is often temporary because of the lack of resources to support another person, and because of the shame associated with being rejected by the husband. In some cases leaving home *is* in fact a strategic choice on the women's part, to escape repeated or extreme violence. But this, the researchers explain, is considered less an indication of agency than the absence of any other options, "The majority suffer silently ..." (Turan et al., 2015, p. 8).

## Housing and property as a deterrent to domestic violence

These situations are an expression of the deep-seated structural insecurity of women and speak to the power relations that underlie violence. The obvious corollary here is the critical role of permanent secure housing in preventing domestic violence. Older research in the United States, assessing the comparative success of various abuse prevention strategies (job training and employment, training in independent living skills, legal support and other interventions) found they all lacked the power of secure housing to prevent further victimization (Webscale and Johnson, 1998). More recent research confirms the comparatively disappointing results of social interventions, and increasingly, homelessness prevention and rapid rehousing programmes (HPRP) are gaining ground as responses to domestic violence.

There is also a growing body of work on the complex links between domestic violence, home ownership and property rights from the global south. Women's property and inheritance rights vary widely between regions and from country to country. But even where laws are in place, they are not necessarily implemented in a gender-blind way, as research in Kenya demonstrates. Even though women there have legal rights to property, they hold an estimated 1 per cent of all titles (Gaafar, 2014). Where southern research exists on the topic, it shows the considerable protective potential of property ownership and housing security for women. For a woman to have her own place can add substantially to her capacity to negotiate violence, and the risks can be significantly reduced. In Kerala, India, for example, among a sample of over 500 urban and rural women, of those who owned both house and land, 7 per cent experienced physical violence from their spouses. For those who owned neither, the figure was 49 per cent. The difference was even greater for psychological aggression. Property ownership in this context offered more protection than either education or employment (Panda and Agarwal, 2005). The same links have been found in South Africa, Uganda and Bangladesh. By strengthening women's exit options, property ownership improves their bargaining position within a marriage. It could be hypothesized that once women have property, they cease to be property.

Research on issues other than violence also supports the link between property ownership and women's control over their own lives. In Peru, for example, when squatters were given property rights, fertility rates declined, but only in those households where the woman's name was on the title along with her husband's (Field, 2004). Women's empowerment, by whatever means, is important. But their power to control their personal space and that of their children appears to have disproportionate weight. Men's more common control of this space is a critical component of the power relations between men and women which underlie so much of the violence that then rebounds on children.

## Neighbourhood conditions

High rates of violence at home often co-exist with high levels of community violence, and the links between them deserve consideration. The Young Lives researchers point, for instance, to how frequently children who experience harsh treatment at home are also enduring it at school, and they note that the occurrence of violence in multiple settings can normalize the experience for children (see for instance Guerrero and Rojas, 2016). Ambient neighbourhood violence can also contribute to higher levels of stress at home, and to a higher likelihood of conflict among family members. It can also stimulate a more instrumental use of corporal punishment with children – when neighbourhoods are violent, chaotic places with high levels of social disorder, parents may turn to more coercive methods to control and protect their children from danger and bad influences. Trevor Noah, brought up in South Africa on the margins of turbulent post-apartheid neighbourhoods, describes how central such discipline was to his experience: "My mom never gave me an inch", he says.

> Anytime I got in trouble it was tough love, lectures, punishment and hidings. Every time for every infraction. You get that with a lot of black parents. They're trying to discipline you before the system does. "I need to do this to you before the police do it to you." Because that's all black parents are thinking from the time you're old enough to walk out into the street.
>
> (Noah, 2016, p. 227)

Noah notes that this was seldom effective in keeping him out of trouble, but also acknowledges how few options may be open to parents who are fearful for their children. There is also the sense that being beaten toughens a child to cope with adversity, a not insignificant consideration when there is no real protection from the harshness of the world out there.

Think back to the parents in Sierra Leone who, when asked to list the major harms for children, included child rights in their list. When corporal punishment was taken off the table as an option, these parents felt hampered in their capacity to protect their children from harm. Here, and in several other African sites, an interagency research network has focused on gaining a better understanding of community-based child protection norms and practices. Part of this involved clarifying exactly what communities perceived to be the harms that children most needed to be protected from. Earlier in the chapter, I mentioned that harsh discipline barely made it on to the radar as a protection concern in these ethnographic studies.

What comes through instead as a primary anxiety for parents in all these settings – in both rural and urban Kenya, in Sierra Leone, in a Rwandan refugee camp, among refugee groups in urban Uganda – is whether their children are in school or not. In Uganda, for instance, this was a worry for 88 per cent of the respondents, while only 6 per cent listed child beating. The other concerns that took priority included early sexual activity and pregnancy, sexual abuse, drug and alcohol use. Hunger was also a major concern in rural Kenya, and discrimination ranked high for urban refugees. But overwhelmingly, parents worried about children being out of school, and about the delinquencies or dangers related to their exposure to influences outside of home. When children were in school, parents reasoned, they were probably safe from these dangers in the community; when they dropped out they were considerably more vulnerable. In this context, far from being a child protection issue, beating children was seen as one of the few strategies for exercising protection. When a child missed school intentionally in Mombasa, the parents' first response was to beat him "thoroughly" – and then pass him on to elders and the police to be beaten again (Kostelny et al., 2013).

What also comes through here is the public–private distinction. The concerns that these communities identify are largely things that happen outside of home in the public domain. The children at risk are distinctly "community children" in Mead's terms – not knee children, not even yard children. Their problem behaviours contribute to and reproduce social disorder, making the local neighbourhood a more dangerous chaotic place for everyone. Appropriate child protection from the perspective of these parents becomes community protection as well, another link in the inescapable ties between children's welfare and that of the communities they are embedded in.

But meanwhile, protection concerns for young children take a back seat. Yet the violence that happens at home, both more accepted and more hidden, is almost always the more corrosive and damaging experience for both children and women. Recall the Nepali children who were more frightened of their drunken fathers than of the Maoist combatants responsible for bombings and abductions. For these more private issues to become an acceptable focus of community concern requires considerable mutual trust and a different perspective. Other mechanisms for establishing and nurturing that kind of trust become necessary – and my argument, to be taken up later in the book, is that collaborative community attention to improving housing, service provision and common space can provide a practical entry point for these more sensitive issues.

## Children in residential care

The United Nations estimated in 2006 that for over 8 million children, home was a residential institution of some kind (Pinheiro, 2006). Because of gaps in record-keeping, and because so many institutions remain unregistered, the actual number is very uncertain. A recent report notes a dramatic rise in the numbers of such institutions, however, the majority of them without approval or monitoring (Chaitkin et al., 2017). Although there is a growing trend in many countries towards family-based care for children who might otherwise be institutionalized, the number of children in institutions remains very high in some parts of the world, and studies have shown that they are far more likely to experience violence than children in family-based foster care (Csáky, 2009).

The great majority of young children in living in institutions around the world, even those in orphanages, are not in fact orphans. An estimated 80 per cent of those in residential care have at least one living parent (LUMOS, 2015). In most cases, poverty is indisputably what drives institutionalization. Parents who cannot afford to provide properly for their children see these institutions as a chance for them to have a better life. Children with disabilities also continue to be institutionalized in large numbers because of the lack of access to adequate support systems and services in most places. Only a small proportion of children in residential care are there because of abuse or neglect. In some countries, agencies encourage children's placement because of the profits that can be made from donations, many from outside the country.

The quality of residential care varies considerably. Adequate care is certainly possible, but conditions in these often poorly resourced institutions can also be so grim that they put children's lives and health at risk. Accounts stress the frequent overcrowding, poor hygiene, lack of toys and play facilities, and time spent confined to cots and cribs. Added to this is the all-important lack of responsive attention from consistent caregivers and, in the worst cases, children's vulnerability to severe neglect and to abusive treatment both by staff and other children (Csáky, 2009). A review of the studies available points to a pervasive problem of abuse in residential institutions.

The great majority of the studies that have looked at developmental outcomes for children point to both cognitive and social delays (Sherr, Roberts and Gandhi, 2017). The youngest children especially are at risk of long-term developmental damage as a result of these conditions. Blackburn and Epel point to studies indicating that the longer children have spent in an orphanage, the shorter are their telomeres (2012). The Bucharest Early Intervention Project, a long-term comparative study in Romania, examined the effects on the development of young children, and found that institutionalized children were at dramatically higher risk for a range of abnormalities compared to children both in foster care and with their own families. These children had significantly lower IQs and brain activity than the norm, were far more likely to have behavioural and social problems, and were seriously stunted physically. Removing them from institutions and placing them in foster care improved their development, but the earlier this happened, the better it was (Bucharest Early Intervention Project, 2009).

A telling indictment of residential care comes from the alternative report to the Committee on the Rights of the Child by a coalition of Russian NGOs in 2013.

(The periodic reports that governments are required to submit to this Committee are often accompanied by these alternative reports, which often shed more light on actual conditions for children within a country than the formal government reports.) According to this group of NGOs, the number of institutionalized children in Russia was close to 400,000 in 2013, down somewhat from 2002, but only, they thought, because the overall child population had declined. These children, they noted, many of them with disabilities, were largely handed over by their parents as a temporary measure. The annual budget for these institutions approached 15 billion euros, and according to the report, "This is enormous Corporation with institutionalized children instead of gas or oil" [sic]. Placement is poorly reviewed, and in many cases children remain until they are passed on to adult institutions for the mentally incapacitated. These children, the report notes, "are brought up without knowledge of such fundamental categories as 'home', 'family', 'meaningful adult', 'private space'." The report cites an investigation revealing that in one Siberian orphanage, older children had been routinely raping younger children over the last ten years (Coalition of Russian NGOs, 2013).

In Kazakhstan, where a 2011 study was carried out in thirty state-run residential institutions for children, both staff and children over 7 were interviewed, their names kept confidential. There were many accounts of violence between children, and towards children by staff. Acts of psychological abuse included breaking children's possessions, locking them in rooms or closets for extended periods, tying or chaining them up, preventing them from using the toilet or giving them burdensome tasks around the institution. About one child in ten had tried to run away; an almost equal number had intentionally harmed themselves. Things were especially bad for children with severe disabilities – in their case, almost a quarter of the staff reported incidents of harsh abuse, and more than half felt that corporal punishment was warranted with these children (Haarr, 2011). In Zambia, where street children are often rounded up and placed in residential care, an assessment of a sample of seventy-four children, age 7 and up, classified 75 per cent as having mental health problems, more than half of them "behavioural/conduct disorders" (Imasiku and Banda, 2015). This may simply be a way of saying that these children were unwilling to be there and were actively displaying that fact.

There are undoubtedly situations where institutional care can provide a valued alternative for children, but the potential for abuse, underpinned by the very nature of the living arrangement, makes this an untenable solution.

## References

Bartlett, Sheridan (1997) No place to play: Implications for the interaction of parents and children, *Journal of Children and Poverty* 3(1), 37–49

Bartlett, Sheridan (1998) Does inadequate housing perpetuate children's poverty? *Childhood* 5(4), 403–420

Blackburn, Elizabeth H and Elissa Epel (2012) Telomeres and adversity: Too toxic to ignore, *Nature* 490, 169–171

Bowstead, Janet (2012) Mapping the forced migration of women fleeing domestic violence: Preliminary report on continuing research, Child and Woman Abuse Studies Unit. Available at www.bl.uk/reshelp/bldept/socsci/events/dangerspaces/Bowstead%20FINAL.pdf

Bowstead, Janet (2015) Forced migration in the United Kingdom: Women's journeys to escape domestic violence, *Transactions* 40(3), 307–320

Brownlie, Julie and Simon Anderson (2006) "Beyond anti-smacking": Rethinking parent–child relations, *Childhood* 13(4), 479–498

Brunk, Doug (2011) Housing troubles linked to a spike in child abuse admissions, *Elseview Global Medical News: Notes from the Road*. Available at https://egmnblog.wordpress.com/2011/05/03/housing-troubles-linked-to-a-spike-in-child-abuse-admissions/

Bucharest Early Intervention Project (2009) *Caring for orphaned, abandoned and maltreated Children*. Available at www.crin.org/docs/PPT%20BEIP%20Group.pdf

Chaitkin, Samantha, Nigel Cantwell, Chrissie Gale, Ian Milligan, Catherine Flagothier, Claire O'Kane and Graham Connelly (2017) *Towards the right care for children: Orientations for reforming alternative care systems Africa, Asia, Latin America*, Luxembourg: Publications Office of the European Union

Coalition of Russian NGOs (2013) *Alternative report 2013 on children's rights by a coalition of Russian NGOs*. Available at http://groups.rightsinrussia.info/archive/right-of-the-child/alternative-report-2013

Csáky, Corinna (2009) *Keeping children out of harmful institutions: Why we should be investing in family-based care*, London:Save the Children

Devries, K *et al.* (2011) Violence against women is strongly associated with suicide attempts: Evidence from the WHO multi-country study on women's health and domestic violence against women, *Social Science and Medicine* 73(1), 79–86

Dong, M *et al.* (2005) Childhood residential mobility and multiple health risks during adolescence and adulthood, *Archives of Pediatrics and Adolescent Medicine* 159(12), 1104–1110

Evans, Gary W, Jeanne Brooks-Gunn and Pamela Kato Klebanov (2011) Stressing out the poor: Chronic physiological stress and the income-achievement gap, *Pathways* Winter, 16–21

Evans, Gary W and K English (2002) The environment of poverty: Multiple stressor exposure, psychophysiological stress, and socioemotional adjustment, *Child Development* 73(4), 1238–1248

Evans, Gary W, S J Lepore and K M Allen (2000) Cross-cultural differences in tolerance for crowding: Fact or fiction? *Journal of Personality and Social Psychology* 79(2), 204–210

Farrell, Susan *et al.* (2000) *Describing the homeless population of Ottawa-Carleton: fact sheets of selected findings*, Ottawa: University of Ottawa, Centre for Research on Community Services

Field, Erica (2004) *Fertility responses to urban titling programs: The role of ownership security and the distribution of household assets*, Harvard University, mimeo, cited in A V Banerjee and E Duflo (2011) *Poor economics: A radical rethinking of the way to fight global poverty*, Philadelphia: Public Affairs

Gaafar, Reem (2014) *Women's land and property rights in Kenya*, Landesa: Center for Women's Land Rights

Garbarino, James (1977) The human ecology of child maltreatment: A conceptual model for research, *Journal of Marriage and the Family* 39, 721–735

Guerrero, G and V Rojas (2016). Understanding children's experiences of violence in Peru: Evidence from young lives, Innocenti Working Paper 2016–2017, Florence: UNICEF Office of Research

Guo, Xiamei, Natasha Slesnick and Xin Feng (2016) Housing and support services with homeless mothers: Benefits to the mother and her children, *Community Mental Health Journal* 52(1), 73–83

Haarr, R N (2011) *Violence against children in state run residential institutions in Kazakhstan: An assessment*, Kazakhstan: Commissioner for Human Rights in the Republic of Kazakhstan and UNICEF

Horn, Rebecca *et al.* (2013) *Community based child protection mechanisms amongst urban refugees in Kampala, Uganda: An ethnographic study*, Columbia, New York: Child Protection in Crisis Network for Research, Learning and Action, Columbia University Mailman School of Public Health

Hume, Mo (2004), "It's as if you don't know, because you don't do anything about it": Gender and violence in El Salvador, *Environment and Urbanization* 16(2), 63–72

Humphreys, Cathy and Ravi Thiara (2002) Mental health and domestic violence: "I call it symptoms of abuse", *British Journal of Social Work* 33(2), 209–226

Iltus, Selim (1994) Parental ideologies in the home safety management of one to four year old children, Dissertation, Environmental Psychology Program, The Graduate School and University Center of the City University of New York

Imasiku, Mwiya Liamunga and Serah Banda (2015) Mental health problems of street children in residential care in Zambia: Special focus on prediction of psychiatric conditions in street children, *Journal of Clinical Medicine and Research* 7(1), 1–6

Jeyasingham, Dharman (2016) Place and the uncanny in child protection social work: Exploring findings from an ethnographic study, *Qualitative Social Work*, 1–15, doi:10.1177/1473325016657867

Jirapramukpitak, Tawanchai, Melanie Abas, Trudy Harpham and Martin Prince (2011) Rural–urban migration and experience of childhood abuse in the young Thai population, *Journal of Family Violence* 26, 607–615

Kostelny, K, M Wessells, J Chabeda-Barthe and K Ondoro (2013) *Learning about children in urban slums: A rapid ethnographic study in two urban slums in Mombasa of community-based child protection mechanisms and their linkage with the Kenyan national child protection system*, London: Interagency Learning Initiative on Community-Based Child Protection Mechanisms and Child Protection Systems

Kostelny, K, M Wessells and K Ondoro (2014) *Community-based child protection mechanisms in Kilifi, Kenya: A rapid ethnographic study in two rural sites*, London: Interagency Learning Initiative on Community-Based Child Protection Mechanisms and Child Protection Systems

Krienert, Jessie L and Jeffrey A Walsh (2011) My brother's keeper: A contemporary examination of reported sibling violence using national level data, 2000–2005, *Journal of Family Violence* 26, 331–342

Lalor, K (2008) Child sexual abuse and HIV transmission in sub-Saharan Africa, *Child Abuse Review* 17(2), 94–107

Lea, Tess and Paul Pholeros (2010) This is not a pipe: The treacheries of indigenous housing, *Public Culture* 22(1), 187–209

Linnan, M *et al.* (2012) Child drowning: Evidence for a newly recognized cause of child mortality in low and middle income countries in Asia, Innocenti Working Paper 2012–2007, Florence: UNICEF Office of Research

LUMOS (2015) Children in institutions: The global picture. Available at https://wearelumos.org/sites/default/files/1.Global%20Numbers_2_0.pdf

Marcus, Rachel (2013) Poverty and violations of children's right to protection in low- and middle-income countries: A review of the evidence. Available at www.odi.org/sites/odi.org.uk/files/odi-assets/publications-opinion-files/9309.pdf

Mclennan, J D (2000), To boil or not: Drinking water for children in a peri-urban barrio, *Social Science and Medicine* 51(8), 1211–1220

Meth, Paula (2003) Rethinking the "domus' in domestic violence: Homelessness, space and domestic violence in South Africa, *Geoforum* 34, 317–327

Meyer, Silke (2016) Examining women's agency in managing intimate partner violence and the related risk of homelessness: The role of harm minimisation, *Global Public Health* 11(1–2), 198–210

Morrow, V and R Singh (2016) Understanding children's experiences of violence in Andhra Pradesh and Telangana, India: Evidence from Young Lives, Innocenti Working Paper 2016–2019, Florence: UNICEF Office of Research

Nallari, Anupama Reddy (2014) The meaning, experience, and value of "common space' for women and children in urban poor settlements in India, Doctoral dissertation, Graduate Center, City University of New York

NCCPR (2011) Child abuse and poverty, *National Coalition for Child Protection Reform Issue Paper 6*. Available at www.nccpr.org/reports/6Poverty.pdf

NNEDV-NLCHP (2007) Lost housing, lost safety: Survivors of domestic violence experience housing denials and evictions across the country, National Law Center on Homelessness and Poverty

Noah, Trevor (2016) *Born a crime*, London: John Murray

Pain, Rachel H (1997) Social geographies of women's fear of crime, *Transactions: Institute of British Geographers* 22, 231–244

Panda, Pradeep and Bina Agarwal (2005) Marital violence, human development and women's property status in India, *World Development* 33, 5

Pankhurst, A, N Negussie and E Mulugeta (2016) Understanding children's experiences of violence in Ethiopia: Evidence from Young Lives, Innocenti Working Paper 2016–2025, Florence: UNICEF Office of Research

Patel, Vikram and Arthur Kleinman (2003) Poverty and common mental disorders in developing countries, *Bulletin of the World Health Organization* 81, 609–615

Pelton, Leroy (1994) The role of material factors in child abuse and neglect, in Gary B Melton and Frank D Barry (eds) *Protecting children from abuse and neglect: Foundations for a new national strategy*, New York: Guilford Press, 131–182

Pelton, Leroy (2015) The continuing role of material factors in child maltreatment and placement, *Child Abuse and Neglect* 41, 30–39

Pinheiro, P (2006) *World report on violence against children*, New York: United Nations Secretary General's Study on Violence against Children

Ramírez Hernández, Nashieli (2012) In their own words: How young children in Ciudad Juárez experience urban violence, *Early Childhood Matters* 19, 13–17

Ritterbusch, Amy (2012) From street girls to "VMC' girls: Empowering strategies for representing and overcoming place-memories of violence in Colombia, *Children, Youth and Environments* 23(1), 64–104

Ruiz-Casares, Monica and Jody Heymann (2009) Children home alone unsupervised: Modeling parental decisions and associated factors in Botswana, Mexico, and Vietnam, *Child Abuse and Neglect* 33, 312–323

Shdaimah, Corey S (2009) "CPS is not a housing agency"; Housing is a CPS problem: Towards a definition and typology of housing problems in child welfare cases, *Children and Youth Services Review* 31(2009), 211–218

Sherr, Lorraine, Kathryn J Roberts and Natasha Gandhi (2017) Child violence experiences in institutionalised/orphanage care, *Psychology, Health and Medicine*, doi:10.1080/13548506.2016.1271951

Thornhill, R and C L Fincher (2011) Parasite stress promotes homicide and child maltreatment, *Philosophical Transaction of the Royal Society B; Behavioural Sciences* 366, 3466–3477

Turan, Janet M, Abigail M Hatcher, Patrizia Romito, Emily Mangone, Modupeoluwa Durojaiye, Merab Odero and Carol S Camlin (2015) Intimate partner violence and forced migration during pregnancy: Structural constraints to women's agency, *Global Public Health: An International Journal for Research, Policy and Practice* 11(1–2), 153–168

UNICEF (2012) Inequities in early childhood development: What the data say. Available from www.unicef.org/publications/index_61802.html

UNICEF (2014) Hidden in plain sight: A statistical analysis of violence against children. Available at www.unicef.org/publications/index_74865.html

UNICEF (2015) Annual results report 2015: Social inclusion. Available at www.unicef.org/publicpartnerships/files/2015ARR_SocialInclusion.pd

Velonis, Alisa *et al.* (2015) Strategizing safety: Theoretical frameworks to understand women's decision making in the face of partner violence and social inequities, *Journal of Interpersonal Violence* 0886260515598953 [Epub ahead of print]

Vu, Thi ThanhHuong (2016). Understanding children's experiences of violence in Viet Nam: Evidence from Young Lives, Innocenti Working Paper 2016–2026, Florence: UNICEF Office of Research

Wachs, Theodore (2010) Viewing microsystem chaos through a Bronfenbrenner bioecological lens, in G Evans and T Wachs (eds) *Chaos and its influence on children's development: An ecological perspective*, Washington DC: American Psychological Association, pp. 97–112

Webscale, N and B Johnson (1998) Reducing woman battering: The role of structural approaches, *Social Justice* 24(1), 54–81

Wessells, Michael (2015) Bottom-up approaches to strengthening child protection systems: Placing children, families, and communities at the center, *Child Abuse and Neglect* 43, 8–21

Wessells, M and K Kostelny (2012) An ethnographic study of community-based child protection mechanisms and their linkage with the national child protection system of Sierra Leone, Interagency Learning Initiative. Available at www.savethechildren.org.uk/sites/default/files/docs/Ethnographic_Phase_Report_Final_7-25-11_1.pdf

Wessells, Mike, Neil Boothby *et al.* (2013) A rapid ethnographic study of community-based child protection mechanisms in Somaliland and Puntland and their linkage with national child protection systems, Columbia Group for Children in Adversity. Available at Final-ethnographic-report-Somaliland-and-Puntland.pdf

WHO and UNICEF (2008) *World report on child injury prevention*, Geneva: World Health Organization

Zuravin, Susan (1986) Residential density and urban child maltreatment: An aggregate analysis, *Journal of Family Violence* 1(4), 307–322

# 4

# NEIGHBOURHOOD

Children's drive to explore, discover and interact socially begins to call for a larger world quite early in life, and ideally they are able to expand their range into the local neighbourhood. The age when this happens depends on the place and the circumstances. Traditionally, children of 6 or 7 have been considered old enough to enlarge their sphere of independent activity beyond home. In some places, even younger children are independent agents within a limited range, or they follow their older siblings around the local area. In Margaret Mead's classification, children over 6 or 7 are certainly considered to have moved from being "yard children" to becoming "community children". Across cultures, the neighbourhood has been considered the natural territory for children this age. In many places, however, this freedom of movement is becoming a rather quaint notion.

Ideally, the move from home into the neighbourhood is gradual and seamless for children, both in terms of scale and independence. But the nature and intensity of a child's engagement beyond home, even the possibility that it will happen at all, are determined in large part by where they live, the quality of their neighbourhood spaces, and the socially constructed boundaries and meanings that are embedded those spaces. Many children of 6, 7, 8 – or even older – are restricted from becoming community children by safety concerns, insecurity and the threat of violence. John McKendrick points out that a good neighbourhood is one where children's poverty or poor housing does not necessarily define their overall experience, but where there are opportunities available that go beyond the scope and reach of their families and homes (McKendrick, 2014). For too many children around the world, neighbourhood does little or nothing to realize this transformative role.

The violence in these neighbourhoods can take many forms, and can cover the full spectrum, from everyday tensions between neighbours to a pervasive climate of lawlessness and violence that leads people to fear for their very lives. In too many places, neighbourhoods might as well be war zones. Fear and insecurity can pervade people's lives through endemic street crime, drug trafficking, gang activity and state sanctioned violence that is perpetuated in the name of security. The World Health Organization distinguishes between community violence and collective violence, and includes in the latter all those forms of violence that have a larger agenda, whether social, political or economic. Collective violence can include war, political violence, ethnic violence, organized crime, terrorist activities and mob violence, and it can be perpetrated by groups of individuals or by states. By contrast, WHO puts gang activity into the realm of community violence (WHO, 2002).

These classifications can be confusing, though, because there are so many areas of overlap and so many charged relationships between violence at different levels. Local forms of violence can, as Arjun Appadurai argues, be "fractal replicas" of larger struggles (Appadurai, 2006). All of these categories of violence, however, have very local impacts, which affect the quality of the neighbourhood world and the lives of families and young children. Michael Taussig made this point in the context of Colombia: "… far too much attention is spent on the headline-grabbing drama of the state versus the guerrilla. For the more fundamental issue in many ways is the sordid everyday one of grinding poverty, street crime, and the nightmare life of kids" (Taussig, 2003, p. 197).

For the purposes of this discussion, I consider neighbourhood violence less in terms of its genesis or agenda and more in terms of the impact that it has on the lives of children and their families. When local violence is endemic, regardless of its source, it can be difficult to shelter children from it effectively. The need to accommodate to some level of danger and insecurity is a routine part of the lives of many children and adolescents, and it is felt by their younger siblings as well. Even when violence outside of home is not inflicted directly on young children, it can have a profound impact on their experience through its effects on those around them, and through the dark mental imagery that accounts of violence may generate in their minds.

## Tensions over shared space

Violence does not have to be extreme to restrict the neighbourhood opportunities for small children. Because they are limited in their range, even the animosity between neighbours, often generated by the physical constraints in environments of poverty, can limit children's chances to get out into the larger world. This in turn can add to the strains at home, which can rebound on children.

Research by Anupama Nallari in Bangalore, India, shows just how restrictive these kinds of tensions can end up being for children. In one slum settlement she studied, where there were no open spaces, when children tried to play in the cramped narrow lanes outside their shacks, neighbours would shout at them. These lanes, too narrow to meet the multiple spatial needs of people living in tiny shacks, caused constant fights between residents. One mother said that she grew so tired of her neighbours' chronic irritation and hostility that she would no longer allow her children to leave the house. "I didn't have a choice but to keep calling them home and then finally forbidding them from playing outside. And with that they just forgot how to play … then got used to not playing. And then they just got used to not going here and there and just staying at home" (Nallari, 2014, p. 159). In densely populated and underserved settlements, every water tap or patch of space can become a point of contention. The resulting tensions add to the more general stress and further limit possibilities for children – even to the point of diminishing a drive as powerful and critical as a child's need for play.

In another neighbourhood in Bangalore, this one an upgraded settlement where the basic conditions were far better, Nallari found that shared facilities were still a source of conflict. One of the women described her frustration with the inadequate water supply:

> There are at least twenty houses that take water from this tap. Water comes only from 2pm to 4pm and everybody gets into fights saying "you have taken more, no you have taken more water!" Then these fights get out of hand. Sometimes they will be hitting and pulling hair and talking bad about the other person's families and all that. Sometimes the water comes very slowly and everybody gets impatient.
>
> *(Nallari, 2014, p. 177)*

Given the increasing water scarcity in the region, the women were sure these squabbles would only get worse.

In an apartment building in the same upgraded settlement, families continued to share toilets, although only with two or three other households rather than with the fifty or sixty who commonly use community toilet blocks. Even so, the sharing of this common facility created discord.

> "The toilet is a big problem!" explained one woman. "People from the other apartments do not keep it clean. We're always fighting with them because of this. We clean up when we use it … they should also do that, right? But they never do … they always leave it dirty and smelly. The men drink and come in at night and dirty up the toilet. Then in the morning all the women fight saying 'Your husband did this! Your husband did this!'" This is how the fights start.
>
> *(Nallari, 2014, p. 178)*

Within these fraught settings, opportunities can become ever more restricted for children as adults attempt to control common spaces. When they first moved into this new apartment building in Bangalore, children enjoyed playing together on the roof terrace and gathering to eat there in the evening. It didn't take long for adults to decide that this was a nuisance and to forbid rooftop access to children. Initially, the children also played behind the building in a small triangle of vacant land. But very quickly that area was seized by local men as a place to park motorcycles and scooters. These kinds of restrictions can hardly be considered the equivalent of violence. But when children tap into adult frustrations, as they naturally do, things can become unpleasant for them as well. Just as living in overcrowded households can encourage harsher control by parents, frustrations over common space in a densely crowded neighbourhood can result in a generally hostile attitude towards children and their play. Boys attempting to play cricket or football in tight spaces, for example, can stir up irritation that sometimes erupts into angry confrontations. One boy described the problem this way:

> Before, we used to play here [in the open areas between apartment buildings], and they would not shout at us so much. But then we started to break glass and all that and then one mother would complain to another and then the mummies would get into fights and then the daddies would get into fights and it used to get very bad. So they are very strict now and they don't let us play anymore.
>
> *(Nallari, 2014, p. 346)*

Given the profound importance of play to every aspect of children's development, these kinds of restrictions constitute in themselves a kind of violence. It is not accidental that Cindi Katz poses play as a kind of counterweight to the structurally violent "willed wasting" of children's lives (2011).

These tensions and disputes among neighbours are not targeted only at children. They come out around all kinds of perceived violations of norms on the use of local space – dogs being left outdoors to bark, trash being placed too close to a neighbour's house, dishwater being thrown into an alleyway. In the recorded narratives of young people from the former Yugoslavia, it is revealing how frequently conflict is sparked by these kinds of physical and spatial violations: neighbours arguing over who painted the graffiti on a building, women fighting over chickens crossing a property line, anger about a man taking more than his fair share of parking space (Daiute and Lucić, 2008). Do these events generate conflict, or are they simply an occasion to express it? When these clashes are endemic and are accompanied by more deep-seated tensions, as in the former Yugoslavia, or in settlements where ethnic groups live side by side in an uneasy peace, there is always the fear that small irritations may flare into actual violence. And young children are often the first to feel the effects of that escalation. Children's natural need to shout and run and explore – or just to *be* somewhere filling up limited and contested space – can become a focal point for hostility.

Physical conditions unquestionably play a role in the formation and erosion of social bonds. Evidence from the United States, for example, demonstrates the connections between the strength of these bonds and child maltreatment. In the 1990s, Robert Sampson and his colleagues in Chicago looked at the level of "collective efficacy" within neighbourhoods and pointed to three aspects critical to the welfare of children: the links between adults and children within a community, the intensity of interaction among adults on child rearing issues, and the level of informal control of and support for children. These aspects are compromised, they argued, in areas where disadvantage is concentrated and where families are isolated from supportive resources. Even personal ties may not be enough to overcome the concentration of distrust that can accumulate in the context of material hardship. This makes it hard to develop the kind of shared expectations and collective action for children that can be strongly protective (Sampson, Morenoff and Earls, 1999). Although this body of research is USA-based, it is clearly relevant to the behaviour observed in India and in Yugoslavia, and to the implications for young children, whose harassment and restriction in the neighbourhood is so closely tied to the frayed social capital that accompanies dense living and limited common space.

A related body of research elaborates on the chronic "mental fatigue" that can accompany life in noisy crowded urban settings (Kaplan, 1987). People living in poverty are arguably at the highest risk of this kind of fatigue, since even their most commonplace concerns can require endless problem solving and attention. Constant demands on attention, combined with a stressful environment, can heighten levels of irritability and aggression. These stresses also appear to lower the capacity for the kind of collaborative problem solving that is so fundamental to creating the supportive neighbourhoods children need. In three communities in India, researchers found a significant relationship between the intensity of environmental hardships (especially the presence of garbage, traffic and crowding) and the degree of personal stress that residents experienced. The researchers identified three ways that people coped in these communities – through problem solving, helplessness and acceptance. For people in the most environmentally stressful neighbourhoods, problem solving was the strategy least likely to be employed in response to local concerns (Siddiqui and Pandey, 2003).

The research on mental fatigue is closely related to work investigating the restorative quality of natural environments, which finds that regular exposure to vegetation causes blood pressure to drop and levels of stress to fall. In a series of studies over several years with low-income residents from housing projects in Chicago, Frances Kuo, William Sullivan and their colleagues explored the effects of proximity to vegetation. They were able to compare residents of public housing blocks that were surrounded by trees and lawns to those living in identical buildings where landscaping efforts had not taken root. Because these public housing residents had been randomly assigned to buildings, the situation was in effect a natural controlled experiment. The focus of the research was on the positive impact of green environments – but looking at the issue from the flip side can be just as informative. The researchers found that residents in the buildings without greenery were less outgoing, less likely to know their neighbours and less likely to experience social support. There were also more reports of both violent crime and property crime, more aggression, higher rates of domestic violence and fewer constructive interactions with children in those buildings than among the residents in the green buildings – even after controlling for income and other differences. These multiple studies point again to some of the impacts of the mental fatigue associated with stressful environments (Kuo et al. 1998; Kuo and Sullivan, 2001). Frances Kuo provided the following summary: "Just as rats and other laboratory animals housed in unfit environments undergo systematic breakdowns in healthy, positive patterns of social functioning, so too do people" (Kuo, 2010).

Physical conditions can exacerbate stress and hostility in a neighbourhood. But it can also work the other way around. In situations where particular groups of people are discriminated against, this discrimination often takes the form of spatial restrictions. Discrimination against dalits in India and Nepal, for instance, is now illegal, but continues to be manifested spatially in many communities by a refusal to allow dalits access to water sources, temples and other community spaces – and sometimes by violent treatment of those with the effrontery to challenge those spatial boundaries. Despite the advances made by many dalits as a result of their social reform movement and affirmative action quotas, discrimination still remains deeply woven into everyday life for many. In a village in Siraha, Nepal, one dalit mother described the challenges she faced to my Nepali colleague: "They say we're dirty, but they don't let us fetch water. Our children bathe with buffalos in the pond – there's not a child without skin problems and infections. They want their own children to be educated, but they want our children to herd their cattle" (Bartlett et al., 2004, p. 9).

Changes for the better can also be very place-specific. In this same village, for instance, discrimination was not permitted in the NGO-supported day-care centre. The teacher knew that she would lose her job if all the children, including dalit children, weren't treated with equal respect. Higher caste parents seemed to accept this basic ground rule with equanimity, even with enthusiasm. They said they liked seeing their children experience a more inclusive social world. One small boy, however, described what happened when he went to his teacher's house to pay his school fees. "She told me just to throw it down near her ... She didn't invite me in, and she didn't want me to touch her while she was eating, because her mother-in-law was there. But the next day, she touched me and washed my face at the center" (p. 48).

## Service provision, amenities and disamenities

The dearth of basic services within neighbourhoods can heighten tensions between neighbours, but can also have direct implications for the safety and emotional welfare of children, adolescents and women. When children from four low-income neighbourhoods in Johannesburg assessed their local environments, most of the problems they identified highlighted links between the provision of basic services and their personal safety. They talked about broken crossing lights that resulted in long waits to get across busy streets, exposing them to harassment; streets without adequate lighting and parks without security measures that limited recreational possibilities and compromised their safety; inadequate waste removal systems that encouraged open spaces to be taken over for drug dealing and clandestine sex, limiting children's options to use these sites for play; inadequate public transport that forced them to rely on often predatory taxi drivers, and the presence of bars and liquor stores on every corner that made it necessary to negotiate their way past drunks to reach home (Kruger and Chawla, 2005). These same complaints are repeated by boys and girls around the world. Nadan and colleagues refer to these kinds of problems as "disamenities" – the undesirable conditions in a neighbourhood like blighted housing, alcohol outlets, crime and drug trafficking, which, when concentrated, have been correlated to higher rates of child maltreatment (Nadan, Spilsbury and Korbin, 2015).

Obstacles to getting around safely are fundamental to children's sense of risk. In Tanzania, children pay only a fraction of the adult ticket price on buses, and because of this, drivers can be reluctant to take them on board. As a result, girls may feel unable to turn down the sexual overtures of drivers and conductors if they want to reach school (Mabala and Cooksey, 2008). A survey in four cities (Kampala, Delhi, Hanoi and Cairo) found that on average fewer than 10 per cent of girls felt safe using transportation services, and over half reported sexual harassment (in Hanoi, it was 77 per cent). For some the harassment was occasional, but some girls said it happened all the time (Plan International, 2015). Harassment and sexual abuse are also routine for women attempting to move around their cities and settlements, whether on buses and subways, walking down streets without adequate lighting, or navigating dark, lonely lanes.

The absence of adequate provision for sanitation is one of the most common reasons for heightened fear about violence and abuse. In Nairobi's informal settlements, for instance, where less than a quarter of households have private toilets, most people have to walk for several minutes to reach a public latrine. Girls and women interviewed there by Amnesty International said that using the public latrines at night was out of the question because of the ever-present danger of rape (Amnesty International, 2010). In the Mukuru slum, Doris, a local resident, pointed to the cramped alleyways between shacks in her settlement, flooded and filthy, where women and children were forced to relieve themselves at night. "Getting to the toilet at night is very difficult. They are closed, so you have to get an alternative. So we come to the bush, and it is very risky. You have to get two or three women to escort you. If you do not come with two or three people, it is a rape case and it will never be reported. Some women fear to escort you ... As women we are in a very, very risky place" (SDI, 2013). In a peri-urban settlement outside Johannesburg, girls told me that they always arranged to accompany one another to the local latrines, and were especially fearful after dark.

In India, millions of women and girls in both rural and urban communities wait until the hours before dawn, when few people are likely to be around, to go relieve themselves, whether in community toilets, in nearby fields or on the railway tracks. In her description of conditions in Bangalore slums, Anu Nallari details the frustration, shame and fear that both women and their young daughters experience because of the simple need to relieve themselves. Girls spoke of the dangers of squatting in the open, their humiliation when they had to dispose of sanitary napkins, and the verbal harassment they endured. "If we tell our problems to anyone," said one girl, "no-one cares ... Our parents don't say anything because they are scared they will get into fights and they will be outcast." According to a mother: "With the older girls we are always scared that something will happen. I go with them sometimes, but sometimes they have to go by themselves. Who knows who will be hanging around outside? Till now nothing has happened, but these are bad times, and if something happens, these girls' lives will be ruined forever!" (Nallari, 2015).

Once reputations have been tarnished by rape, as this mother suggests, girls' prospects can be destroyed. Celine d'Cruz and Patience Mudimu of Shack Dwellers International point to the same anxiety:

> The young girls on the pavements of Byculla or the daughters of Khayelitsha in Cape Town and Payatas in Manila and in settlements all over Asia, Africa and Latin America face the same vulnerabilities: harassment, provocation, early pregnancies or worse. Their parents are constantly worried even at work and within their limited options they try to find a safe haven for their girls. The most common solution is to marry them off very young.
>
> *(d'Cruz and Mudimu, 2013, p. 37)*

And so the prospect of harassment or rape contributes to the perpetuation of another child protection concern, that of early marriage with all that it entails in terms of health, educational opportunity and a young woman's capacity for control over her own life.

For children especially, acutely sensitive to the world around them, one of the most challenging aspects of poverty is the degree of shame they feel about their material conditions. Using a filthy public toilet can be frightening, but it can also be humiliating. Piles of uncollected trash, bad smells and run-down surroundings are often experienced by children as painful reflections of their own worth. The experience of stigma can certainly be a potent source of stress. Whether it can be considered a form of violence is another question. To the extent that this discussion includes the structural violence endemic to inequitable systems, stigma is indeed a crucial consideration.

Jill Swart-Kruger described the experiences of children in an unserved squatter camp on a small patch of vacant land in central Johannesburg. The squatters were blamed for a spike in local crime and a fall in surrounding property values. Children described the disgust and anger directed at them by neighbours of all races around the settlement. This made them reluctant to use whatever scarce local amenities there were. Some children tried to clean themselves in bathrooms at a local shopping centre, but had to do so furtively. Those who attended local schools were careful not to reveal where they lived, fearful of ridicule and rejection (Kruger, 2001). When this community was later evicted and relocated to barren land miles away from the city, water had to be trucked in, and residents were often without a water supply for days at a time. A film documenting the children's lives (*Children of Thula Mntwana*) makes it clear how mortifying it was for them to be unable to wash. One boy explained that when there was no water, he could not attend school because it would be so shameful to arrive in the classroom unclean. In Kathmandu also, children who lived in a squatter settlement by the Bagmati River spoke to me about their reluctance to reveal where they lived for fear of facing contempt and harassment.

What these children experience, often with shame than seems deeper than that of adults, is the sense of being less than fully human by virtue of their surroundings. These children literally embody deprivation. Systems over which they have no control dictate that they live in sub-human conditions, ergo they must be sub-human and can expect to be treated as such. Their foul surroundings, by some perverse reasoning, explain and justify their treatment as the despised other. Those filthy people, by this same ugly logic, do not deserve to have their waste collected or to have access to working toilets. The sense of exclusion is only heightened by the fact that for those living in unserved settlements, addressing basic needs can even become criminalized – as residents collect water illegally from wells belonging to others, dispose of waste illegally or tap illegally into municipal power lines.

This sense of stigma does not come only from outsiders. Contempt can also come from people who themselves live in these communities. Children and young people in a low-income barrio in Buenos Aires spoke of how judged they felt by their neighbours when they hung out with friends on the corner (la esquina), behaviour that adults associated with gang members. Children acknowledged that gang members did hang out on street corners, but there was no other place where they could socialize with their friends. Standing around on the corner, they insisted, did not necessarily mean they were up to no good (Hardoy et al., 2010). The same response comes from young people in Northern Ireland: "When we're on the corners we're just gettin' together, havin' a laugh. But straight away they see it as a threat … Just bein' together with your pals is targeted as anti-social. You want to tell them that you're bein' social, not anti-social. They wouldn't get it!" (McAlister, Haydon and Scraton, 2013, p. 14).

## Hot spots, environmental design and a note of caution

Even in neighbourhoods plagued by insecurity and violent incidents, problems are often quite place-specific. Crimes do not happen randomly, but because specific opportunities present themselves in particular places – dark paths and lanes, isolated bus stops, public latrines and other "hotspots". One neighbourhood "disamenity" that appears, for instance, to have distinct effects for children's sense of safety is the local bar. Over and beyond the effects on life at home, there is the pall that can be cast on neighbourhood life. Children in both north and south have pointed to their fear of passing bars and alcohol outlets. In Philadelphia, in the USA, for instance, children's perceived safety on the walk to school was inversely related to the density of alcohol outlets along the way (Wiebe et al., 2013).

The theory that features of the physical environment can contribute to criminal or violent behaviour has been around for a long time. Considerable research links specific features of local space and anti-social behaviour. Two classic and influential contributions are Oscar Newman's work on "defensible space" (1972), and Jane Jacobs' insights into the quality of safe urban neighbourhoods (1961). Newman's research pointed to such factors as building height, layout and the number of people sharing a common entrance, all of which he claimed could affect the level of ownership and control that people feel over their space, and with it the incidence of crime. Jacobs stressed the danger of areas that do not allow for informal surveillance or "eyes on the street". By contrast, she argued, windows that face the street, neighbourhood enterprises, well-lit streets and well-kept public spaces all increase the control that people have over their surroundings, contributing to an active community presence and to more constructive interaction. Active street-level commercial activity can also help ensure the steady flow of people in an area, increasing security for all.

A note of caution is in order here. These theories are intuitively compelling, but they are not consistently supported by the empirical findings. An overly simplistic or deterministic stance regarding these physical features can be misleading. Incidents may tend to be clustered in particular hotspots, but the constellation of influences can be difficult to untangle. Some research, for example, finds that adequate street lighting can reduce incidence of crime, and indeed my introduction opens with this assumption. Yet a large study in London in 1991 found no evidence that lighting reduced either crime or people's sense of safety (Atkins, Husain and Storey, 1991). Nor are people's perceptions of unsafe hotspots always related to actual events. Public housing residents in Baltimore, for instance, identified a place where young people gathered to drink and play music as the most dangerous spot in the area, yet no crime had ever actually occurred there (Wilson and Kelling, 1982).

The Marcus Garvey Village in the Brownsville neighbourhood of New York City is an example of the complexity of the issues. This was one of the more celebrated applications of Newman's principles – carefully designed low-income housing built in the 1970s, consisting of over 600 apartments that had little in common architecturally with most of the crime-ridden public housing projects in the city. Apartment doors opened to the outside, and there were both communal courtyards and private backyards – features that were considered to support precisely the sense of control that Newman felt was absent in most housing projects. But these features also served the interests of gang members, and the housing became a notorious home base for criminal activity. Brownsville was always poor, and it is now poorer than ever. Ginia Bellafante, who reported on the project in the *New York Times*, pointed out that "Mindful design can accomplish little divorced from broad, aggressive strategies to fight social inequality" (2013). Design features can affect people's behaviour, but there are no hard and fast connections with the occurrence of local violence. In low-income countries the discussion of "CPTED" – or "crime prevention through environmental design" – has tended, importantly, to emphasize the way that disparities in living conditions can contribute criminal activity, and the importance of achieving greater spatial integration.

Despite some caution around overly simplistic applications of the CPTED approach, there are some measures that continue to be found effective in lowering levels of crime and insecurity in a community: features that maximize visibility and support surveillance; symbolic and real barriers that deny access; territorial behaviour and indications of ownership. But a reliance on these principles is best mediated by the close involvement of residents. There is a fine example from Delhi, where municipal authorities decided on a courtyard design for resettlement housing on the fringes of the city. Housing around a central courtyard has been a traditional solution in India, as in many other places, since it provides small-scale shared space separated from the larger public domain, and a protected place where small children can play while women work. This pattern is compatible with CPTED principles. But during a workshop arranged by local NGOs, women and young girls rejected this plan. They argued that they were unwilling to share enclosed courtyard space with unfamiliar neighbours. Resettlement is often accompanied by the loss of jobs and there is a far greater incidence of unemployment and idleness. They felt their chances of being harassed by drunken men, who usually stayed home during the day, were much higher than they would be if their houses opened onto the street. And so the plan was changed (Chatterjee, 2007). The point is that environmental features *can* affect social relations and behaviour, but that solutions must build on the specificities of local experience rather than just generic principles about space.

A related approach to CPTED, also controversial, is the "broken windows" theory, according to which social disorder is reflected in disrepair in the physical environment, whether garbage in streets, graffiti or general dilapidation, which can stimulate vandalism and even lead to higher rates of crime and violence. A 2008 study appears to offer a justification for this connection. This study, from the United States, which examined children's responses to photographs of houses and neighbourhoods, notes that the appearance of dilapidation and disrepair summons up moral attributions and assumptions about potential danger, even in quite young children. Among more aggressive children, these more physically deteriorated environments can become a cue for justifying more provocative and retributive behaviour (Pitner and Astor, 2008).

This broken windows theory has led to a good deal of "zero tolerance" policing in the United States, which some observers argue has resulted in significant improvements in levels of property and violent crime in some cities. But there has been considerable disagreement on the actual reasons for these improvements. Robert Sampson and Stephen Raudenbush tested the association of systematically observed disorder, social and physical, with officially recorded crime rates in Chicago. They demonstrated that these phenomena are not related in a cause-effect way, but rather are both expressions of underlying factors – specifically the degree of concentrated structural disadvantage in an area, and the lower levels of collective efficacy that were the result. Their conclusion was that "attacking public disorder through tough police tactics may thus be a politically popular but perhaps analytically weak strategy to reduce crime, mainly because such a strategy leaves the common origins of both, but especially the last, untouched" (Sampson and Raudenbush, 1999, p. 638). They did argue, however, that collective efforts among residents to address disorder and disrepair can strengthen local ties and thus end up over the long run in lowering rates of violence – a rather different process. To be avoided, from their perspective, are approaches that identify the slum as the culprit, rather than the failure to provide for the slum.

## Spatial segregation and the "architecture of fear"

There are many reasons why poor neighbourhoods tend to have significantly higher rates of crime and violence. While being poor does not in itself cause people to be violent, inequalities between groups and the inequitable distribution of resources and services have a strong impact on levels of conflict and violence. Especially in areas of concentrated poverty, the absence of markets, employment, amenities, institutions and capital all restrict opportunity and contribute to frustration.

These inequities are especially visible in places where various forms of spatial segregation separate the affluent from the poor. In many parts of the world, urban space is increasingly reorganized in response to crime and violence and to a lack of confidence in the state's capacity to provide security. In growing numbers of cities, the wealthy live in private gated communities, enclosed neighbourhoods or fortified enclaves, surrounded by private security systems. These hard spatial boundaries reinforce inequalities and concentrate privilege in archipelagos. People in these enclosed spaces no longer make use of public space – or they co-opt it for private use. Meanwhile, public disinvestment contributes to the deterioration of whatever is outside these areas. More than ten years ago, Dennis Rodgers described a network of high speed roads in Managua connecting the residential, commercial and leisure worlds of the rich. This highway system ripped through large areas of the city for the exclusive convenience of the rich, leaving the remainder of Managua to crumble into dystopic, neglected, unpoliced slums where people went out as little as possible (Rodgers, 2004). The same strategy in many cities has left both public and private spaces less safe, increasing fears, deepening segregation, often undermining social cohesion in poorer areas.

This segregation is not always enforced through hard physical boundaries. In Rio de Janeiro, for instance, where the favelas of the poor rise up on steep hills above the wealthy neighbourhoods below, there are no walls or gates to keep people out of more affluent streets and shopping malls. Social distance here appears to be just a part of the city's geography. Yet children in these hundreds of favelas are as effectively cut off from the rest of the city by social barriers as they would be by fences of barbed wire (Fraser, 2011). Responses to the material environment are not always to its actual properties but to the symbolic interpretations of these properties and of relational arrangements they embody.

In the mid-1990s, anthropologist Teresa Caldeira described the more general effects of this kind of segregation:

> In the materiality of segregated spaces, in people's everyday trajectories … in their appropriations of streets and parks, and in their constructions of walls and defensive facades, social boundaries are rigidly constructed. Their crossing is under surveillance. When boundaries are crossed in this type of city, there is aggression, fear and a feeling of unprotectedness, in a word; there is suspicion and danger. Residents of all social groups have a sense of exclusion and restriction. For some, the feeling of exclusion is obvious, as they are denied

access to various areas and are restricted to others. Affluent people who inhabit exclusive enclaves also feel restricted; their feelings of fear keep them away from regions and people that their mental maps of the city identify as dangerous.

*(Caldeira, 1996, p. 324)*

This spatial division contributes to the normalization of violence and insecurity in the daily life of many communities, as illegal activities and markets become more concentrated in poorer areas. The violence and criminality so well guarded against by the wealthy can become directed against the poor themselves. Ailsa Winton explains how this segregation contributes to a self-reinforcing process:

> ...violent spatial processes of segregation, gentrification and forced relocation, and spatial polarization all have a profound effect on social structures. This spatial violence, the dual expulsion–concentration of the socially excluded, is compounded by the (symbolically violent) social stigmatization of these spaces. Exclusionary processes thus become self-reinforcing: in such spaces it is more likely that gangs emerge and also that they gain legitimacy as social institutions, and therefore become more institutionalized. Once such spaces are constructed as "deviant" as a result, it becomes possible to wage a territorial war on crime and violence (i.e. gangs).

*(Winton, 2014, p. 408)*

Fear and insecurity begin to pervade people's lives through street crime, drug trafficking, gang culture and police violence, and what Taussig called "terror as usual" can have far reaching implications for trust among communities and individuals (Taussig, 1989).

Often this spatial segregation is formally constituted by illegality. More than a third of urban dwellers globally, primarily those in poverty, live in settlements that are not officially recognized as part of the city. Inherent in the informal status of these settlements and their residents is the potential for additional forms of exploitation and violence, as people with connections work the situation for their own gain, whether as political strongmen, landlords or purveyors of basic services. The very informality of the situation offers scope for contention and creative speculation. Sometimes, this same illegality means not just segregation but elimination, as entire neighbourhoods of the poor are simply bulldozed into oblivion on the assumption that out of sight is out of mind. The growing phenomenon of evictions will be discussed in the next chapter.

Sometimes these destructive spatial divisions are not just between the rich and the poor, but are based on political or ethnic enmity. Debbie Bonnin explains the history of spatial divisions in one South African community, Mpumalanga Township in Natal, as an expression of allegiance to opposing political parties. Outbreaks of politically-based violence increasingly began to determine the geography of the area, as specific residential areas became identified with political affiliation, an identification that then became self-perpetuating. As in the case of wealth inequities, the creation of what are in effect spatial enclaves can mean greater security within these neighbourhoods, but also more rigid demarcations that limit access to a range of facilities and destinations. For many residents, it was these physical boundaries, rather than their political loyalties, that ended up defining where they could go and what they could do, often dividing families, restricting access to work, destroying assets of all kinds, and limiting opportunities for children (Bonnin, 2004).

These kinds of divisions remain evident at a country-wide level in Northern Ireland, where even in the post-conflict context there is a continued legacy of place-based identity, separation and violence. Housing, services, schools, leisure facilities all remain segregated by religious affiliation, and there are reportedly more "peace walls" dividing neighbourhoods now than there were before the ceasefires. Violent outbreaks are sporadic but not uncommon. Young children remain "cocooned" within their local neighbourhoods, while older children report feeling imprisoned in areas with few opportunities, unable to negotiate safely through areas occupied by the other community. "Those working closely with young people," according to researchers, "note a lack of purpose, identity and belonging which manifests itself in violence towards others or the self" (McAlister, Haydon and Scraton, 2013, p. 10). The ever-present undercurrent of violence, along with "buried trauma", spills over into family relationships, resulting in aggressive parenting and domestic violence which is, according to one community member, just "part of a way of life".

Scott Bollens in 2001 referred to the organized hatred expressed through these spatial divisions in many cities – including at that point Sarajevo, Berlin, Jerusalem and Nicosia. Some of the cities have changed, but Bollens' analysis is no less relevant. These boundaries, he says, whether buffer zones, walls, no-man's lands, razor wire fences or less physical, more symbolic, barriers, are fault lines in a society, both manifestations of contested space and historical records of violence. They more often than not signify deep economic disparities as well as political or ethnic differences. The expression of identity and difference through place can perpetuate hostility by anchoring it to the concrete reality of physical territory and markers of past violence. The violence is not just the product of antagonistic identities; it can also be the way that identity is produced and confirmed.

This spatially entrenched violence is especially evident in occupied zones. Jason Hart points out that the risks faced by Palestinian children are related not so much to conflict as it is generally understood, but to the fact of Israel's occupation, enclosure, concentration and sometimes destruction of their living space. Between 2007 and 2011, he explains, nearly 1,000 children were made homeless when their houses were destroyed because they lacked the permits which were in any case largely unobtainable. "Assumptions about the ability of family and community to secure the most immediate space of children's lives and afford them protection, which lie at the core of the spatialised approach, are clearly questionable in light of such experiences" (Hart, 2012).

## Power, insecurity and fragile cities

Police vigilance can be more intensive in these excluded neighbourhoods. But it is also common for lower levels of police protection to go hand in hand with an absence of provision on every other front. Ailsa Winton's research in some violent low-income Guatemalan neighbourhoods, for instance, revealed that one community had been in existence for twenty-six years before a police station was established (Winton, 2007).

Even where there is a police presence, the relationship can be ambiguous and conflicted. A young woman from Barrio San Jorge in Buenos Aires, for instance, describes her neighbourhood as safer than it used to be – but this is clearly in spite of the police, not because of them.

> Before you couldn't go into the barrio alone, but now you can, everything is OK, it's more quiet. Before, taxis wouldn't come in because of fear of being robbed. When the neighbour got out at his or her house, the driver would get robbed. Today, the ambulance has problems getting in because of the state of the roads. If it does come in, it comes with three police cars to guard it. The police don't walk much around the barrio. A while back they were posted outside the barrio to control the robbed cars coming in. But they aren't stealing so many cars now, so the police have left. If there are robbed cars still coming in, it's from outside people who have arrangements with people within the barrio to dismantle the car. It would be great if we could all help each other and defend ourselves because police officers often can't do anything.
>
> *(Hardoy et al., 2010, p. 374)*

The ambiguity is understandable. Police responses can include everything from the welcome monitoring of anti-social or threatening activity to selective repression and even disappearances and torture. What for some citizens is valued protection, for others might be the source of anxiety or even extreme fear. A mother in Mangueirinha, Brazil, explains that in her neighbourhood, violence is associated primarily with the police.

> When the police aren't there, there is no problem. You don't see any guns, nothing. Everyone's just playing normally. My eldest son says, "I'm young, but it won't be long until they start wanting to beat me up." Because that's the way it is, when you live in the community, you are a suspect. My children tell me that where we live is a horrible place, a place where they feel like prisoners, they have no freedom.
>
> *(Santos, 2012, p. 20)*

In New York City, the notorious "stop and frisk" policy, which the police commissioner credited with bringing the crime rate to a new low, involved over 1.2 million stops over a two-year period, 88 per cent of them young men of colour in poor neighbourhoods. The rationale was the higher rates of crime in these neighbourhoods – yet less than 1 per cent of the stops turned up a weapon, and for the tens of thousands of boys and young men involved, and for their families, the repeated stops make neighbourhood life a source of anger and chronic anxiety (Siegel and Glasser, 2013). In many places, these New York excesses would be considered mild. Stops have plummeted since litigations in 2013, yet crime levels have continued to drop.

The complexity of policing has been well illustrated in Rio de Janeiro in the lead up to the FIFA World Cup in 2014 and again before the 2016 Olympics. Rio has long been known for extraordinarily high levels of police violence, but through the UPP programme, "police pacification units" were intended to replace the usual militarized raids in the favelas with a new focus on community policing and gaining local trust. This initially resulted in safer streets and lower homicide rates, but it didn't last. According to Human Rights Watch, excessive police violence dropped initially, but rapidly started to rise again. Unlawful police killings in the city reached over 600 in 2015 and have continued to climb. These unlawful killings confirm community distrust and make neighbourhoods less secure for everyone. During the alleged "shootouts" reported from 2013 through 2015, Rio police killed five times as many people as they injured, the reverse of what one would expect (Human Rights Watch, 2016a). Robert Muggah, a Rio-based expert on urban violence, relates these rates to the police officers' own experience of violence, citing a study that showed a quarter of them had been victims of violent assault as children, and almost a third had a friend or family member who had been murdered (Muggah, 2016). These fraught relationships with police are not inevitable. The genuinely community-based police panchayats in Mumbai and Pune, India, for instance, have managed to build a successful community–police collaboration to compensate for the absence of police protection in informal communities. These will be discussed in more detail in the responses section.

When police protection in these segregated neighbourhoods is absent it can be simply a function of state neglect. There are other situations, though, where in the absence of legitimate governance, whole settlements become no-go zones, outside the reach and control of formal security forces and governance structures, as parallel structures take over and the authority of gangs or militia groups is consolidated. Robert Muggah describes the phenomenon of the "fragile city" where the level of civic violence can be on a par with armed conflict and where there has been a serious rupture of the social contract (Muggah, 2014).

The distinctions, in fact, between armed conflict and these other forms of urban violence may be somewhat moot, as the lines between war, insurgency, struggles over land, organized crime, gang activity become more blurred. Today's wars, argue Reid-Henry and Sending, are increasingly likely to be civil conflicts that take place in urban areas (2014). All conflict has to happen somewhere – even the largest wars have local manifestations. But as armed violence becomes a more urban phenomenon, growing numbers of children are likely to come within its orbit. The destruction of local habitat for large numbers of people is increasingly the face of current conflict, which frequently ignores the sanctity of hospitals, schools, residential neighbourhoods. In Syria in recent years, this has reached a horrific crescendo. UNICEF reminds us of the thousands of children killed in their own neighbourhoods, in schools, homes and playgrounds, of the families living under siege, of children malnourished and terrified, of the 70 per cent without reliable access to water, the resurgence of formerly controlled diseases, the damage and closure of more than a quarter of the country's schools, the children as young as 7 recruited by parties to the conflict (UNICEF, 2016).

## The impact of violent neighbourhoods for children's opportunities

Comparatively few children in the world experience violence on a parallel with that in Syrian neighbourhoods under siege. Yet accommodating to chronic fear is the norm for far too many. The most immediate outcome of local violence for children is a restriction in mobility, either imposed on them by parents or chosen themselves. In low-income settlements in Guatemala City, children and young people revealed to Ailsa Winton that, other than going out for school or work, they spent almost no time away from home. In the context of pervasive gang activity, their options were "avoidance, compliance or engagement". Avoidance was the simplest choice for those who chose not to become gang members themselves, and on average, these young people were in public space for less than an hour a day (Winton, 2007). Jenny Parkes in South Africa quotes a young girl. "There's just nothing good because on every corner there's gangsters and we're very scared to walk past them now and I don't want to play actually outside … there's no safe place to play" (2007, p. 406).

In a challenged neighbourhood in New York City back in 2000, Caitlin Cahill reported that,

> Every student's neighborhood description was saturated with stories of the drug culture and the dangers associated with it, including the "weird" or violent people who deal or use drugs, and crime. Both girls and boys discussed the limitations on their freedom in the neighborhood imposed by the drug culture, race issues, police surveillance, the dearth of places to go where they felt welcome, and fear, which restricts their movement, often keeping them at home.
>
> *(Cahill, 2000, p. 262)*

These constraints on mobility are especially severe for girls. In much of the world, north and south, rural and urban, the independent range permitted to girls tends to be more constrained, and a common refrain is that there is nowhere girls can go to socialize together. Their vulnerability to sexual violence is most often the rationale. But Fatma El Nahry argues that these kinds of restrictions are specifically intended to control girls' and women's access to public space. It is, she says "an institutionalized system of violence that functions to police women's participation, freedom of movement, and behaviour in public spaces. It is not how women behave in the public sphere that makes them vulnerable to street harassment; it is that they have chosen to enter the public sphere at all" (El Nahry, 2012).

Even in places where more explicit gender discrimination and taboos have started to disappear, the presence of local violence can be sufficient to ensure its de facto persistence. The dangers do not have to be extreme for girls to be restricted. In the context of violence, the street can be constructed as the site of masculine power, with women and girls expected to stay away. The sense that girls are behaving inappropriately simply by being in the public domain, especially once they reach puberty, may increase their risk. When toilets, water sources, schools, markets are at a distance, this can create a difficult bind. Younger girls, even if they have not yet experienced this harassment, have watched older sisters, mothers and neighbours facing this kind of systematic discrimination and restriction.

Despite the constraints and anxieties, many children and adolescents do continue to make use of their less than safe neighbourhoods, drawing on a range of strategies that help them feel safe. Cahill's young New Yorkers developed rules for negotiating their local surroundings. Cahill discusses their "street literacy" and the "language of street practices and strategies for staying safe, or more importantly, for enabling them to at least feel safe". The "mind your own business" rule, for example, was fundamental to staying safe. You don't meet people's eyes.

Researchers from Belfast and South Africa also write about the sophisticated street knowledge that is necessary for children to be able to manage risk and stay safe in fraught areas (Leonard, 2010; Parkes, 2007). In cities or areas where there is conflict along group lines, whether ethnic, religious or related to some other source of difference and tension, it is commonly in the "interface" areas, where the territories of different groups adjoin one another, that children are most likely to feel at risk, and they are careful to avoid the more fraught locations. Although the negotiation of local space becomes more of an issue as children get older and are permitted greater mobility, the vigilance begins far earlier. By the age of three, children in Irish interface areas are reportedly able to distinguish between Catholics and Protestants. Focusing on neighbourhoods of concentrated poverty in Lisbon, Carvalho also describes quite young children demonstrating their "astute" awareness of local violence and the physical and social disorders surrounding it (including broken streetlights, fights in bars, easy access to drugs and weapons) (Carvalho, 2013).

Within home neighbourhoods, even these very young children may have a fine-tuned sense of when the situation is safe. Bree Akesson explores the meaning of this kind of contested local space for young children in the occupied Palestinian territories. Their neighbourhood access, she says, is constantly moderated by changing circumstances from day to day. During periods of "fragile calm", children of all ages play freely in the streets, often without adult supervision. When violence erupts, they peer through barred windows. They are, in Akesson's words, "constantly negotiating access to places by testing boundaries and engaging in creative placemaking despite the restrictions of caregivers and the restraints of conflict settings" (2012, p. 6). Street play for these children, when it is possible, becomes not only a way to meet the more common needs of childhood, but also a way to process the particular conditions they live in, both venting emotions and trying through make-believe play with other children to make sense of the violent events that they see taking place around them.

Research from the favelas of some Brazilian cities has pointed to mistaken efforts on the part of NGOs to get children off the street as a safety measure. The favelas are essentially the retail marketplace for the cities' crack cocaine business, keeping this criminal enterprise off the streets of wealthier neighbourhoods that house most of the drug clients. These researchers argue that even drug dealers and gang leaders respect children's street play in their own neighbourhoods, and that removing children from this community space that has always been the locus for local social life runs the risk of making it more rather than less likely that violence could be happen there (Da Silva and Shaw, 2011).

In too many cases, though, there are more blanket restrictions on children's mobility. In Ciudad Juarez, Mexico, drug trafficking has resulted in extremely high levels of violence, hijacking public space and blighting community life. Frustrated by the failure of city statistics to communicate the experienced realities of these children, a local organization interviewed nearly 5,000 children under 8 and many of their mothers. They found children were well aware of the violence and were frightened and anxious, despite efforts by adults to keep them from seeing what was going on right outside their doors. ("Interviewer: What does she think when she sees what's going on? Mother: Nothing, because we cover her up so she can't see it. We tell her not to look because she's very young ", p. 15.) Even if they were allowed to go outdoors, say many children, they wouldn't want to. Adding to the anxiety here is the fact that many of these children, even very small ones, are left alone at home while their mothers work because childcare is so hard to arrange. As noted in the last chapter, work hours in the maquiladora assembly plants change at least weekly, complicating childcare arrangements, and it is not unusual for mothers to have leave their often fearful children alone for at least three hours a day. The local organization, as noted earlier, found significant delays and regression in the development of many of these children (Ramírez Hernández, 2012).

One of the most powerful accounts of the day-to-day realities of living in an extremely violent neighbourhood as a young child is still Alex Kotlowitz's now classic account of the lives of two young brothers and their 4-year-old triplet sisters in neglected and run-down Chicago public housing, an area which gang activity had turned into the equivalent of a war zone. Kotlowitz describes the bloodstains on the stairwell, the bullet holes in the living room curtains and in the boys' bedroom windows, the narrow interior corridor where the boys and their mother and the triplets take refuge during night-time gun fights from high-rise to high-rise between rival gangs. He recounts the sheer terror of 9-year-old Pharoah [*sic*], walking home from school when fighting breaks out; he bangs on the door to be let in, but cannot be heard over the noise of the gunfire. This child takes refuge from his terrifying environment by refusing to acknowledge it. When he has free time, he walks to a more affluent building complex nearby and lies with his eyes closed on the green lawn, imagining a better world. The 4-year-old triplets do not have even this freedom (Kotlowitz, 1991).

## The attraction of violence

Many of the researchers who document the restrictions and anxieties for children in violent neighbourhoods also discuss another side of this difficult relationship. Jenny Parkes speaks of the complexity of the emotions for children who participated in her South African study. They felt repulsed, fearful, helpless in the face of the incidents that occurred so routinely around them – but also excited sometimes and even attracted to the dangerous association of violence and masculinity. Violence disempowers and restricts them, but it is also seen as a form of capital that can potentially offer a level of control and belonging (Parkes, 2007). As in the case of divided Belfast, children are drawn to reproduce the social relations that characterize their near surroundings. If you can't fight them, join them. Also in South Africa, Trevor Noah explains that the slum townships had always been a source of shame for his friends at school. Then those same townships became a badge of honour when hip hop music from the United States rendered them cool. It gave the children street cred – they were no longer from the township, they were from the "hood". Noah found excitement in the sheer electricity of many of these segregated areas. "It's a hive of constant human activity, all day long, people coming and going, gangsters hustling, guys on the corner doing nothing, kids running around. There's nowhere for all that energy to go, no mechanism for it to dissipate, so it erupts periodically in epic acts of violence" (Noah, 2016, p. 205).

Carvalho explains, in the context of Lisbon, that "For many children, violence and delinquency play a functional and instrumental role, providing attractive and rewarding forms of socialization, which vary from what they consider to be just child's play, and fulfilling the need to obtain recognition in socially stigmatized areas" (2013, p. 20). The same attraction, starting early, was described by Barbara Fraser with reference to Rio de Janeiro.

> "Drug traffickers flaunt their physical and economic power with flashy motorcycles, multiple girlfriends, and guns that kids begin to crave." She quotes Gaspar, a grassroots community worker: "For many young people, who lack a broader perspective and never go far from the favela, the world becomes reduced to the favela, and they want to be like that … Some start to think the violence is normal."
>
> *(Fraser, 2011, p. 1735)*

The lens of glamour that some children hold up to local violence can contribute to its perpetuation. The slums of Kibera and Korogocho in Nairobi are characterized by high levels of violence and by an equally violent resolve on the part of the state to deal with arms and those that carry them. A few years ago, the Minister for Internal Security ordered a shoot-to-kill strategy for people in possession of arms or in the company of armed gangs, with no opportunity for trial. Many men were brutally executed in these slums in broad daylight, and many children witnessed these bloodbaths. Irene Karanja, who lives and works in Nairobi, wrote to me about this:

> They grow up associating these events with Hollywood movies, and celebrate the fallen men as heroes who are mighty and powerful enough to command the state machinery to come to the settlement. A couple of weeks ago I attended a burial of a friend's 23 year old son. To my amazement, many girls and boys came to the grave, chanting "Oh Daddy, you were our hero!", "You died a soldier!", "You have molded us and shown us the way", "You are an elder!". When a young man who has chosen a criminal way of life survives even into young adulthood, he is considered an elder. My friend's son was an elder in this sense, and the fifty young people were there to pay their respects to a fallen leader.

Karanja notes that slum upgrading and the work of the urban poor federations in Nairobi have in many cases become a way for young criminals to become involved with constructive and tangible alternatives and to identify themselves with responsibilities that allow them to "abandon the gun for a bigger course".

Trevor Noah, again, explains another way that crime is normalized and accepted:

> The hood made me realize that crime succeeds because crime does the one thing the government doesn't do; crime cares. Crime is grassroots. Crime looks for the young kids who need support and a lifting hand. Crime offers internship programs and summer jobs and opportunities for advancement. Crime gets involved in the community. Crime doesn't discriminate.
>
> (Noah, 2016, p. 209)

Where there are not clear alternatives, local gang activity is not only "normal" but understandably linked to the aspirations of many children and young people. This can become the case especially where, as in Nairobi and Rio and numerous other cities, gang membership may be perceived as an honourable alternative to the violence of the authorities. The sense of belonging and security that gang membership can provide is also a powerful incentive for many young people. Often family violence pushes young men to leave home, join gangs and turn to drugs, eroding local trust and social capital even further. As one young man explained, "I joined the guerrilla so I could get a gun, so I could shoot my father, and stop him beating up my mother" (Moser, 2009, p. 82). While gang membership may not be an issue for most young children, the conditions that cause their elder siblings to gravitate to this form of belonging, and to an acceptance of violence as the norm, are there early in life.

The online world is another domain that exerts its attraction. Although not a place in the conventional sense, it is increasingly an important part of children's "neighbourhoods" and research findings point to its contribution to the risks facing children. More than a third of Internet users in the world are estimated to be children, and there has been a steady increase in use, among even poor communities in the global south. A four-country survey of more than 2,000 children over the age of 9 found children's online concerns included disturbing news, ugly gossip, virtual bullying, hurtful interactions and unwanted sexual content. Between 2 and 11 per cent had been subjected to overt sexual solicitation. More than one child in three had had contact online with people they didn't know, although most had not had subsequent contact with these people – except in South Africa where more than half had gone on to face-to-face meetings (Byrne et al., 2016). There is no way to know currently what the overlap is between children who run the risk of harmful experiences online and those who experience routine violence in their communities. This overlap is important given the significance of accumulated risk factors for children's well-being, and ideally future research will shed more light on this contribution to children's more general exposure to harm.

## Violence at school

It is all too easy to associate school violence with the rash of school shootings in the United States or the large scale kidnappings that have occurred in Nigeria. These horrifying events are relatively rare, however, and it is the far more common everyday concerns that are of interest here. Schools, like homes, are supposed to be safe places for children. Yet they are one of the community settings where violence is most commonly experienced, whether from other students or from teachers.

For the young children who are the primary focus of this discussion, this violence is most likely to be experienced through the high levels of physical punishment that still characterize school in many countries. The international Young Lives study, for example, found that four out of five 8-year-olds in Ethiopia, Peru and Vietnam reported that they had been hit once or twice in the last week by their teachers; in India, numbers were still higher, and a third of 8-year-olds there said they experienced corporal punishment most of the time. Rather than sharpening children's attention, this has the effect of reducing their engagement with school – for instance, in three of these four countries there is a significant negative correlation between corporal punishment and children's scores in mathematics (Pells and Ogando, 2015). In settings as different as Nepal and Zanzibar, I have observed teachers as a routine matter holding switches in their hands as they teach, a default reality that seems to call for no explanation. Many young children are reluctant to start school because of the stories they have heard from older siblings and their fear of the teachers.

Beyond the fact that schools are a distinct physical setting, it might be stretching the case to attribute this common practice to material conditions in schools, although the challenge of dealing with overly large classes in crowded conditions does appear to predispose teachers to use the stick as a method of classroom management. But material conditions can in fact contribute in other ways to the likelihood that children will be punished in school. According to one young girl in Kenya, "It's very cruel. You can be beaten for anything: if you are feeling sleepy in class, or you are late, or dirty, or you have not done your homework, or you are given a test and you fall below the average, you may be beaten" (Human Rights Watch, 1999, p. 34). When children are late, it is often because of distance from school; when they are unable to finish homework, it can be because carrying water and other household chores take so much time, or because studying is difficult without lights or in crowded noisy homes; when they are dirty, it is generally because of the difficulty obtaining water; when they fail tests, it may be related to the diminished concentration and cognitive functioning that accompanies intestinal worms – and so on.

There are clear links between physical discipline in schools, often officially sanctioned, and other forms of school violence. Bullying by other children, for instance, often takes place against a background of corporal punishment and a tendency among teachers to humiliate children. A growing body of literature has pointed to high levels of bullying, harassment and violence among students, with the bullies often coming from the most difficult home environments (Menesini and Salmivalli, 2017). Although bullying tends to peak among somewhat older children, it can also be a significant part of the school experience for many younger children – among the Peruvian cohort of the Young Lives study, for instance, over 47 per cent of 8-year-olds reported being bullied (Pells, Ogando and Revollo, 2016).

In recent decades, the literature, much of it from Africa, has also pointed to high levels of emotional and sexual harassment and abuse by teachers, in addition to physical punishment. These concerns appear to be keeping many girls in particular out of school, in both rural and urban areas, and often placing those who attend at high risk (Jones et al., 2008). Schools can be insecure spaces within a larger context of violence and poverty, where abuse and intimidation can easily take place. In Nairobi, for instance, over 20 per cent of school-going children in the slums reported sexual advances from teachers compared to 6 per cent of non-slum children. The same study noted that weapons were common within slum schools, with no disciplinary action being taken by often intimidated teachers (Mudege, Zulu and Izugbara, 2008).

Violent behaviour by students within schools is astonishingly widespread. A survey of schools in thirty-seven countries found that over a quarter of children had been victims of violence from other students in the last month, and almost half reported that friends had experienced violence. Teachers had trouble teaching because of threats to their safety and that of their students. Although the study found national rates of school violence were higher in low-income countries, this was unrelated to more general patterns of violence within the country and to the factors that usually predict higher crime rates. Rather, it was the quality of the schools themselves that affected the level of school violence. National school systems that created a high level of disparity among students based on academic results were found to be more vulnerable to violent behaviour on the part of students, pointing to the role of frustration with inequity (Akiba et al., 2002).

Links have been found in different places between the physical condition of schools and the type and severity of violence that occurs there. Crowding and run-down, uncomfortable conditions often accompany higher levels of violence, and as with neighbourhoods more generally, violent episodes tend to occur in specific and predictable locations – stairways, hallways, eating areas, playgrounds, parking lots and other places that lack an adult presence and that tend to be undefined and unowned. Titman argued almost thirty years ago from the UK that the boring, barren and often hostile-feeling concrete playgrounds of many schools are the perfect breeding ground for bullying (1988).

Schools can also be taken over as controlled areas for gangs, where drug sales and recruitment of gang members can easily take place. Human Rights Watch explained that schools become "territorial prizes" in effect, providing gangs the controlled area they need for selling drugs or recruiting new members (2001). School toilets, empty classrooms, long hallways all become sites for assault, abuse and exposure to gang violence and robbery. The high level of intimidation interferes with academic work, making a culture of learning impossible to achieve, and children are also cheated on this front.

According to Plan International in West Africa, despite the tradition of secrecy around sexual assault in schools, a growing body of testimony by 2008 from both students and teachers suggested that the problem might be pervasive. In Niger, of fifty teachers interviewed, 88 per cent acknowledged that there were "sexual incidents" between teachers and students at their schools. Often this is a transactional event – an exchange for grades or other favours. But the problem is not limited to teachers. In Ghana, a quarter of all boys interviewed admitted they had raped a girl, either alone or as part of a group assault (Plan International, ODI, 2008). The school environment can be an insecure space where, in a larger culture of violence, these acts can easily take place. Girls interviewed in Cape Town found the most unsafe places to be the gates of the school, where former students would harass them, the toilets, where they were subject to assaults from gangs of boys, and the male teachers' staff room, where girls sent on errands would be raped by teachers during their free time (Human Rights Watch, 2001).

Although much of the relevant research is African, and the problem appears especially pervasive there, it is not unique to Africa or even to low-income countries. In the USA, the majority of girls responding to a 2011 online survey said they had experienced some form of sexual harassment at school that year (Hill and Kearl, 2011). Jones and colleagues cite copious evidence from Latin America. In the Caribbean, for instance, over 60 per cent of children had seen violence in their schools, and associated their absenteeism and school drop out with this violence; in Ecuador over a third of those responsible for the rape of girls were teachers. There is less evidence from Asia. In India, for instance, most violence occurs under the guise of discipline, and there is a general failure to recognize as problematic anything that is not extreme. Sexual harassment that falls short of rape or death, for instance, is dismissed as just "eve-teasing". In Pakistan too, where corporal punishment and discrimination are endemic, and where there is no legal prohibition against the sexual abuse of a child, only the most severe incidents draw attention (Jones et al., 2008).

Violence in schools is an expression of a constellation of structural factors – the sanctioning of male aggression, the underpayment of teachers who see themselves as deserving of something more, the poverty and scant opportunities of girls who accept transactional sex. But there are also characteristics of the often hostile physical environments of these schools that can contribute to what goes on within their confines. Schools are the settings, microcosms, within which these larger social power relations are played out, pitting teachers against students, more powerful students against the less so, in ways that reflect and reinforce accepted norms and local practices. In Brazil, where three public schools were compared to determine how neighbourhood quality affected the levels of violence within the schools, researchers found, as expected, that the school in the most disadvantaged neighbourhood had the highest rates of violence, gun availability and substance abuse, and pointed out that schools are part of a cycle of violence within neighbourhoods, both contributing to the larger milieu and affected by it (Stelko-Pereira and de Albuquerque Williams, 2013).

Often students are more exposed to violence at the school gates or on the journey to school than in the school itself. Getting back and forth, as already discussed, is complicated for many children and is a key reason why girls especially drop out or are forbidden to attend school in the first place. Those who live far from school and easy bus routes, for instance, may feel forced to accept rides from men in return for sexual favours. In conflict-affected settings, the risk of sexual assault is intensified by the presence of soldiers or militias and by a climate of fear where rape tends to go unpunished. It is an unfortunate irony that dropping out of school, so often the effect for girls of violence in school or on the way, exposes them to a higher likelihood of intimate partner violence later in their lives.

Beyond the violence within or around schools that can stem from "everyday" issues, there is the growing problem of the occupation of schools by parties to armed conflict, turning schools in effect into legitimate military targets, as documented for instance in the Ukraine. There can be extensive and often repeated damage and months of lost classroom time (Human Rights Watch, 2016b).

## Violence at work

Since this is not as significant an issue for young children, it is described here in brief. The absence of data makes it difficult to report on the extent of the violence in the workplace, but the vulnerability of millions of children extends not only to the physical conditions of their work, and to their treatment by employers but to the behaviour of co-workers, police, customers and others.

The conditions of work can themselves constitute violence, and the ILO estimates that over 90 million children globally under the age of 11 are working in hazardous conditions, using dangerous tools and equipment, being exposed to toxic substances, or carrying overly heavy loads (IPEC, 2013). Whether they are working in mines and quarries, managing forges or crushing stone, children sometimes as young as 5 or 6 may be dealing with extremely hazardous, exhausting conditions.

Frightening conditions can extend beyond what are typically considered "workplaces". Consider the combination of conflict, wildlife and parental violence that had to be faced by many children in Nepal during the civil war there:

> When we go to the forest to graze the goats, sometimes we hear bomb blasts and we run home crying. My parents say not to go to such dangerous places. But I always have to graze the goats early in the morning, and sometimes it makes me late for school because I don't know what time it is. I get so scared when I'm with the goats and I hear leopards roaring. One time a leopard took two of my goats, so my father shouted at me and my mother beat me. But now if I say I don't want to go out with the goats, they say the leopard doesn't come to the same place twice, and I have to go.
>
> *(Bartlett and Sunar, 2007, p. 13)*

Even when workplaces are not this dangerous, they can expose children to abusive treatment. Consider the millions of children worldwide who work as domestic servants. This work is often rationalized on the basis of kinship ties – children work for wealthier relatives or connections who in return guarantee their safety and promise an education. This can work out well in theory, offering a good entry point to migrating children. But the physical setting of this situation, out of the public eye, is also widely recognized to provide the context for physical and sexual abuse. Available figures are estimates at best, but of the more than 15 million young people estimated to be working in this sector, almost a quarter are considered to be between 5 and 11 years of age, and most of them are performing work designated as hazardous, either by virtue of chronic sleep deprivation or the physical conditions under which they live and work (IPEC, 2013). The isolation of these children is in some cases compounded by virtual incarceration, with children confined to kitchens and even locked in when their employers are out. The ambiguity of the circumstances can result in the youngest and most at-risk children being overlooked by agencies, which are more likely to target somewhat older paid domestic servants. Girls and boys as young as 7 and 8 are vulnerable not only to beatings, humiliation, physical and psychological abuse from employers, but also to sexual violence and harassment.

In many cases children's work exposes them to life on the street, with consequent exposure to hazards of various kinds, whether traffic, harassment or sexual abuse. In Nigeria, for instance, out of a group of 100 girls between 8 and 15 who were engaged in street-hawking, half reported being raped or seduced while working; by comparison "only" 9 per cent of a non-working group had been sexually coerced while running errands or walking to school (Ebigbo, 2003). Even 9 per cent is of course an appalling number, a reminder of the seriousness of the challenges facing so many children moving around their own communities, even in the normatively more ideal context of attending school.

An awkward reality around discussing work for underage children is the very fact that this normative discourse on childhood may not align with children's own viewpoints and those of their families. The values that drive many rights-based policies and determine the child protection agenda prioritize children's school attendance and dependency within nuclear families and frame most child work as a violation of rights. But in many well-documented cases these norms may not be viewed as practical survival solutions by the children and families concerned. Young girls working as housemaids may be exploited and isolated; but many of them will say that this is better than working as unpaid labour on drought stricken family farms, or having nothing to do there and little hope of a better life. This issue becomes especially controversial around the blurred boundaries between child trafficking and intentional migration for work, as will be discussed in the next chapter.

## References

Akesson, Bree (2012) The concept and meaning of place for young children affected by political violence in the occupied Palestinian territories, *Spaces and Flows: An International Journal of Urban and ExtraUrban Studies* 2(2), 245–256

Akiba, Motoko, Gerald K LeTendre, David P Baker and Brian Goesling (2002) Student victimization: National and school system effects on school violence in 37 nations, *American Educational Research Journal* 39(4), 829–853

Amnesty International (2010) *Insecurity and indignity: Women's experiences in the slums of Nairobi, Kenya*, London: Amnesty International Publications

Appadurai, Arjun (2006) *Fear of small numbers: An essay on the geography of anger*, Durham and London: Duke University Press

Atkins, S, S Husain and A Storey (1991) The influence of street lighting on crime and fear of crime, Crime Prevention Unit (Paper No. 28), London: Home Office

Bartlett, Sheridan, Udayalaxmi Pradhananga, Pashupati Sapkota and Narmaya Thapa (2004) *Everyone counts: Dalit children and the right to education in Nepal*, Kathmandu: Save the Children

Bartlett, Sheridan and Basanti Sunar (2007) *Finding hope in troubled times*, Kathmandu: Save the Children US and Norway

Bellafante, Ginia (2013) A housing solution gone awry, *New York Times*, 1 June 2013

Bollens, Scott A (2001) City and soul: Sarajevo, Johannesburg, Jerusalem, Nicosia, *City* 5(2), 169–187

Bonnin, Debbie (2004) Understanding the legacies of political violence: An examination of political conflict in Mpumalanga Township, KwaZulu-Natal, South Africa, Working Paper 44, London: LSE, Crisis States Programme

Byrne, J, D Kardefelt-Winther, S Livingstone and M Stoilova (2016) Global kids online research synthesis, 2015–2016, UNICEF Office of Research Innocenti and London School of Economics and Political Science

Cahill, Caitlin (2000) Street literacy: Urban teenagers' strategies for negotiating their neighbourhood, *Journal of Youth Studies* 3(3), 251–277

Caldeira, Teresa P R (1996) Fortified enclaves: The new urban segregation, *Public Culture* 8, 303–328

Carvalho, Maria João Leote de (2013) Childhood, urban violence and territory: Children's perceptions of place and violence in public housing neighborhoods in Portugal, *Children, Youth and Environments* 23(1), 124–154

Chatterjee, S (2007) Children's role in humanizing forced evictions and resettlements in Delhi, *Children, Youth and Environments* 17(1), 198–221

Daiute, Colette and Luka Lucić (2008) What matters to youth in the aftermath of war? Paper presented at ISCAR, International Society of Culture and Activity Research, San Diego, CA

Da Silva, R de C and K Shaw (2011) *Cartography of the favela: Community resources to resist violence in Recife and Olinda*, Florianópolis and Santa Fe: Shine a Light

d'Cruz, Celine and Patience Mudimu (2013) Community savings that mobilize federations, build women's leadership and support slum upgrading, *Environment and Urbanization* 25(1), 31–45

Ebigbo, P O (2003) Street children: The core of child abuse and neglect in Nigeria, *Children, Youth and Environments* 13(1)

El Nahry, Fatma (2012), She's not asking for it: Street harassment and women in public spaces, Gender Across Borders: A Global Voice for Gender Justice. Available at www.genderacrossborders.com/2012/03/20/shes-not-asking-for-it-street-harassment-and-women-in-public-spaces/

Fraser, Barbara (2011) Growing up in Rio's favelas, *The Lancet* 377(9779), 1735–1736

Hardoy, Jorgelina, Guadalupe Sierra, Andrea Tammarazio, Gabriela Ledesma, Lucas Ledesma and Carolina García (2010) Learning from young people and from our own experiences in Barrio San Jorge, *Environment and Urbanization* 22(2), 371–387

Hart, Jason (2012) The spatialisation of child protection: Notes from the occupied Palestinian territory, *Development in Practice* 22(4), 473–485

Hill, C and H Kearl (2011) *Crossing the line: Sexual harassment at school*, Washington, DC: American Association of University Women

Human Rights Watch (1999) *Spare the child: Corporal punishment in Kenyan schools*, New York: Human Rights Watch

Human Rights Watch (2001) *Scared at school: Sexual violence against girls in South Africa*, New York: Human Rights Watch

Human Rights Watch (2016a) *Brazil: Extrajudicial executions undercut Rio security*. Available at www.hrw.org/news/2016/07/07/brazil-extrajudicial-executions-undercut-rio-security

Human Rights Watch (2016b) *Studying under fire: Attacks on schools, military use of schools during the armed conflict in eastern Ukraine*. Available at www.hrw.org/report/2016/02/11/studying-under-fire/attacks-schools-military-use-schools-during-armed-conflict

IPEC (2013) *Ending child labour in domestic work and protecting young workers from abusive working conditions*, Geneva: International Labour Office, International Programme on the Elimination of Child Labour

Jacobs, Jane (1961) *The death and life of great American cities*, New York: Random House (reprinted 1993)

Jones, Nicola, Karen Moore, Eliana Villar-Marquez with Emma Broadbent (2008) *Painful lessons: the politics of preventing sexual violence and bullying at school*, ODI/Plan International. Available at www.files.ethz.ch/isn/92501/wp295.pdf

Kaplan, S (1987) Mental fatigue and the designed environment, in J Harvey and D Henning (eds) *Public environments*, Edmond, OK: Environmental Design Research Association, pp. 55–60

Katz, Cindi (2011) Accumulation, excess, childhood: Toward a countertopography of risk and waste, *Documents d'Anàlisi Geogràfica* 57(1) 47–60

Kruger, Jill Swart (2001) Children in a South African squatter camp gain and lose a voice, in L Chawla (ed.) *Growing up in an urbanizing world*, London: Earthscan/UNESCO, pp. 83–100

Kotlowitz, Alex (1991) *There are no children here*, New York: Doubleday

Kruger, Jill Swart and Louise Chawla (2005) "We know something someone doesn't know" ... children speak out on local conditions in Johannesburg, *Children, Youth and Environments* 15(2), 89–104

Kuo, F E, W C Sullivan, R L Coley and L Brunson (1998) Fertile ground for community: Inner-city neighborhood common spaces, *American Journal of Community Psychology* 26(6), 823–851

Kuo, Frances E and William C. Sullivan (2001) Aggression and violence in the inner city: Effects of environment via mental fatigue, *Environment and Behavior* 33(4), 543–571

Kuo, Frances Ming (2010) Parks and other green environments: Essential components of a healthy human habitat, Research Series 2020, National Recreation and Park Association. Available at www.nrpa.org/uploadedFiles/nrpa.org/Publications_and_Research/Resea rch/Papers/MingKuo-Summary.PDF

Leonard, Madeleine (2010) Parochial geographies: Growing up in divided Belfast, *Childhood* 17, 329–342

Mabala, R and B Cooksey (2008) Mapping adolescent vulnerability to HIV/AIDS in Dar es Salaam: Results of an exploratory study, Joint Learning Initiative on Children and AIDS (JLICA) Learning Group 4: Social and Economic Policies. Available at www.jlica. org.

McAlister, Siobhán, Deena Haydon and Phil Scraton (2013) Violence in the lives of children and young people in "post conflict' Northern Ireland, *Children, Youth and Environments* 23(1), 1–22

McKendrick, John (2014) Geographies of children's well-being: In, of, and for place, in Asher Ben Arieh, Ferran Casas, Ivar Frønes and Jill Korbin (eds) *Handbook of child well-being: Theories, methods and policies in global perspective*, Dordrecht: Springer, pp. 279–300

Menesini, Ersilia and Christina Salmivalli (2017) Bullying in schools: The state of knowledge and effective interventions, *Psychology, Health and Medicine*, doi:10.1080/13548506.2017. 1279740

Moser, Caroline (2009) Safety, gender mainstreaming and gender-based programmes, in Ana Falu (ed) *Women in the city: On violence and rights*, Santiago de Chile: Women and Habitat Network of Latin America, pp. 77–99

Mudege, Netsayi N, Eliya M Zulu and Chimaraoke Izugbara (2008) How insecurity impacts on school attendance and school dropout among urban slum children in Nairobi, *International Journal of Conflict and Violence* 2(1), 98–112

Muggah, Robert (2014) Deconstructing the fragile city: Exploring insecurity, violence and resilience, *Environment and Urbanization* 26(2), 345–358

Muggah, Robert (2016) How did Rio's police become known as the most violent in the world? *The Guardian*, 3 August 2016

Nadan, Yochay, James C Spilsbury and Jill E Korbin (2015) Culture and context in understanding child maltreatment: Contributions of intersectionality and neighborhood-based research, *Child Abuse and Neglect* 41, 40–48

Nallari, Anupama Reddy (2014) The meaning, experience, and value of "common space" for women and children in urban poor settlements in India, Doctoral dissertation, Graduate Center, City University of New York

Nallari, Anupama Reddy (2015) "All we want are toilets inside our homes!" The critical role of sanitation in the lives of poor adolescent girls in Bengalaru, India, *Environment and Urbanization* 27(1), 73–89

Newman, Oscar (1972) *Defensible space*, New York: Macmillan

Noah, Trevor (2016) *Born a crime*, London: John Murray

Parkes, Jenny (2007) The multiple meanings of violence: Children's talk about life in a South African neighborhood, *Childhood* 14(4), 401–414

Pells, Kirrily and Maria Jose Ogando (2015) Corporal punishment in schools, Innocenti Discussion Paper 2015–2002, Florence: UNICEF Office of Research

Pells, Kirrily, Maria Jose Ogando and Patricia Espinoza Revollo (2016) Experiences of peer bullying among adolescents and associated affects on young adult outcomes: Longitudinal evidence from Ethiopia, India, Peru and Viet Nam, Innocenti Discussion Paper 2016–2003, Florence: UNICEF Office of Research

Pitner, Ronald O and Ron Avi Astor (2008) Children's reasoning about poverty, physical deterioration, danger, and retribution in neighborhood contexts, *Journal of Environmental Psychology* 28, 327–338

Plan International (2015) Because I am a girl urban programme – global baseline analysis report, Plan International Headquarters, Women in Cities International, and UN-HABITAT. Available at www.sustasis.net/Assiago%20Munive.docx

Plan International, ODI (2008) Increasing visibility and promoting policy action to tackle sexual exploitation in and around schools in Africa: A briefing paper with a focus on West Africa, West Africa Regional Office, Plan International. Available at www.unicef.org/wca ro/Rapport_plan_LWF_web_(3).pdf

Ramírez Hernández, Nashieli (2012) In their own words: How young children in Ciudad Juárez experience urban violence, *Early Childhood Matters* 19, 13–17

Reid-Henry, Simon and Ole Jacob Sending (2014) The "humanitarianization" of urban violence, *Environment and Urbanization* 26(2), 427–442

Rodgers, Dennis (2004) Disembedding the city: Crime, insecurity and spatial organization in Managua, Nicaragua, *Environment and Urbanization* 16(2), 113–124

Sampson, Robert J, Jeffrey Morenoff and Felton Earls (1999) Beyond social capital: Spatial dynamics of collective efficacy for children, *American Sociological Review* 64, 633–660

Sampson, Robert J and Stephen W Raudenbush (1999) Systematic social observation of public spaces: A new look at disorder in urban neighborhoods, *American Journal of Sociology* 105(3), 603–651

Santos, Hermílio (2012) "This isn't what I dreamt about": A mother's experience in Mangueirinha, Brazil, *Early Childhood Matters: Community Violence and Young Children: Making Space for Hope* 119, 17–21

Siddiqui, Roomana N and Janak Pandey (2003) Coping with environmental stressors by urban slum dwellers, *Environment and Behavior* 35(5), 589–604

Siegel, Norman and Ira Glasser (2013) Bloomberg and police stops, *New York Times*, 1 May 2013

Slum Dwellers International (SDI) (2013) SDI Dispatch: Women and sanitation in Nairobi's slums, 4/26 2013. Available at http://us6.campaign-archive2.com/?u=6129216e3782d 400b7dde136d&id=431604e466

Stelko-Pereira, Ana Carina and Lucia Cavalcanti de Albuquerque Williams (2013) School violence association with income and neighborhood safety in Brazil, *Children, Youth and Environments* 23(1), 105–123

Taussig, Michael (2003) *Law in a lawless land: Diary of a limpieza in Colombia*, Chicago: The University of Chicago Press

Taussig, Mick (1989) Terror as usual: Walter Benjamin's theory of history as a state of siege, *Social Text* 23, 3–20

Titman, Wendy (1988) Adult responses to children's fears, in Delwyn Tattum and David Lane (eds) *Bullying in schools*, Stoke on Trent: Trentham Books

UNICEF (2016) *No place for children: The impact of five years of war on Syria's children and their childhoods*, Amman, Jordan: UNICEF

WHO (2002) *World report on violence and health*, Geneva: WHO

Wiebe, Douglas *et al.* (2013) Fears of violence during morning travel to school, *Journal of Adolescent Health* 53(1), 54–61

Wilson, J Q and G E Kelling (1982) Broken windows: The police and neighborhood safety, *Atlantic Monthly* 249(3), 29–38

Winton, Ailsa (2007) Using "participatory" methods with young people in contexts of violence: Reflections from Guatemala, *Bulletin of Latin American Research* 26(4), 497–515

Winton, Ailsa (2014) Gangs in global perspective, *Environment and Urbanization* 26(2), 401–416

# 5

# LOSING HOME AND NEIGHBOURHOOD

An estimated 100,000 children and adolescents crossed Europe in 2015 without their families. One of them was 11-year-old Wasil from Afghanistan, who was interviewed a year later by journalist Lauren Collins. Wasil's father had fled Afghanistan, and soon afterwards Wasil was kidnapped by his father's adversaries. He was released after government troops stormed the compound where he had been held for a month, but his mother decided it was unsafe for him to remain at home. Hoping that Wasil might reach her brother in England, she paid a smuggler to see him through the first stage of a gruelling 4,000-mile trip. Wasil was alone for most of his journey and fearful always about his mother's safety back home. He spent a month squatting in a derelict railroad station, some time in prison, ten days wandering in a forest. He walked day after day until he reached the Jungle, the appalling refugee camp in Calais, France. Collins lists the dangers there: vermin, faeces-contaminated water, petty crime, bullying, violence, sexual abuse and diseases ranging from scabies to tuberculosis. Half of the unaccompanied children examined there by a team of doctors had sexually transmitted diseases – the going rate for sex with a young Afghan teenager was 5 to 10 euros. After the Jungle was demolished, Wasil was housed along with 1,500 other children and young people in shipping containers. After being transferred to a juvenile centre in France, Wasil finally made it to England late in 2016, but was still in detention two months later when the article was published, possibly facing deportation (Collins, 2017).

More and more children and families are uprooted every year – fleeing conflict or persecution, escaping from drought, driven by the need for work, pushed out by eviction. Refugee numbers are at an all-time high and there is growing pressure from climate-related disasters and hardships. Economic migration has also been climbing in recent years, and evictions displace more people than conflict and disasters combined. Forced displacement has grown globally by almost a third over the last decade, and about one child in forty-five is estimated to be on the move.

This mobility is not always triggered by violence, but the situations that develop out of these moves can generate violence, and can mean harm and turmoil for children. Economic migrants generally move after careful consideration, which is not to say that the process is untroubled. But refugees, disaster victims and those who are forcibly evicted most often leave home in a hurry and often have little or no control over the process. The implications can be profound, and rebuilding a life may be as daunting as the events that prompted the exodus.

Mindy Fullilove, a psychiatrist, refers to the suffering associated with displacement as "root shock" and she defines this as "the traumatic stress reaction to the destruction of all or part of one's emotional ecosystem" (Fullilove, 2005, p. 11). Her work has focused primarily on the long-term effects of urban renewal on the African-American population in the United States. Compared to the trials endured by Wasil, or the hardships associated with mass movements of people in the context of war or disaster, the experience of urban renewal in the 1950s and 1960s might be considered relatively innocuous. People's neighbourhoods were destroyed to make room for new development, and in most cases this did not result in death or homelessness. Yet Fullilove documents the deeply unsettling impacts of this neighbourhood dismemberment, which continue to reverberate forty and fifty years later as people and communities fail to recover from being uprooted and to recreate the daily patterns of connectedness that make the difference between residing in a place and truly dwelling there. Fullilove argues that displacement is the big problem that the twenty-first century needs to solve, as people are shunted from one place to another. "In cutting the roots of so many people, we have destroyed language, culture, dietary traditions, and social bonds. We have lined the ocean with bones, and filled the garbage dumps with bricks" (p. 5). Over a decade later, Fullilove's analysis is still timely.

The various categories of displacement can overlap in ways that are difficult to peel apart. Conflict, for instance, can be underpinned by climatic conditions, especially by drought, as in Sudan or Yemen. There are many increasingly dry places where living off the land is no longer a viable option, and where competition over scarce water can feed bitter hostilities. When people respond to slow moving events like these entrenched droughts, it can also be hard to draw the line between economic migration and forced displacement. This is true also where rising sea levels coupled with stronger storms are gradually driving vulnerable people from their homes, whether in Bangladesh or Louisiana. These people are not classified as disaster victims and do not qualify for the kinds of assistance that might be available to those experiencing more sudden calamities, but their displacement is hardly voluntary. These categories matter, precisely because of the kinds of supports that may or may not be made available. The children crossing in waves into the United States a few years ago to escape endemic and worsening violence in El Salvador and Guatemala were viewed as illegal migrants, but they might more reasonably have been considered candidates for asylum. The blurred edges of all these categories should be kept in mind in what follows.

## Migration and trafficking

Migration happens at every scale – people cross boundaries to distant countries in large numbers every year to find work, sometimes with formal documentation, sometimes hidden in the back of trucks. By 2015, an estimated 244 million people were living outside of the country where they were born. But even more people move from their home villages to district centres forty or fifty miles away or from there to the nearest large city, part of the huge global trend towards urbanization that involves around 40 million migrants every year. Some migrants also go in the opposite direction, but less attention is given to that. The scale and direction of this movement is mostly explained by hardship at home and the location of economic opportunity. Whether temporary or long-term, internal or international, migration plays a key role in the adjustment of households to changing economic and physical conditions.

Children are far more often included in the internal migration to towns and cities than in the international flows. These internal migrants are not a homogeneous group, and their migration may be more or less straightforward. But it is fair to say that most of them take time to adjust to the upheaval and to find a foothold. Assimilation can be very challenging. There are seldom systems in place to ease their transition. In fact, out of 185 countries in 2013, 80 per cent had policies specifically designed to discourage rural-to-urban migration, more than double the number in 1996 (United Nations, 2013). Often these policies mean that migrant households lack all the rights of citizens.

Not all migrants are poor – sometimes it is the more well-to-do in a village that can afford to make this gamble – but many households and individuals are driven to migrate by declining incomes and accumulating debt. Once living at their destination, they are often among the poorest of the poor, living in the grimmest settlements, working in the least secure informal sector jobs, lacking local supports and safety nets, often remaining in debt for extended periods. "First generation" slums are less likely to have electricity, water connections or sanitation and residents are more likely to live in tents and leaky hovels or, in some places, to rent rooms in rundown tenements, vulnerable to the whims of unregulated landlords (Tacoli, McGranahan and Satterthwaite, 2015). There are obvious implications for young children. They face higher survival risks, they are more likely to be malnourished, less likely to attend school and more likely to face discrimination. "When young children move to cities," notes an observer of migrant brick factory workers in Hyderabad, India, "it is as if they become alien citizens in their own country" (Daniel, 2013, p. 28).

Similar difficulties apply for the children of seasonal migrant farm workers, who typically live in appalling conditions. In Turkey, for example, of a sample of over 600 seasonal agricultural workers, a quarter had to defecate in the open fields, only about half had electricity in their rundown shelters, and that for only part of the time, and there was no regular running water. Only 15 per cent ever saw a health professional. In the absence of childcare, more than 40 per cent took their young children to the fields each day, exposing them to the dangers of pesticides and heavy equipment and often the impatience of supervisors; about 10 per cent of young children were left back at their shelters alone. Despite growing attention to child labour laws, many of the older children still worked long hours every day (Artar, 2013).

A burning protection issue is the exploitation and abuse that can face the many children who migrate unaccompanied by their families every year. This phenomenon is far from new, although it has achieved greater prominence in recent years as the focus of a relatively new line of research. For many years, research and programming were far more oriented towards street children and child workers. This change reflects a transformation less in the actual realities for children than in the way the issue is conceived. Many of those street children and child workers who were the subject of research, as Roy Huijsmans points out, were undoubtedly child migrants themselves (2015). Surveys of working children and adolescents in urban areas have revealed that a great many are recent migrants, often without any accompanying family. In Ethiopia, for instance, only 17 per cent of children and young people working in the informal sector were living with their parents; in Thailand only 12 per cent (Yaqub, 2009).

In sub-Saharan Africa, the waves of unaccompanied minors explain a demographic oddity – the relatively larger share of young people within the urban population. Marc Sommers argues, based on his in-depth research in several countries, that most children and young people in the region who do not already live in urban areas certainly plan to make this move. For most of them, migration is the inevitable route to social mobility, independence and adulthood. The social implications of staying at home in the village can be more disagreeable to these young people than the very serious hardships they are likely to face in the city (Sommers, 2010).

Several years ago, a child protection professional from an international agency told me a story that highlights the complexities of the situation. In an attempt to stem migration to the city by young rural girls, as part of a larger protection programme, she travelled to a village accompanied by girls from an urban rehabilitation project that provided some respite from street life and opportunities for job training. The idea was that these city girls, who had seen it all, would be able to talk to their rural peers and stress the dangers of migration more persuasively than any protection officer could. The girls had what appeared to be a very productive exchange – it was an excellent example of young people's participation in action. But when the programme officer woke up the next morning, ready to drive back to the city, she found that the urban girls had taken off at dawn, accompanied by several village girls who were eager to experience the city for themselves.

The concerns do not apply just to young people on the threshold of adulthood. Sommers points out that the independent migrants in sub-Saharan Africa include many young children, and that most of the trends that apply to urban youth in the region can equally be applied to their younger counterparts. In my own informal discussions with girls 8- or 9-years-old in villages along the Kenyan coast in 2010, there was little uncertainty in their minds about whether they would move to the city in the next few years – that part was taken for granted. Their questions were more about where they would go. Should they move to Malindi, not that far away, or to Mombasa, the really big city? They also debated what they would do once they had children – raise them in the city or leave them back in the village with their grandparents.

Mainstream migration statistics do not report on independent child migrants, but Shahin Yaqub's excellent 2009 overview cited relevant information from studies in many countries, pointing to how young many of these young migrants there actually are. In Nepal, for instance, 8 per cent of all children between 5 and 14 became independent migrants; in Burkino Faso over 9 per cent of those between 6 and 17; in Benin, 22 per cent of those between 6 and 16, their average age 10 or 11. In one rural district in South Africa, an estimated 21 per cent of all children migrated, four out of five of them independently. In Cambodia, about a quarter of all the children between 10 and 14 in one village had migrated to Thailand for work without family. In India, around half of all the sampled child workers in Mumbai were migrants under 12. Of a similar sample in El Salvador, about 41 per cent were migrants, almost half of them under 12 (Yaqub, 2009). Most young migrants would no longer consider themselves children, but for many children aged 6 or 7 or 8 around the world, this is the future they contemplate, and often the not-so-distant future.

Concern about these independent young migrants was for a number of years couched in terms of child trafficking. Human trafficking certainly deserves attention as a spatial expression of exploitation and violence – it is in fact considered the third largest criminal enterprise in the world, after drugs and counterfeiting, and according to United Nations figures, a third of all victims are children (UNODC, 2014). The ILO estimated in 2002 that 1.2 million children were trafficked every year, a figure that UNICEF still uses as the benchmark (IPEC, 2002). Yet little systematic research has been done on the topic and some experts think these kinds of figures may be significantly inflated (Godziak, 2008).

While trafficking is a serious problem, conflicting understandings of both childhood and exploitation call into question the valid application of this category. Most of the identified victims are over 16 and, as noted, they do not think of themselves as children. Many of them, once identified, choose to remain in the city working at their jobs. The classification of all those under 18 as children accords with the Convention on the Rights of the Child, but it bears little relevance to the culturally understood roles of young people who are well advanced in their transition to adulthood. Depending on the agenda of the observer, the same young person might be defined as either a child or a youth, and normative expectations vary considerably depending on the term actually used. A growing literature demonstrates that many ostensibly trafficked "children" – perhaps the majority – are in fact purposeful migrants taking advantage, with the endorsement of their families, of work and life opportunities not available near their homes. They may make use of recruiters, but these agents are not generally seen by the children and their families as traffickers. Yaqub makes the point that most of these young people leave home with a good idea of what faces them and many are in fact repeat migrators. They report practical reasons for their choices, and in most cases they see migration as having improved their socio-economic situation and their position within their households.

This is not to say that there are no protection issues involved. Children of 9 or 10, regardless of cultural framings, are seldom fully equipped to tackle all the issues of survival on their own. And while most children leave home to expand their opportunities, a substantial number are attempting to avoid abuse or early marriage at home, or possibly the threats presented by conflict. Daunting conditions generally face them at their destinations, where many end up living on the street, as will be discussed in the next section, or coping with the strong likelihood of exploitation in whatever work they find, whether as domestic servants or market vendors, as discussed in the previous chapter. There remains, however, little evidence that, in most cases, anti-trafficking policies and programmes do more than address a symptom of structural failure, and often in ways that may do children more harm than good.

Neil Howard's critical examination of child trafficking policies in Benin, an area of West Africa considered to be the hub of child trafficking and exploitation, finds a considerable disconnect between official perceptions and the larger realities that underlie children's migration for work. International declines in the price of cotton, he argues, played havoc with the rural economy, and the decision for children to leave home has clearly been a strategic one, carefully considered. "Protection" in this context can end up penalizing both children and families. In a setting where 6-year-olds routinely care for younger siblings and help around the house or in the fields, it is not considered extreme for older children to find opportunities further afield when there is no paying work at home. When asked what NGOs and government *should* be doing rather than attempting to prevent their migration, the response from most young people is that they should be providing alternative options for employment nearer to home, and ensuring that those who have to migrate can do it safely (Howard, 2012).

This is increasingly the direction that is being taken. The programmatic focus, as Huijsmans details, has moved from an anti-trafficking stance and towards the protection of children on the move, whatever their age. The demographic reality of adolescent and child migration to cities will persist, and there is little evidence of young people willingly returning home. A growing body of research indicates the need for more nuanced understandings of children's migration as well as more care in developing protective responses, making sure that there are systems in place to ensure that the needs of unaccompanied children are addressed at all stages of their journeys (see for instance Verdasco, 2013).

These needs can be manifold. Some unaccompanied children travel with other people and are connected to relatives or familiar people at their destinations, but this is not true for all. For children, obtaining important formal registration documents at their destinations may be even more difficult than for adults – and without work permits, health cards and the like they may be penalized in terms of their options. They may be afraid of being reported to authorities and indebted to employers who have agreed in advance to take them on – leaving them less able to change jobs when that seems called for because of harsh treatment or exploitation. Without adults, they have more limited access to housing and many end up living on the street. Some, mostly girls, are pushed to rely on transactional sex for survival. Yaqub cites a study of a sample of migrant children in South Africa, some as young as 7. Many had been assaulted trying to cross the border. Some survived by selling on the street, some by collecting plastic bottles, some by begging or relying on a welfare organization. Only one in three went to school, despite their plans to do so. What they felt they most needed was help getting into school and finding better jobs. Despite the hardships, most of them continued to feel that their lives at their destination would be better than the situations they had left behind (Yaqub, 2009).

## Children on the street

Many of these young migrants join the more than 100 million young people estimated to be living and working on the streets of towns and cities around the world, drawn to particular urban centres by the prospects available there, and making use of the survival opportunities that present themselves. Whether they come from a distance or from nearby slums, however, these young people face high levels of risk in the interconnected environments they occupy. A global report on street children and violence, drawing on commissioned papers from sixty-nine representative countries, points to the accumulated experience of abuse and violence that is routine for many of these children (Thomas de Benitez, 2007). Many are on the street in the first place to escape abuse at home. Just as violence often precipitates home-lessness for women, abusive treatment can often result in children running away or being driven to the street.

Although the majority of these children on the street are older than the age group that is the primary focus for this book, there are also quite young children who end up in this situation, and certainly there are many who see their elder siblings leave home, whether because of abuse, conflict, local poverty crises or family breakdown. A Ugandan study of almost 300 children showed over a third had left home because of abuse, about a quarter primarily because of poverty, and about 20 per cent because of the death of a parent. Less than 4 per cent reported that they were drawn primarily by the allure of the city streets (Van Blerk, 2004).

Once on the street, children are exposed to multiple risks that can lead to further abuses, including routine brutality by police in many places, robbery, violence among groups of children, and exposure to sexual abuse and harassment. Children living and working on the street also run the risk of being rounded up in efforts to "clean up" a city, often prior to large international events or visits by dignitaries. Those who then end up in detention centres or shelters of various kinds can be exposed to further neglect and abuse. In Zambia, as noted in an earlier chapter, an assessment of street children taken into residential care reported that the majority suffered from mental ill-ness, in most cases manifested as behavioural or conduct disorders (Imasiku and Banda, 2015). There was no indication in this report of the routes by which these children ended up in care, and it is possible that these conduct disorders might have been, as much as anything, an expression of their resistance to being where they were. Children drawn to the street are often those who prefer the hardship of living rough to the loss of control over their own lives. Even when offered free transportation back to their families, for instance, these children will most often opt to remain where they are.

While children on the street are often viewed primarily as victims, many researchers see them as resourceful agents, creatively using street space to avoid abuse at home or at the hands of authorities or predators on the street. Matthew Davies describes the world of street children in a Kenyan town, where they occupied a hidden stretch of mud road in the town centre behind the main commercial buildings – an area filled with rubbish and open sewers and considered to be both filthy and dangerous. The children found this place relatively free from harassment because of its reputation, which they then manipulated to ensure their own safety. Townspeople had ceded them this space, knowing that otherwise they would be an undesirable presence on the rest of the town's streets (Davies, 2008).

Also from Kenya, Ivan Droz describes another way of conceptualizing children on the street as belonging to "street families" rather than being "street children", an approach that stresses their strong ties to one another and often to adults as well, and that acknowledges the street as a genuine social environment and a "home" rather than just an expression of homelessness. This apparently more progressive way of viewing these material realities, however, has also been used to "euphematize" the situation, in Droz's words, normalizing harsh realities that have been forced on children by their deep poverty and the absence of effective supports (Droz, 2006).

Amy Ritterbusch's account of the experience of young girls living on the street in Bogota, Colombia, highlights many of these harsh realities. Their lives are defined by the constant dangers that characterize the street spaces they occupy, never comfortably but always balancing the need for survival, companionship, autonomy with the inevitability of violence, whether from gender-based hate crimes, social cleansing or the by-products of drug use and prostitution. No place feels safe, they say. Their constant movement through the city, Ritterbusch explains, is "haunted by place-memories of violence" (2012, p. 65). Yet they insist on their self-determination, rejecting the term "street girls" because this category effectively disempowers them, allowing the spatial referent to simplify and overshadow what they feel are more complex identities.

## Evictions

Forced evictions affect millions of households globally every year. They are most often targeted at people living in informal settlements without legal tenure – the situation for a large and growing percentage of urban dwellers. In some cities, this can include more than half the population. Although China stands out for the scale of its evictions, they also take place in large numbers in countries with democratic governments like India, South Africa and the Philippines, and not infrequently they involve the excessive use of force.

An Indian slum dweller describes the experience of being a parent in this situation:

> When you live in a slum the threat of eviction is always around you. Most of the time it is like a shadow in the night. You sense its presence but you convince yourself that everything will be OK. But at other times it is a real danger. And when the eviction happens it is an explosion of fear and anger, sorrow and disbelief. Imagine what it is like to watch your children witness your total powerlessness as police tear down their home, trash their belongings, beat them with batons and hound them with teargas.
>
> *(SDI, 2013)*

The available information, incomplete as it is, indicates, as noted above, that even more people are displaced each year by development-related evictions than by conflict and disasters combined (Kothari, 2015). A conservative estimate is that 15 million people a year are displaced by public sector development projects alone. (This does not include all the evictions related to development by the private sector.) About 1.5 million were evicted, for instance, just as a result of Beijing's preparations for the 2008 Olympic Games. These evictions occur in both urban and rural areas for a range of projects, which can include dam building, urban renewal, new highways, large sporting events – or simply the decision to clear an aspiring world city of unsightly slums. These evictions are generally presented as being for "the greater good". But they can have dire results for families, with the loss of property and livelihoods, community breakdown and long-term upheaval, entrenching the poverty of those already hard pressed. Because the people affected are frequently deemed to be illegal residents, there is often no warning, no recourse, no compensation and no alternatives for relocation. Alternatives *can* realistically be developed, however, as has been made clear by the numerous occasions on which federations of the urban poor have negotiated peaceful relocations with municipalities on terms that are mutually acceptable and beneficial (see for instance Patel and Bartlett, 2009).

These evictions are not only a matter of greed or indifference. Gautam Bhan details in the context of Delhi the language used within the courts, the media, the policy environment, the general public discourse, which defines who does and does not have rights. People squatting illegally are not spoken of as "citizens" – they are "encroachers" who are essentially stealing the city's land from its more deserving residents, polluting it and undermining the capacity for more aesthetic development. As thieves, encroachers, polluters, they can hardly expect sympathetic treatment (Bhan, 2016). Arjun Appadurai, writing about the "us" and "them" dichotomy that underlies so much violence, refers also to the hostility engendered by the notion of state-provided entitlements for undesirable populations – whether to housing, health or sanitation (2006). The fear of "the other" surely underlies the violent methods so often undertaken to wrest land, possessions and stability from people.

When resettlement after eviction is part of the deal, it is often to distant peripheral areas where people have no access to jobs, schools or services. Many relocated households, unable to survive, end up abandoning the new site and heading back into the city, taking their chances. In the case of rural people displaced by dams and reservoirs, the long-term outcomes may also be dire. Both India and China keep records of these kinds of resettlements, and in both countries, large proportions of those resettled (46 per cent in China, 75 per cent in India) remained impoverished two decades after their removal (IDMC, 2016).

It is not only governments that are at fault here. A year-long examination by an international team of investigative journalists pointed in 2015 to 3.4 million people displaced over the previous decade by World Bank-supported projects, with the Bank routinely failing to live up to its own policies for protecting those displaced. The Bank in theory forbids sudden forceful evictions and requires that families be compensated and resettled in improved conditions, yet it has repeatedly been complicit in displacements that have violated these guidelines. It is also increasing its support for the large-scale projects that are the most problematic. A letter from advocacy groups around the world in 2012 urged the Bank not only to strengthen its own guidelines, but to undertake detailed assessments of the likely impact for children, and the potential in particular for violence and exploitation. The Bank's response, however, has included no specific plans on that front (Chavkin et al., 2015).

The details of individual evictions, usually from news reports, can be harrowing. In Kathmandu, Nepal, in May 2012, over 2,000 police were deployed to assist in the eviction of almost 1,000 people, including more than 400 children under 15. Families were awakened at 5 a.m. and told to gather their belongings and leave their homes. There was too little time to gather up cooking utensils, bedding, citizenship papers and other essentials, and women were beaten when they tried to go back for more of their belongings. Police used rubber bullets and tear gas while bulldozers levelled almost 250 shacks. Those injured were prevented from accessing medical treatment until the end of the day. This demolition was presented as the first step in the removal of multiple squatter settlements along the bank of the Bagmati River to make way for road improvements (Housing and Land Rights Network, 2012).

Government officials claimed that they had posted warning notices in newspapers, but most residents were illiterate and the eviction came as a surprise. Pabitra Magar told a reporter a few years later that it had been the most frightening day of her life. She and her 9-year-old daughter watched as the brick home they had built bit by bit over eight years was demolished. The family slept under trees near the ruins of the settlement for several months along with other residents, and then they all started cautiously to erect huts out of bamboo and plastic sheets. There was no resettlement plan, and a few years later, most of the evicted households were still living there illegally in these temporary shelters. The government had offered them grants of USD 250 to leave the area, but most had nowhere to go and they relied on this location for access to local jobs. "The eviction was partially successful," said an official, "but people again started building temporary huts. They are still staying there illegally. A stern step has to be taken to remove them." As road construction plans failed to materialize, the dangers of flooding were offered as an updated justification for the eviction, although still without alternative solutions (Manandhar, 2014).

Sometimes these evictions involve tens of thousands of people at a time. The violent November 2016 eviction of waterfront fishing families in the community of Otodo Gbame in Lagos, Nigeria, involved an estimated 30,000 people. According to Amnesty International, Lagos authorities claimed in advance that these demolitions were necessary because of the rise in kidnappings in the city – the irregular structures were seen as a security threat (Amnesty, 2016). In the early morning hours on 9 November, fires were set by a gang of boys with ties to a powerful family. The fires were spread further by police when they arrived soon afterwards, and an estimated 10,000 residents were left homeless in a matter of hours. The destruction continued the following night. According to a young woman in the community, "Police came again after midnight with caterpillar and started breaking everywhere, putting fire on people's houses. They are seriously beating our people and threatening to shoot unless we leave. All of us are on top of water now, there is nowhere to go" (Housing and Land Rights Network, 2016). This happened despite an injunction a few days earlier from the High Court of Lagos State. Just a year earlier, over 10,000 residents of the Badia-East community in Lagos had also been forcibly evicted, and many of them, according to Amnesty, remain homeless and dependent on family and friends. Given that over half the population in Nigeria is under 18, we can assume that almost a quarter of those affected would have been young children, those least able to cope with this physical and emotional assault.

Perhaps the most dramatic example of eviction in recent decades was the systematic Operation Murambasvina (or "drive out trash") in 2005 in Zimbabwe, when President Robert Mugabe, in the aftermath of elections, called in the bulldozers on slum settlements where people had voted in large numbers for the opposition. Not surprisingly, these were also areas coveted for redevelopment. Over 700,000 people were forcibly displaced, and those who resisted were shot, beaten or arrested. Tens of thousands of children dropped out of school because they were forced to move to areas without enough schools or because the impact on family finances made school impossible to afford. Twenty-eight per cent of all the children lost more than a year of school and many of them were out for more than three years, or never went back. Many of the children who continued their schooling were in poorly equipped informal schools set up by their families after the evictions (Amnesty, 2011).

Given how common evictions are, there has been astonishingly little formal research into the impact for children. One qualitative study in the late 1990s described interviews with evicted children from Manila, Phnom Penh and Mumbai, who spoke of their panic in the confusion of the evictions and the fear around having no place to go and having to sleep outdoors. Picking up the pieces afterwards and regaining any kind of stability had been difficult. Friends were lost, parents' jobs were lost, children dropped out of school. Many continued to have nightmares, headaches and panic attacks over subsequent months (Rahmatullah, 1997).

There have also been a few follow-up studies of cases where children were relocated after a forced eviction. Jill Swart-Kruger followed a group of children after their eviction from a squatter settlement in central Johannesburg to a distant relocation site outside the city with no basic service provision. This site was also the setting for a few of the situations discussed in previous chapters: the children who felt unable to attend school, given the indignity of arriving unwashed; and the paraffin poisonings of some small thirsty children, who had mistaken the colourless fuel for water when trucked deliveries failed to arrive when scheduled. Kruger noted more generally that the relocation had in effect replaced the challenges of living in a congested inner city squatter settlement with a brand new set of difficulties that included the complete disruption of access to livelihoods, thus entrenching the poverty of these children and their families (Kruger, 2001). More recently, Sudeshna Chatterjee worked with children in Delhi, who were also forcibly moved from a central squatter settlement to a peripheral relocation site (2007). Like Kruger, she noted that the already trying conditions that families had been dealing with at their original sites became far more challenging in the new settlements, as access to everything became more difficult. In Delhi, the impact for some of the children was somewhat mitigated by their active involvement in advocating and negotiating for certain outcomes, as will be discussed further in the final chapter. More research is sorely needed on the long-term impact for young children of these increasingly common and entirely preventable events, especially in situations where children and families endure repeated evictions and are driven into ever-deeper poverty.

A lack of legal tenure does not necessarily result in eviction. Many communities worldwide, even without tenure, may have a measure of *de facto* security. But hundreds of millions of these households live in constant fear of forced removal. The vigilance can be so extreme that it may entail a look-out child staying at home all day while older household members go off to work – as was the case for pavement dweller families in Mumbai. The child's function is to stay alert to any threats, and to grab important papers and run to warn family members if yet another eviction gets underway. Anxiety aside, the possibility of eviction has other significant implications. Families are far less willing to invest their time or limited resources in housing that may be taken from them, and this means that the gradual incremental improvements that generally characterize the housing of the poor tend not to happen.

The phenomenon of market-driven evictions, not by large external developers but often within slums themselves, is also worth remarking on here. In many places a combination of policy and pressure from organized communities can make forced evictions difficult to carry out. What often happens instead is that owners of slum land and structures evict tenants and then replace their housing with cheaply built multi-storey tenements that, informal as they are, ignore any building regulations.

The evicted tenants may be able to return to these buildings if rents do not go up too steeply, but safety is a real issue, and rapidly increasing density expands the risks for all in a settlement. In Nairobi slums, the problem is acute. Slums occupy 2 per cent of the city's land, but house half of its population. A resident comments: "There are disasters in waiting ... Have you seen those houses? They are buildings but they almost look bent. We are waiting on time bombs. If you go to something cheap and then your life is gone, it's expensive" (Lines and Makau, 2017, p. 81).

## Refugees and internally displaced people

Around the world, millions of people each year are forced to start living as refugees, uprooted from their homes and communities because of conflict or persecution. The most recent figures, for the end of 2015, estimate the number of these displaced people at 65.3 million, an all-time high. This is one human being out of every 113 in the world, more than the population of France or the United Kingdom. About 21 million of these displaced people are classified as refugees proper – those who have crossed borders into other countries. The remaining majority, 40 million plus, are IDPs, or internally displaced people. As of September 2016, the Syrian conflict alone had displaced over 11 million people, more than half of them IDPs.

There are also of course the many irregular international refugees and migrants, those not officially accounted for, but part of what UNHCR (the UN refugee agency) describes as "mixed migration flows", people who may or may not gain formal asylum, whether they are Sudanese crossing the Mediterranean to escape drought and conflict or young Guatemalans attempting to find refuge from gang violence. These are estimated to be anywhere from 10 to 30 per cent of the documented international flows of people (UN Population Division, 2013).

For many displaced people, the situation is prolonged. The Dadaab camp in Kenya, for instance, larger than most of the cities in the country with a population of about 330,000, has been home to many Somali refugee families for over twenty years. In many countries, such as the Democratic Republic of Congo, Iraq or Sudan, numbers have flat-lined as displacement remains a chronic state of affairs. In other countries where conflict has escalated in the last few years, such as Nigeria, Syria, Yemen, there is the risk that it will become endemic and endlessly protracted.

About half of these uprooted people are children, many of them separated from their families. For many of these children, displacement is all they have ever known. UNICEF offers some shocking statistics. The number of child refugees, they say, has risen 77 per cent in just five years; 28 million children have been displaced by violence; in Nigeria alone, Boko Haram has led to the displacement of 1.4 million children (UNICEF, 2016). The figures are numbing. It almost doesn't matter how high the millions climb, they quickly become unthinkable. And these figures do not include the huge number of people who are displaced by disasters. In 2015 alone, there were over 19 million new disaster displacements – more than twice as many as those newly displaced by conflict over the same period (IDMC,

2016). The numbers displaced by any one event can be enormous – for instance, in just one week at the end of June 2012, over 6 million people were forced by monsoon rains to leave their homes in Assam and other states in northeastern India (IDMC, 2012). In many cases, those who are displaced cannot head home for prolonged periods and can be highly vulnerable to the next round of weather disasters.

Displacement because of floods or droughts or earthquakes is not an effect of violence, as in the case of war or forced eviction. Yet it is widely accepted that there is no such thing as a "natural" disaster. Putting initial causes aside for the moment, a number of factors determine whether an event actually becomes a disaster or not: the prior vulnerability of those affected, the level of preparedness, the effectiveness of responses and the quality of reconstruction or resettlement. Far from cutting across social differences, these disasters tend to lay bare and deepen existing inequities. Those most profoundly affected by climate change, which contributes to many of these events, often have barely perceptible carbon footprints.

The massive scale of displacement worldwide and the limited resources allocated to this rapidly growing problem raise grave protection issues for children. "Consider," says Stuart Lustig, "the destabilizing impact of one's family suddenly uprooting, often violently, from everything familiar (friends, neighbourhoods, cherished places, favourite activities) and transplanting themselves, sometimes as a unit but potentially in fragments, in an entirely unknown world …" (2010, p. 241). Research from both global north and south points to the distress, frustration and despair that can accompany displacement, whether through refugee status or the loss of home through disaster. Aside from deepening poverty and its many implications for health and survival, there are the acute social and emotional pressures.

Specific risks have been pinpointed for young children. There are all of the issues related to mental and physical health, but increased rates of child abuse have also been associated with factors that become more prevalent after upheaval – such as maternal depression, increased poverty, loss of property or a breakdown in social support. Research in the United States in the six months following a hurricane found that in areas most severely affected by the storm, rates of traumatic brain injury in children under two rose sharply. Five times as many children were admitted to hospital with inflicted brain injuries as in the previous six months. There were also ten times as many accidental brain injuries, considered to be due to the presence of environmental hazards in emergency shelters and damaged or temporary housing, as well as reduced parental supervision. In other words, both abuse and neglect were at issue here (Keenan et al., 2004).

No similar research from the global south points so precisely to increased rates of maltreatment. However, there is a growing body of evidence on the toxic conditions of displacement, whether in camps or in the process of longer-term resettlement. In the aftermath of the event that precipitates displacement, children's capacity to cope can be closely related to the settings they end up in. Research from Croatia, for instance, after the war there, compared displaced children whose families were resettled with host families with those who were placed in collective shelters.

Those in the shelters showed considerably higher levels of stress, manifested through such indicators as eating disorders, difficulties with sleep, nightmares, physical problems, emotional and behavioural problems (Ajdukovic and Ajdukovic, 1993).

Post-disaster and refugee camps are often grim places where the frequent shortages of clean water, food and medical care, along with exposure to infectious disease, can result in illness and acute malnutrition, especially for young children. The camps are generally uncomfortable and overcrowded, with little provision for privacy in spaces that may be shared by multiple families. Concerns about theft, violence, deteriorating shelters, insufficient latrines and washing facilities, long lines for water, an absence of adequate lighting, may all contribute to the more general stress and anxiety. Deprived of their own space, of the routines of home and a sense of control over their lives, people sitting idle for the most part may experience a breakdown in the social controls that normally regulate household and community behaviour.

Sexual violence is frequently reported, and there have been numerous accounts of children and women enduring repeated abuse. Girls in a Vietnamese detention camp for boat people explained that at night, once the doors to their dormitory huts closed, the sexual predators would take over, secure in the knowledge that no one would risk the violent reprisals that would result from reporting them (Garbarino, 2008). Research from Colombia also details the increased rates of domestic abuse experienced by women who have been displaced – almost one woman in two (Profamilia, 2011). Sexual exploitation has become a survival mechanism for many refugee families, and inadequate food rations in camps can encourage young girls to engage in sex to help their families. Parents often believe that marrying off their daughters can reduce the chances that they will be victimized. The UN report on conflict-related sexual violence makes the point that the fear of rape can also lead to displacement, as women and girls in some places flee to avoid becoming victims of sexual violence by armed groups (UNSG, 2012).

Depression and anxiety can be widespread, and high rates of post-traumatic stress disorder (PTSD) as well as more common mental disorders have been identified among camp populations (Kane et al., 2014). Among Syrian refugees in Jordan, clinical depression and PTSD were both commonplace, and people reported worries about missing relatives and about the violence that is so common within camps. This violence can become both a cause and a consequence of despair. "The violence gets internalized as men and families are not earning incomes, the tensions rise … so kids are experiencing high levels of violence in their families and not just having to cope with their past experiences and what they've lived through now as a result of very difficult circumstances" (Jay, 2016). In the Vietnamese boat people's detention camp, two thirds of the children, primarily girls, described spending entire days in their bunks. This was in part an effort to remain unnoticed by predators, but certainly depression played a role. One girl noted that she could see forests in the distance that reminded her of home, but had not actually been outside the camp for over two years (Garbarino, 2008).

Ethnographic work in the Gihembe and Kiziba refugee camps in Rwanda provides details from residents on their concerns. These camps are each home to about

15,000 residents, over half of them under 17 years of age. Housing is semi-permanent, mud walls with plastic or tin roofs, and too small to accommodate the frequently large families. Little shacks known as ghettoes are often added outside to accommodate older boys. Residents rely mostly on food aid for survival, although there are some economic activities, including the sale of their food rations both within and outside the camp. According to mothers, the most serious harm facing children is the risk of early pregnancy; according to fathers, it is being out of school. These concerns are closely followed by worries about delinquency and prostitution. Other harms, ranked lower, were also listed by these parents: malnutrition, the lack of living space, sexual abuse, abandonment and the lack of healthcare, entertainment and opportunity. One woman explained the situation: "… we've got a very huge problem in this camp … outside, children cultivate and do other things, but here if they don't have something to do they come up with weird things … girls become uncontrollable and prostitutes. They do some bad things due to the bad conditions they are living in" (Prickett et al., 2013, p. 43). Children were being pushed into delinquency (theft, drug and alcohol use, violent behaviour) by poverty, neglect and abuse at home, and the violence of the older boys, in turn, terrorized others in the camp. "When they take drugs," said one young woman, "those children become very dangerous. They fight, destroy things, injure people; they cause insecurity in the camp" (p. 51).

An estimated half or more of all refugees and IDPs choose not to go to camps, but take their chances instead in cities, mostly in the hope that this will mean more opportunities for work and a better chance to rebuild their lives. Although this decision may moderate some problems, it creates others. In many cases, humanitarian services and food rations are only dispensed in camps and those who take the city route are expected to fend for themselves. They may also be forced to live hidden marginal lives. The opportunities may be greater in cities, but people who have already experienced profound loss may also face contempt and rejection from local residents who fear the influx of strangers and the implied competition for jobs, state entitlements and resources.

A companion piece to the research in the Rwandan camps looked at conditions for both Congolese and Somali refugees in slums in Kampala, Uganda. Here, resident parents also felt that the most significant harm faced by children was a lack of access to formal education, but this was followed by their experience of discrimination. For the Congolese, rape and inadequate housing followed in the list of significant harms for children; for the Somalis, drug abuse and child trafficking were more important. Both communities saw younger children as less vulnerable to harm because they were more closely supervised (Horn et al., 2013).

Gillian Mann describes the situation of Congolese refugee children in slums in Dar es Salaam, who experienced their exclusion, fear of exposure and abject family circumstances as more devastating than the dangers they faced in the context of war back at home. "You are no longer a person," explained one boy. "You have lost not only your land, your things and your country, you have lost yourself." A young girl echoed his sentiments: "Here we live like chickens, caged up … circling around, never knowing if we will be released. In Congo, it was different, I had a life. I was a person" (Mann, 2012, p. 451). In the context of displacement, as in the case of the more routine survival strategies of life in poverty, children frequently identify the assaults on dignity and personhood as the most draining aspect of their complicated lives.

## Everyday violence and distress

It is increasingly clear that for many displaced people, the most challenging aspect of the experience is the long, slow, exhausting process of putting life back together again, and often the sheer impossibility of regaining a solid foothold on life. Wessells and Kostelny note that there are usually not clear boundaries between conflict and post-conflict periods, or between acute traumatic events and more ordinary forms of distress. "These everyday sources of distress lack the salience of traumatic events and often go unattended, yet can have significant, cumulative impact" (Wessells and Kostelny, 2012, p. 641). The challenges are often reflected in much higher mortality and malnutrition rates for young children. Children who are born in conflict-affected countries are twice as likely to be malnourished and twice as likely to die before they reach the age of 5 (World Bank, 2011).

For both the Somali and Congolese refugee groups in Kampala, the discrimination they experienced did not improve with time. The Somali population in the Kasaato slum settlement, for instance, had been there since 1993, but over twenty years later they were still treated with contempt. Children described verbal abuse and assault when they were walking to school or fetching water for their families. Even rape was not unusual, and it was frequently experienced as an expression of contempt on the part of the rapist. The most common strategy employed by refugee households was to avoid Ugandans as much as possible. Parents described accompanying children to school, sending them to fetch water only when everyone else was finished, and even keeping small children locked in the house. Language barriers exacerbated the situation and created a self-perpetuating cycle. Assaults were rarely reported to authorities because they were unsympathetically received, seldom resulted in practical responses, and could mean repercussions. "When you report a person, a Ugandan, he can destroy you," said one Congolese woman, "This is why when things happen we prefer keeping quiet, we go to the hospital … we help our children who are depressed and we stay home together" (Horn et al., 2013, p. 62). Even in cases of rape, girls would often keep quiet for fear of retaliation, and the rape would often be discovered even by their families only if they became pregnant.

The post-conflict situation affects more than just those who are displaced. The legacy of the conflict may be escalating and continuing levels of violence, especially in urban areas. This may be the case especially when the local population has been swollen by an influx of displaced people, straining resources and the capacity to respond. Gabriella McMichael, pointing to the city of Juba in Sudan, acknowledges the role of ex-combatants and unemployed youth in these situations, but also points also to more complex dynamics, often involving inequitable access to land markets and unscrupulous attempts to capitalize on the fluid post-conflict context (2014).

The wreckage of post-conflict lives is often experienced in the most material terms. James Quesada describes the situation of Daniel in Nicaragua, following the revolution. Evicted from their home as a result of changes in property rights after the Sandinista electoral defeat, his family experienced rapidly declining fortunes. After living with friends, they ended up squatting on a hillside in a dwelling of cardboard, plastic and zinc sheets. Daniel and his small brother dug ditches around the house to prevent their dirt floor turning to mud during rainstorms; they fetched water from a spigot half a mile away, washed clothing in a stream, scavenged for food and fought to maintain their leaking plastic roof while their mother searched for work around the city. It was the sheer constancy of these burdens as much as the recurring crises that led Daniel, at age 10, to confide to Quesada that it would be better if he died. "Look at me, I'm all bones anyway, I'm already dying. I'm too small and I've stopped growing and I am another mouth to feed" (Quesada, 2004, p. 294). These costs to children in the aftermath of violence may be overlooked because they do not constitute an immediate violent threat. But the everyday violence of continued survival may cost children as much or more.

Also important in this context is the "slow violence" that results from the more gradual manifestations of climate change. Millions of people may be forced to move in coming decades, whether from drought-stricken areas or from places where land is slowly disappearing as sea levels rise. International courts have rejected to date the notion that people displaced for reasons of climate change can be covered by the same laws and protections that apply to refugees from conflict.

Even more widespread in their effects are the gradually worsening conditions that do not literally displace people. They may not be losing home and neighbourhood, but they are losing ground in a more metaphorical sense as their often-precarious toehold on life is threatened. Longer dry spells mean lower water tables, failing crops, higher food prices. More frequent and intense rainfalls mean flooding and standing water, landslides on heavily built hillsides, the destruction of fragile assets. When families are barely getting by, even minor changes can be completely destabilizing.

When I lived in Kathmandu, I spent time along a stretch of riverside in an illegal settlement there. Higher water levels each year during monsoon rains meant people's shacks were more routinely flooded, and families had to take refuge for a month or more each year under plastic sheets up by the roadside. By the time the heaviest rains had passed, a foot or more of foul-smelling mud had been deposited in their shacks. Everything had to be dug out and dried out and many possessions could not be salvaged. People living just a stone's throw away and those who passed by each day on the bridge nearby noticed the higher waters but were unaffected. This community of a hundred-odd families, however, was more impoverished each year, as were hundreds of other households also squatting in settlements along the river. They didn't dare go to the authorities for assistance because eviction would have been the most likely response and they had nowhere else to go.

Here as in so many places it is the poorest families and communities that are most affected – those who lack secure tenure, who build on flood plains, who have no storm drains, who can't count on water supplies, who have the least capacity to prepare, adapt and protect themselves. These more gradual changes in communities around the world can mean rising prices for basic supplies, more precarious livelihoods, more demands on time and energy to cope with increasingly difficult surroundings and daily routines – further to go to find firewood, more time in line to fetch water. This equation by which the world's most affluent people displace the cost of their lifestyles onto the countries and communities and households that have done the least to contribute to changing climates is the most extreme global manifestation of the violence inherent in inequity. And by the same logic, when things get worse, children are often where the costs accumulate. Instead of being physically displaced, they are the end point of this displacement of costs.

Consider the simple metric of calories and their allocation. Research from Bangladesh looked at the way food was distributed within households. After first calculating individual energy expenditures and calorie needs for everyone in the family, researchers found that when there were enough calories to meet everyone's needs, the excess was generally given to children. When there was not enough to go around, adults took priority and children received less than they needed (Cockburn, Dauphin and Razzaque, 2009). This makes sense in immediate terms. If wage earners are not fed, it threatens their capacity to support the entire household enterprise. But the costs for children are long-term. In fact, a powerful measure of poverty, along with all the other multi-dimensional indicators that are used, would be the extent to which parents are forced to draw from their children as opposed to being able to invest in their well-being and their future.

Children's nutrition is not the only cost in the context of these kinds of pressures. All too often in situations of extreme need, children are, in effect, the means by which adjustments are made to maintain family stability. Even if they are not explicitly targeted in terms of nourishment or added work burdens, when families face more pressure than they can reasonably adapt to, neglect and abuse can easily follow.

These disproportionate impacts for children are not exclusive to the context of climate change. But this consideration of extensive and everyday risk is not really the detour here that it may appear to be. It is basic to understanding why this slow violence over so much of the planet has to be taken as seriously as the more extreme events that cause displacement. There is growing evidence that the cumulative exposure to these everyday hazards is having a wider and deeper impact than the more dramatic large disasters (Adelekan et al., 2015). Mindy Fullilove suggests that displacement is the big global problem of the twenty-first century. This is so much more the case if we include as a form of displacement the relentless erosion of people's capacity to preserve their roots, maintain community and nurture their children.

# References

Adelekan, I, C Johnson, M Manda, D Matyas, B Mberu, S Parnell, M Pelling, D Satterthwaite and J Vivekananda (2015) Disaster risk and its reduction: An agenda for urban Africa, *International Development Planning Review* 37(1), 33–43

Amnesty International (2011) Left behind: The impact of Zimbabwe's mass forced evictions on the right to education. Available at www.amnesty.org/en/documents/AFR46/019/2011/en/

Ajdukovic, Marina and Dean Ajdukovic (1993) Psychological well-being of refugee children, *Child Abuse and Neglect* 17, 843–854

Amnesty International (2016) Nigeria: Tens of thousands at risk of imminent mass forced evictions in Lagos, 13 October 2016. Available at www.amnesty.org/en/latest/news/2016/10/nigeria-tens-of-thousands-of-residents-of-waterfront-communities-at-risk-of-imminent-mass-forced-evictions-in-lagos

Appadurai, Arjun (2006) *Fear of small numbers: An essay on the geography of anger*, Durham and London: Duke University Press

Artar, Müge (2013) Seasonal migrants' realities: A study of 686 Turkish households, *Early Childhood Matters: Children of Seasonal Migrant Workers* 121, 20–23

Bhan, Gautam (2016) *In the public's interest: Evictions, citizenship and inequality in contemporary Delhi*, Delhi: Orient Black Swan

Chatterjee, S (2007) Children's role in humanizing forced evictions and resettlements in Delhi, *Children, Youth and Environments* 17(1), 198–221

Chavkin, Sascha, Ben Hallman, Michael Hudson, Cécile Schilis-Gallego and Shane Shifflett (2015) How the World Bank broke its promise to protect the poor, *Huffington Post*, 15 April 2015

Cockburn, John, Anyck Dauphin and Mohammad A. Razzaque (2009) Child poverty and intra-household allocation, *Children, Youth and Environments* 19(2), 36–53

Collins, Lauren (2017) Europe's child-refugee crisis, *The New Yorker*, 2 February 2017. Available at www.newyorker.com/magazine/2017/02/27/europes-child-refugee-crisis

Daniel, Umi (2013) A healthy and safe environment for young migrants at urban Indian worksites, *Early Childhood Matters: Children of Seasonal Migrant Workers* 121, 27–30

Davies, Matthew (2008) Anthropological study of street children in northwest Kenya, *Childhood* 15, 309–331

Droz, Ivan (2006) Street children and the work ethic: New policy for an old moral, *Childhood* 13, 349–363

Fullilove, Mindy Thompson (2005) *Root shock: How tearing up city neighborhoods hurts America, and what we can do about it*, New York: Ballantine Books

Garbarino, James (2008) *Children and the dark side of human experience: Confronting global realities and rethinking child development*, New York: Springer

Godziak, Elzbieta (2008) On challenges, dilemmas, and opportunities in studying trafficked children, *Anthropological Quarterly* 81(4), 903–923

Horn, Rebecca, David Bizimana, Scholastica Nasinyama, Lilia Aporo, Emmanuel Kironde, Mark Canavera and Lindsay Stark (2013) Community based child protection mechanisms amongst urban refugees in Kampala, Uganda: An ethnographic study, Child Protection in Crisis Network for Research, Learning and Action, Columbia University Mailman School of Public Health. Available at www.alnap.org/pool/files/cbcpms-uganda-final-6-december-2013.pdf

Housing and Land Rights Network (2012) Forced eviction and demolition of 248 homes in Kathmandu, Nepal. Available at www.hlrn.org/img/cases/np-ddfe-080512.pdf

Housing and Land Rights Network (2016) Urgent action appeal: Fire, bulldozers and demolitions on Lagos Lagoon, Lagos, Nigeria. Available at www.hlrn.org/img/cases/ua_nig_16112016.pdf

Howard, Neil (2012) Protecting children from trafficking in Benin: In need of politics and participation, *Development in Practice* 22(4), 460–472

Huijsmans, Roy (2015) Children and young people in migration: A relational approach, in C N Laoire *et al.* (eds) *Movement, mobilities and journeys, geographies of children and young people*, New York: Springer, pp. 1–22

IDMC (2012) North-east India: 6 million internally displaced by monsoon floods and landslides. Available at www.unhcr.org/refworld/publisher/IDMC.html

IDMC (2016) GRID 2016: Global report on internal displacement, Internal Displacement Monitoring Centre. Available at www.internal-displacement.org/globalreport2016/pdf/2016-global-report-internal-displacement-IDMC.pdf

Imasiku, Mwiya Liamunga and Serah Banda (2015) Mental health problems of street children in residential care in Zambia: Special focus on prediction of psychiatric conditions in street children, *Journal of Clinical Medicine and Research* 7(1), 1–6

IPEC (2002) *Every child counts: New global estimates on child labour*, Geneva: International Labour Office

Jay, Martin (2016) Depression, mental illness endemic amongst Syrian refugees, DW News. Available at www.dw.com/en/depression-mental-illness-endemic-amongst-syrian-refugees/a-19076642

Kane, Jeremy, Peter Ventevogel, Paul Spiegel, Judith K Bass, Mark van Ommeren and Wietse A Tol (2014) Mental, neurological, and substance use problems among refugees in primary health care: Analysis of the Health Information System in 90 refugee camps, *BMI Med* 12, 228

Keenan, Heather T, Stephen W Marshall, Mary Alice Nocera and Desmond K. Runyan (2004) Increased incidence of inflicted traumatic brain injury in children after a natural disaster, *American Journal of Preventive Medicine* 26(3), 189–189

Kothari, Miloon (2015) *The global crisis of displacement and evictions: A housing and land rights response*, New York: Rosa Luxemburg Stiftung

Kruger, Jill Swart (2001). Children in a South African squatter camp gain and lose a voice, in L Chawla (ed.) *Growing up in an urbanizing world*, London: Earthscan/UNESCO, pp. 83–100

Lines, K and J Makau (2017) Muungano nguvu yetu (unity is strength): 20 years of the Kenyan federation of slum dwellers, IIED Working Paper, London: IIED

Lustig, Stuart (2010) An ecological framework for the refugee experience: What is the impact on child development? in Evans, Gary W, and Theodore D Wachs (eds) *Chaos and its influence on children's development: An ecological perspective*, Washington DC: American Psychological Association, pp. 239–251

McMichael, Gabriella (2014) Rethinking access to land and violence in post-war cities: Reflections from Juba, Southern Sudan, *Environment and Urbanization* 26(2), 389–400

Manandhar, Shilu (2014) Evicted once, Nepali squatters living in the ruins of a razed river settlement fear a recurring nightmare, *Global Press Journal, Asia*, 5 November 2014. Available at https://globalpressjournal.com/asia/nepal/evicted-once-nepali-squatters-living-in-the-ruins-of-a-razed-river-settlement-fear-a-recurring-nightmare/

Mann, Gillian (2012) Beyond war: "Suffering" among displaced Congolese children in Dar es Salaam, *Development in Practice* 22(4), 448–459

Patel, Sheela and Sheridan Bartlett (2009) Reflections on innovation, assessment, and social change: A SPARC case study, *Development in Practice* 19(1), 3–15

Prickett, Imogen, Israel Moya, Liberata Muhorakeye, Mark Canavera and Lindsay Stark (2013) Community-based child protection mechanisms in refugee camps in Rwanda: An ethnographic study, New York: Columbia University Mailman School of Public Health, Child Protection in Crisis Network for Research, Learning and Action

Profamilia (2011) *Encuesta en zonas marginadas salud sexual y salud reproductiva, desplazamiento forzado y pobreza*, Asociacion Probienestar de la Familia Colombiana, Colombia. Available at www.profamilia.org.co/encuestaenzonasmarginadas/pdf/ezm2011_completo.pdf

Quesada, James (2004) Suffering child: An embodiment of war and its aftermath in post-Sandinista Nicaragua, in Nancy Scheper-Hughes and Philippe Bourgois (eds) *Violence in war and peace*, Oxford: Blackwell, pp. 290–296

Rahmatullah, T (1997) *The impact of evictions on children: Case studies from Phnom Penh, Manila and Mumbai.* New York: United Nations ESCAP and The Asian Coalition for Housing Rights

Ritterbusch, Amy (2012) From street girls to "VMC" girls: Empowering strategies for representing and overcoming place-memories of violence in Colombia, *Children, Youth and Environments* 23(1), 64–104

SDI (2013) Age of zinc: Memoirs of an Indian shack dweller, Slum Dwellers International. Available at http://old.sdinet.org/media/upload/documents/Age_of_Zinc_Book_2_ Memoirs_of_an_Indian_Shack_Dweller

Sommers, Marc (2010) Urban youth in Africa, *Environment and Urbanization* 22(2), 317–332

Tacoli, Cecilia, Gordon McGranahan and David Satterthwaite (2015) Urbanisation, rural–urban migration and urban poverty, IIED Working Paper, London: IIED

Thomas de Benitez, Sarah (2007) *State of the world's street children: Violence*, London: Consortium for Street Children

UNICEF (2016) *Uprooted: The growing crisis for refugee and migrant children*, New York: UNICEF

United Nations (2013) World population policies 2013, New York: United Nations Department of Economic and Social Affairs

United Nations Population Division (2013) International migration policies: Government views and priorities, New York: United Nations Department of Economic and Social Affairs, ST/ESA/SER.A/342

UNODC (2014) Global report on trafficking in persons, New York: United Nations

UN Secretary-General (UNSG), Conflict-related sexual violence: Report of the Secretary-General, 13 January 2012, A/66/657*–S/2012/33

Van Blerk, Lorraine (2004) Journeys to the street: The complex migration geographies of Ugandan street children, *Geoforum* 35, 471–488

Verdasco, Andrea (2013) Strengthening child protection systems for unaccompanied migrant children in Mozambique: A case study of the border town of Ressano Garcia, Innocenti Working Paper 2013–2013

Wessells, Michael and Kathleen Kostelny (2012) Everyday distress: Psychosocial and economic impact of forced migration on children and families, in Rosalind King and Valerie Maholmes (eds) *The Oxford handbook of poverty and child development*, New York: Oxford University Press. doi:10.1093/oxfordhb/9780199769100.013.0035

World Bank (2011) *World development report 2011: Conflict, security and development*, Washington DC: World Bank

Yaqub, Shahin (2009) Independent child migrants in developing countries: Unexplored links in migration and development, Innocenti Working Paper 2009–2001

# 6

# EXPANDING THE CHILD PROTECTION PARADIGM

Over the course of one year, 2016 to 2017, two reports came out of UNICEF's Office of Research in Florence that represent two very different perspectives on the violence in young children's lives. The first describes the findings of a multi-country study on the drivers of violence affecting children, and analyses the way social, cultural, economic, legal, organizational and policy realities interact to shape the violence in children's homes and communities (Maternowska, Potts and Fry, 2016). Drawing on data from four countries, this study describes violence as "a fluid and shifting phenomenon in children's lives" that manifests itself differently from one society to another, and from one place to another.

The second report describes the findings of two reviews of parenting education programmes, currently the dominant approach globally for responding to the violence in young children's lives. These reviews focus specifically on the effectiveness of parenting interventions designed and tested in the global north and then imported for use in countries in the global south (Gardner, 2017). The local appropriateness of such imports has generally been considered a matter to take into careful account. This report, however, dismisses cultural suitability as a concern. Based on the evidence, it finds that the effectiveness of these programmes has in fact been highest when interventions from the global north are applied directly in places that are culturally the *most* different. The report notes also that effect sizes are not influenced by the level of child poverty in the country in question, or by the presence or absence of family friendly budgets or policies. The author does not speculate on the reasons for these counter-intuitive findings, but simply recommends the cut-and-paste use of parenting packages prepared and assessed in the global north over any approach less rigorously developed in the country in question.

If we take both these reports at face value, the takeaway message is that, while violence is a complex, shifting phenomenon, deeply sensitive to context, it can be effectively addressed using simple methods that are universal and context free.

I contrast these two reports here because they are indicative of a more general anomaly in the children-and-violence discourse. Attempts to understand the violence in children's lives tend to stress its complexity and contingency. Attempts to respond to this violence often appear to reduce it to a far simpler phenomenon.

This second report is perhaps not fully representative of the thoughtful case that has been made elsewhere for the role of parenting programmes (for instance in Ward et al., 2016). But the fact remains that the primary interventions for responding to the violence in children's lives appear to give little weight to the larger ecology of violence.

The Global Campaign to End All Violence against Children, for instance, gives little explicit attention to this ecology. The major thrust of this campaign is described as strengthening child protection systems globally, with a focus on three specific objectives: legislation, integrated programmes for preventing and responding to violence and access to social services. UNICEF, one of the chief members of this partnership, has specified strategies for eliminating violence against children that also fall within the remit of child protection systems as rather narrowly defined: supporting parents and caregivers to use positive discipline; changing attitudes and norms; providing professional support services for children; implementing laws and policies that protect children; and carrying out data collection and research on violence against children (UNICEF, 2014).

These UNICEF strategies, along with the more general campaign objectives, place the elimination of violence against young children squarely within an institutional space that focuses on parents and on the immediate manifestations of violence rather than the larger structures that underpin and reproduce it. That is fair enough. When your child has diarrhoea, you give her rehydration fluids even if the diarrhoea is the result of poor sanitation and often (if you are a resident of an urban slum) a consequence of your status as an illegal resident. And yet, if the goal is actually to eliminate diarrhoea, something more needs to happen, involving politics and a focus on social justice.

For any large campaign, it is admittedly important to keep the underlying principles clear and simple in order to gain political engagement and commitments. But despite some of the well-reasoned arguments supporting parenting programmes and other related strategies, it is hard not to feel sceptical about the capacity of child protection systems, as they are most often defined, to achieve the goal of actually "eliminating violence against children". This approach risks reducing violence to some of its most immediate episodic manifestations, ignoring the substrate of conditions within which it is embedded.

Not all of the parallel efforts to address the problem have been this anchored to child protection systems and attention to parenting. A related partnership led by the World Health Organization has endorsed the INSPIRE package, a more extensive set of strategies that also recognizes the importance of economic strengthening, supportive education and attention to safe environments, thus drawing in other government sectors (WHO, 2016). This is more compatible with the longer-term efforts of the Special Representative to the Secretary General

(SRSG), who cooperates closely with United Nations programmes, agencies, funds and mechanisms to promote the broad protection of children from violence as a human rights imperative. The SRSG calls for economic and social policies that address poverty, gender and other forms of inequality in child sensitive ways, in addition to promoting national strategies, legal bans and research focused on violence against children, thus functioning as a broad-based policy advocate.

Most recently, the independent Know Violence learning initiative, drawing on the work of a broad interdisciplinary team, has synthesized the available evidence on children and violence, confirming in its global report the need for a more nuanced approach (Know Violence in Childhood, 2017). As described also in a preliminary special journal issue related to this initiative, it views violence not as a series of episodes perpetrated against children, but as a thread that connects different aspects of children's lives, that can involve them in a range of ways and that is deeply entwined with violence against women (Shiva Kumar et al., 2016). The evidence from the global south is thin, but this report draws on it carefully, and it supports the need for a broader, more contextual approach that acknowledges the multiple sources and manifestations of violence in the lives of children and their mothers.

The current children-and-violence landscape is thus far from univocal. Yet for the moment, the predominant global strategy for responding to violence in the lives of young children is through formal child protection systems, with a heavy reliance on parenting programmes. I will discuss the potential of these systems and the evidence for the effectiveness of the programmes before going on to make the case for an expanded paradigm for protection, one that attends to the complexity of the problem of violence by building on the potential of community-driven development. These community responses to material deprivations, I argue, provide a practical bridge between structural violence and the more immediate manifestations of violence in children's lives, as well as a platform for the negotiation of changing norms and values.

## Formal child protection systems and their reach

The World Health Organization, in its 2014 update on violence prevention, reported on the status of child protection systems and efforts in 133 countries, containing over 90 per cent of the global population (WHO, 2014). Most of these countries (71 per cent) report that they have a national agenda for child protection. (To put this in perspective, somewhat fewer countries have plans for addressing intimate partner violence and sexual violence, and fewer still have them for youth violence, gang violence and elder abuse.) These plans are not always accompanied by data, however – only 41 per cent of these countries have conducted national surveys to identify the scale of the child protection problem. Among low-income countries, only 14 per cent have this kind of information.

When it comes to implementation, the numbers drop still further. The programmes most commonly implemented to address the prevention of child maltreatment are parenting education, child sexual abuse prevention and home visits. These pro-grammes are present in about a third of the 133 countries and are limited in scope and scale. In less than 15 per cent of countries do they reach even a third of the target population. There are more countries – 69 per cent – that report having child protection response services (as distinct from prevention), including the identification of potential abuse, screening and referral. But WHO reports that these systems are for the most part spotty, poorly resourced and often even detri-mental to children. They are not widely used, nor are laws widely enforced. For instance, 76 per cent of countries have laws against corporal punishment, but only 30 per cent enforce them.

Although the scope of these child protection systems has almost certainly grown since 2014, coverage remains sparse. If fewer than twenty countries had managed to reach a third of their target populations by 2014, they are a long way from reaching every child by 2030 – even assuming these systems are the way to eliminate violence. Where response services are concerned, research details the endemic failures of bureaucratic and under-resourced systems. In Kenya, for instance, these failures include such travesties as children remaining in over-crowded remand centres for years because the lack of funds for transportation delayed their placement in family homes (Cooper, 2012). A study in Uganda considered the experience of 529 children referred to local child protection ser-vices, based on their disclosure of experiences of violence. Concrete action was taken in 20 per cent of these cases, but only in twenty cases did the responses meet basic criteria for adequacy (Child et al., 2014). This means less than 4 per cent of the children who said they needed help actually received it in a form the system found acceptable.

Closely related to the reach of these child protections systems is of course their cost. Although not as costly as services to individual families, parenting programmes, currently the primary preventive mechanism for responding to the violence in young children's lives, can be prohibitively expensive. The training costs for effective programmes are high even in the context of the global north. In low-income countries they may exceed the annual per capita budget allocation for health (Desai, Reece and Shakespeare-Pellington, 2017). It is clearly still more expensive *not* to prevent violence, but that doesn't speak to the need for the prevention efforts to be as effective and appropriate as possible.

## The effectiveness of the formal systems

Even in high-income countries, where child protection systems are well established and relatively well resourced, there are reservations about how these systems are conceived and what they accomplish. Given that approaches from the global north have tended to be adopted as the paradigm in the south, these reservations deserve attention. Child protection operates primarily on a social work model that focuses in a case-by-case way on the elimination of harm. Preventive efforts like parenting education can reach larger numbers. But when the harm stems from poverty, the supports provided – parenting programmes, home visits – may not in fact be the supports that families most need.

The National Coalition for Child Protection Reform in the United States claims that parents living in poverty are often penalized, rather than supported, for situations they cannot control (NCCPR, 2011). Leroy Pelton, whose work was discussed in an earlier chapter, elaborated on this concern, pointing out that because poor families more often live in less safe environments, they are more often judged to be guilty of neglect.

> If we really intend child safety and child protection to be our goals, we should be concerned about protecting children from harm, no matter what the presumed source. But "child protection" has come to mean, more narrowly, protection of the child from the parent, and from harm that can be attributed to the fault of a parent ... the remedy has frequently been child removal rather than remediation of the environmental hazard.
>
> *(Pelton, 2015, p. 34)*

Parenting interventions do not penalize parents as much as they encourage them, but the environmental hazards and the poverty remain an issue. Pelton also pointed to the findings of an experimental study in the United States indicating that the provision of housing assistance and other material supports was associated with a reduced risk of child maltreatment, while "intensive family preservation services programmes" resulted in no such reduction.

The evidence base from the global north on the effectiveness of most child protection interventions has not been impressive overall. Reviews have either found no conclusive results (Jaycox, 2011) or have noted, at best, effect sizes in the moderate range (Lundhal, Nimer and Parsons, 2006). The most comprehensive review of reviews, synthesizing evidence on almost 300 intervention programmes, judged home visiting programmes, parent education and sexual abuse prevention programmes to be "promising" overall, but the authors point out that this can mean that as few as one or two programmes in that category were found to be unambiguously effective. For other kinds of interventions (like support groups or media efforts), evidence was considered mixed or insufficient. Even the promising programmes were most often judged to be effective based on their reduction of risk factors, not the reduction of actual abuse (Mikton and Butchart, 2009). A more recent overview notes, similarly, that parenting programmes appear to have a positive effect on risk factors, but that there are methodological problems and few long-term follow-up studies (Desai, Reece and Shakespeare-Pellington, 2017). The failure to demonstrate unambiguous success may be a matter of research methodology as much as programme effectiveness. Yet the fact remains that the rationale for exporting these approaches to the global south, especially given their cost, does not appear to be strong.

In the global south, the evidence for the effectiveness of this protection model, and of parenting education in particular, is understandably much sparser. A systematic 2013 review of the benefits of parenting programmes indicates that the validity of most studies is questionable; but that, based on the two largest and highest quality trials, parenting interventions *may* be feasible and effective in addressing parent–child interactions and the prevention of child maltreatment (Knerr, Gardner and Cluver, 2013). The more recent Gardner report (2017) described at the beginning of this chapter, which claims that effectiveness is not constrained by cultural suitability or by larger economic and policy realities, raises questions, as I noted above, about how effectiveness is actually being defined and determined.

Randomized controlled trials (RCTs), considered the gold standard within the development world for their rigour, are increasingly the preferred method for determining whether or not an intervention passes muster. Yet the necessary reduction of complex phenomena to variables amenable to manipulation in a tight experimental trial is problematic. Putting aside for the moment the reduction of "violence" to "parent behaviour", consider just the outcome measures and the effort to capture social change around something as multi-faceted as the maltreatment of children.

A closer look at the assessment of one successful programme is informative on this front. The BPP parenting programme in Jordan has been identified as an effective model for preventing violence towards children in a country where more than half of all children were estimated to be physically abused (Landers, da Silva e Paula and Kilbane, 2013). This major programme, supported by UNICEF and the government, reached more than 70,000 parents and was assessed by external evaluators as having had a significant positive impact.

The actual evaluation was based, as many evaluations are, on before-and-after responses by parents – in this case to statements through a four-point scale designed to shed light on their basic parenting skills and practices (e.g., "I yell and tell him/her to stop doing that: 1 = never, 2 = rarely, 3 = sometimes, 4 = always"). The scores for programme parents, before and after the parenting intervention, went up from 15.8 to 17 points – an effect the researchers describe as "positive but small". (They don't indicate the denominator.) For parents in the control group, with no intervention, scores went up from 15.7 to 16. Given the large size of the sample, this minor difference reached statistical significance. The evaluation was conducted immediately after the completion of the programme, and the researchers acknowledge that responses might have been biased by parents' desire to demonstrate an awareness of the material they had just been exposed to. They also note the limitation of relying only on parents' self-reports (Al-Hassan and Lansford, 2011). In other words, even these very modestly higher scores may not have been a valid or reliable indication of a genuine change to beliefs, let alone to practice. The change may have been statistically significant, but whether it was meaningful as a proxy for reduced violence in children's lives – or even changed behaviour – is a different question. All we can really say here is that this programme resulted in parents responding in marginally preferable ways to a set of statements about their own behaviour.

The programme may, in fact, have had a catalysing effect in the context of a wider campaign on the use of harsh treatment with children. Yet a news report a few years later pointed to rising rates of child abuse in Jordan, which were presumed to be a reflection of growing hardship and poverty. As UNICEF's country representative pointed out to the reporter, "It's not like a vaccination. Having an immunization campaign across the country is not easy – but it is [easy], compared to reducing child abuse in all its forms" (Sweis, 2012). This is precisely the point. How far *can* parenting classes go to alter established patterns of behaviour, especially in the context of the kind of pervasive poverty that arguably contributes to these same patterns?

The questions that are raised here remind me of an experience in Zanzibar, Tanzania, where I spent a few days driving around the northern island of Pemba with the child protection officer from the local office of an international NGO. His job was to manage for this NGO the government campaign to eliminate all corporal punishment from Pemba. He was well trained and articulate about the rationale for this intervention, and he gave compelling presentations about the potential harm to children of more punitive approaches to discipline. I had no doubts about his conviction. But after we had spent a few days together in the car and over meals, discussing the many challenges of raising his ten children, he argued that these new forms of discipline just didn't work. "These Zanzibar children are tough," he said. "The only thing they understand is the strap." He valued his job – he had a large family to support. But he had no interest in applying the new standards of discipline within his own household, and he doubted that the campaign was making much of an impact.

Social norms can be hard to shift. Even in the United States, where there is broad exposure to the principle of non-violent discipline, changing people's beliefs and practices can be a long, slow process. The Vermont women I worked with for my research had all grown up within families where violence was a normal, routine form of control. At the same time, harsh treatment was frowned on by the social services system that their families relied on, and they all knew it could be grounds for removing children from the household – these women had all spent time in foster homes. Now they had their own children and, as part of their delicate negotiations with the formal system, they were fully aware of the standards they needed to maintain. They managed, without apparent conflict, to embrace both disciplinary norms at once as acceptable frameworks for child rearing. You never strike a child, they told me. Except it's different if you're really angry, or if the child is being outrageous or is about to do something dangerous. But you have to be careful that the social worker doesn't hear about it.

In the global south, a far larger proportion the population deals with chronic poverty and exclusion. We cannot state with confidence that this means a higher risk of child maltreatment everywhere. But there is also a far broader spectrum of risks at play, including child labour, ill health, conflict, disaster and high levels of displacement, all in the context of often weak governance institutions. Formal child protection systems, minimal at best and focused on more narrowly conceived objectives, may hardly make a dent. As William Myers and Michael Bourdillon point out, "A major question raised about this social work model is whether or not, when children are at risk from things that face whole communities or societies, such as some form of social exclusion or poverty, they can be protected without looking at the broader issues" (Myers and Bourdillon, 2012, p. 442). Parenting programmes in these contexts may do little to address the pressures that parents and children actually face, and their suitability as the primary tool for combating the spectrum of violence is questionable.

Reflecting on dysfunctional policies and systems and "good protective intentions gone awry", Myers and Bourdillon (2012, p. 442) question whether child protection is even a useful category in this context.

> Does it perhaps encourage single-faceted responses, taking children out of development and indeed out of the societies in which they live? Does it encourage a harmful dichotomy between children and the adult world into which they are growing up? Is the notion of child protection too reactive, responding to threats, and insufficiently proactive in establishing conditions in which children thrive?

A related problem has been the tendency – understandable in the context of limited resources – to focus responses on particular classes of children, such as AIDS orphans, trafficked children, unaccompanied or separated children in the context of displacement. But this ignores the fact that many children in jeopardy fit into more than one category, and it can also distract attention from all those children who fall outside the focus of these more dramatic problems. These categories may also not match well with local understanding or experiences of vulnerability. Patricia Henderson, addressing this issue from the perspective of the attention given to AIDS orphans, questioned whether distinguishing these children might not be "an obsessive fixation on points of violation or personal pain" in a context where there is widespread pain, not only from the impact of AIDS, but from endemic poverty and violence (Henderson, 2006, p. 306). Labelling children this way, she argued, might also have negative implications for their sense of themselves and for the responses of those around them.

Child protection agendas and systems in much of the world, then, might be considered overly ambitious, given their seriously inadequate capacity and resources to deal with the scale of the protection problems they are designed to address. But they might also be considered not ambitious enough, since they are not set up to consider the deeper causes of violence and the multiple endemic sources of risk for children – and their mothers. Nor do they generally see families and communities as potential partners in solving the issues of child safety, but frame them only as beneficiaries of services.

The child protection world is certainly not oblivious to these concerns. Far from it. As Michael Wessells explains, most practitioners are sorely aware that children often face systemic threats that are grounded in histories of inequality and injustice, and that protective factors need to be developed and strengthened at every level within their social ecology (Wessells, 2015). In the absence of local and national governments with the resources and will to address the wide ranging risks that children need to be protected from, other models plainly need to be established, models that are grounded in multiple levels of protection.

Many early childhood specialists agree that violence must be addressed as an integral part of attention to the full range of young children's interrelated needs (Huebner et al., 2016), and Neil Boothby, among others, has been looking at other ways to enhance attention to younger children through family dialogues and problem solving approaches. The strategic plan that Boothby guided for USAID, for instance, stresses the primary need to build strong beginnings for children through integrated attention to health, nutrition and family support, defined in ways that address structural issues, not just parenting behaviour (USAID, 2012).

There has also been steadily growing interest, both within some governments and among international agencies and non-profits, in identifying and supporting traditional and non-formal community-based protection practices and structures, seeing these as a low-cost way to reach more children than would ever be possible through an individual casework or project approach. Other partners within the global protection apparatus have been less enthusiastic about incorporating these parallel local mechanisms, and are sometimes even hostile to the idea.

## Bottom-up approaches to child protection

The objective of the community-based child protection approach is to train, support and build on the involvement of a group of local people, most often volunteers, who make up a community child welfare committee. This committee monitors and ensures the protection of children within a local community or neighbourhood. Some countries, including Sierra Leone and India, have mandated the establishment of these committees at the community level. Horizontal links between the committees in different communities and vertical links with the formal district and national level mechanisms theoretically ensure that they operate within an integrated and supportive framework.

This appears on the face of it to be a practical strategy for addressing the global objectives on behalf of children and, in the context of enormous constraints for formal systems, achieving the kind of coverage that is needed. The arguments in favour of more integrated, place-based, community-driven approaches to development are familiar, and surely they apply to child protection as to other efforts. Both problems and opportunities vary by locality and the most effective solutions to the full range of problems arguably take these variations into account. Communities are also the scale at which sectoral efforts can best be integrated. The investment of local energy and skills is especially critical in resource-poor settings. Local ownership is also the best guarantee of lasting change in a world where governments come and go and project cycles are quickly over. The most compelling reason, though, is that children cannot be adequately protected in the absence of strong stable families and communities, and it stands to reason that protection efforts should involve these families and communities, ideally strengthening them along the way.

But is this approach effective? While an extraordinary wealth of such community-based child protection groups exists on the ground, there has been, as Wessells acknowledged in 2009, slim evidence of their efficacy. In response, he and an inter-agency team undertook an effort to review available documentation on a wide range of diverse community-based groups – 160 of them in all (Wessells, 2009). Most of these assessments were programme evaluations undertaken by implementing agencies, and the inter-agency team found that this evidence on the whole was anecdotal and impressionistic. It was difficult to isolate the impact of the community-based efforts from other local influences and there was also an absence of the well-defined indicators for success that are standard in such areas as health and sanitation (and essential to experimental assessment trials). Positive outcomes and some notable successes were found in seven key areas: reductions in dangerous labour and in trafficking, increased school enrolment; improvements for orphans and other vulnerable children; increased levels of participation for children; reintegration of child soldiers; and increased birth registration. Far less attention had been given to family violence, the problem that contributes the most to the burden of violence for young children. As Wessells pointed out, "Such engagement is always highly sensitive, violates traditional practices in many countries, and raises thorny issues about intrusion into people's homes" (2009, p. 53). And only one of these 160 programmes actually targeted children under 8 years of age.

Another concern expressed in the review was the limited success in stimulating genuine local ownership of these child protection committees. The great majority of the programmes fit into a category that placed communities as partners of external agencies; they were more than just beneficiaries, but they did not fully own or manage the interventions in question. Community-based child protection, the review concluded, remained in many ways a top-down effort on the part of international groups and some governments. A particular problem on this front, and one that is familiar in broader development efforts as well, was the introduction of considerable sums of money before groups had either a strong identity or a clear understanding of, or sense of responsibility for, the problems they were tackling.

Protection efforts in these contexts, Wessells argued, need to be better integrated into the priorities and more general development of local communities. Outside organizations and institutions can provide support but cannot be an alternative to the stable families and organized communities that are essential to genuine protection for children. The concept is simple ("It takes a village") but realizing that concept gets to the heart of the more general challenges posed by successful development and poverty reduction.

There is no lack of "community-driven" initiatives in the development landscape – they have become a staple over recent years, featuring conspicuously, for instance, in the portfolio of World Bank projects. But there are some distinct differences between the more project-oriented externally propelled initiatives, and the longer-term processes that become genuinely driven by local communities (Mansuri and Rao, 2013). Perhaps the most significant difference is in the depth of the social cohesion that emerges, a critical consideration where child protection is concerned.

Subsequent to this report, Wessells and his colleagues carried out a series of rapid ethnographic studies in diverse settings in sub-Saharan Africa for a better understanding of how local communities actually perceive the harms that their children face – a basic step in catalysing ownership by communities rather than by the organizations that support them. I have already referred to these rich, useful studies several times in earlier chapters (Horn et al., 2013; Kostelny et al., 2013; Kostelney, Wessells and Ondoro, 2014; Wessells et al., 2013). Different as the target communities were (both rural and urban, and both refugee groups as well as those not displaced) there were some significant similarities in their concerns. Parents in most of these communities in Kenya, Uganda, Rwanda and Sierra Leone prioritized their concerns about children being out of school and exposed to influences or pressures that could result in early pregnancy, sexual exploitation, drug and alcohol use and general delinquency. The refugee communities were also concerned about discrimination and the rural communities about hunger. But these groups were worried primarily about what was happening with older children outside of home, and how that was contributing to more general social disorder. As in the case of the 2009 evaluation, concerns about younger children – their experience of harsh treatment, their exposure to violence between parents, the neglect that many of them were almost surely experiencing in the context of deep poverty – were not worries that most of the respondents chose to focus on. As Wessells points out, these are sensitive issues, deeply grounded in norms about the parental responsibility to control and discipline children, and in a discomfort with rights-based standards on physical punishment.

One of these ethnographic studies departed from the more general findings, the study from Somaliland and Puntland, autonomous regions in Somalia where both rural and urban areas were investigated (Wessells et al., 2013). Here the extraordinary depth of poverty combined with cultural factors appeared to generate more explicit concern about younger children, about material deprivation and even about the abusive treatment of children by parents and others. Parents spoke about young children having to fend for themselves at home for long hours and about heavy work even for those as young as 4 or 5 years of age. Some young children had drowned while fetching water, others had been injured by passing vehicles while playing on roads in the absence of other play space. Children had also died in fires that spread rapidly from one flimsy shack to another, in some cases because they had been tied to poles to keep them safe while their mothers were out. Parents spoke even about children's profound misery over beatings and scoldings. Sometimes this resulted in children hanging or drowning themselves. It is a heartbreaking account, and the authors make it clear that an effective protection response could not realistically ignore the material context of deprivation.

In most of the communities represented in these ethnographic studies, however, parents' expressed concerns did not provide a natural entry point for attention to the harsh treatment of young children. Their primary anxieties about their children overlapped only partially with the objectives of national child protection programmes and the Global Partnership, bypassing the major emphasis on violence inflicted on children and the need to shift parental norms for behaviour.

There is an acknowledged need here on the part of Wessells and colleagues to find ways to encourage attention to the full spectrum of age-related child protection concerns, while still anchoring these multi-dimensional protection concerns within the ownership of the community, where they belong.

Another approach to developing a more responsive bottom-up model for child protection has been the use of cash transfers and other economic strengthening mechanisms, on the theory that addressing the poverty directly with cash subsidies might limit the potential for abuse, neglect and exploitation. These welfare measures are directed at families and most often have not been integrated into community-based protection processes. Hard evidence on the protection impact of these mechanisms remains thin, since in most cases protection is not the explicit objective of these programmes. These transfers are most often conditional, requiring for instance that children be taken to health clinics or attend school, and there are demonstrated effects for health and nutrition, school enrolment and the amounts that households spend on children (Chaffin and Ellis, 2015); also for intimate partner violence (Palermo, 2015). And there are certainly indications that these mechanisms reduce the harms that are specifically driven by economic hardship – such as transactional sex or child labour. But even in the absence of rigorous experimental research, an expert roundtable in 2016 was able to conclude that these kinds of safety nets, although inadequate to respond to all drivers of violence, could certainly make a difference "through addressing poverty, and particularly mechanisms which allow adults and children to suffer less poverty-related stress, engage in fewer negative coping behaviours, and allow caregivers to spend more time with their children (in protective environments)" (Cook et al., 2016, p. 6).

## Expanding the focus

This chapter so far has provided a brief outline of current child protection systems and approaches, and the models that are primarily under consideration for eliminating violence against young children. It points in general terms to the inadequate capacity of formal systems, especially in the global south, and to their failure to coordinate with efforts to address the larger factors underlying violence. Bottom-up responses appear to be more promising in this regard. Yet it is clear that there have been limitations in most of the documented community-based efforts. These initiatives have tended to overlook both young children and violence within homes, and the ownership aspect has been problematic. Meanwhile, cash transfers and other poverty-oriented responses lack the orientation towards strong communities that is arguably an essential support for the protection of young children, an asset that outside agencies cannot act as substitutes for.

I am suggesting here that a focus on material living conditions through collaborative community-driven development might reasonably supplement and deepen these other child protection approaches. A focus on living conditions speaks to Wessell's argument about the need for child protection to be better integrated into the more general development priorities of local communities. It also highlights the range and complexity of the issues relevant to child protection, and the dependence of children and their families on safe, secure homes and neighbourhoods for stability. It essentially broadens the platform for response, placing child protection squarely within the domain of poverty reduction and community development.

In the introduction to this book, I described a case in South Africa, where young girls in focus groups, organized by a child rights organization, pointed to the lack of streetlights in their neighbourhoods as a problem that made them more vulnerable to endemic sexual harassment and more fearful. Rather than working with the municipality and local community on installing streetlights, the organization's reaction was to hold more focus groups with the girls, stressing the need for caution and the importance of avoiding dark streets. This kind of response is understandable. When we have a hammer, we look for a nail. It is reasonable to assume that people are most effective working in the area of their expertise. But sectoral child protection responses like this, unless they are well integrated with broader efforts, risk becoming simplistic and incomplete.

This is not to suggest that streetlights would have solved the problem either. Responding to a particular environmental issue cannot "solve" the problem of violence, any more than a focus group can. Violence and maltreatment arise out of the interaction of a range of factors that cannot be effectively addressed by focusing on single causes. The streetlights are just an entry point to a more complex process that needs to be set in place. Concerted local attention to getting streetlights installed might have had a catalysing effect in starting to shift the intricate ecology of material and social factors that made the harassment of young girls a default reality in this situation.

Thinking collectively about material conditions encourages more contextual responses to violence and draws attention to fundamental issues of equity. Streetlights, decent housing, adequate provision of basic services, lively common spaces and places for recreation, safe routes to school, adequate security in poor neighbourhoods – these are a few of the basic needs that have been highlighted in this larger discussion of research and experience, and that have been related in various ways to the prevalence of violence.

Improved material conditions can lessen the likelihood of violence and neglect. But just as important, they can reduce the cumulative burden of risk that young children may be facing, and with it the likelihood that their exposure to violence or neglect will sabotage their development over the longer term. The more risk factors children face, the worse their likely outcomes are. By extension, the greater the number of protective factors in their lives, the more likely they are to be buffered from the impact of the harms in their lives. Better material conditions are powerful protective factors and can help build resilience in the very best sense for both children and adults – that is, as a step in the direction of transformation, not just the capacity to "bounce back" and endure more of the same.

But the rationale goes well beyond the substance of these material concerns and their potential impact for equity, violence, neglect and children's long-term developmental outcomes. There are some other important reasons why a focus on material conditions could be an important ingredient of a more community-based approach to child protection.

The first is that anchoring child protection effectively within a community – where it belongs – requires local organization and commitment. But people generally organize to work together only when the changes they need are things they cannot manage to achieve alone. This commitment happens most readily around issues perceived as central to survival and a decent life. There may be disagreements about priorities or solutions, but there is little need to make an argument in favour of better quality housing or sanitation or clean water. These are the concerns that preoccupy communities and are likely to stimulate involvement. People in the most difficult situations often gauge their well-being or their misery in terms of their material conditions. In Mike Wessells' experience, they often expect and demand changes in their material conditions as a requirement for partnering with NGOs. Children's miseries can also be viewed by parents in terms of their material deprivations, rather than their fear or anxiety or humiliation – during the conflict in Nepal, for instance, parents considered children's ragged clothing a more serious indication of their state than the nightmares that were so common.

Once people are attracted and engaged, they need to stay involved – it takes time to build the capacity to organize and collaborate effectively, and it's often a matter of trial and error. It also takes time to shift the social norms and practices that underpin much of the violence that young children experience. Here again, the improvement of material conditions is most likely to keep people involved over the long haul. Significant change on this front can take time, but the objectives are clear and relatively easy to keep in sight. Once structures, processes, relationships have been established to tackle these needs, and once people are animated by their own capacity to collaboratively effect change, it can seem more feasible to apply that experience to other issues. It can also be easier then to start to see those other issues as genuine concerns. As Wessells points out with regard to the more successful community-based child protection responses, "A circular relationship existed between resource mobilization and community ownership. The voluntary participation of diverse people in the work elevated the sense of community ownership, which in turn heightened their desire to devote their time, energy, and resources to supporting vulnerable children" (Wessells, 2015, p. 12).

A second reason is that the discussion of material conditions can be an entry point for raising other concerns that may be considered too private, too sensitive or too secondary to bring up directly in community discussions. In the course of negotiating and planning for material needs, whether it be the layout of housing, the placement of toilets, the need for lighting or more secure transport, women and children especially can be emboldened to point to the situations that frighten and humiliate them, as I describe in the next chapter. Julian Brigstocke, writing about participation, points to the critical importance of "amplifying hidden, whispered truths, truths that testify to experiences that have until now been silenced". These truths rise to the surface more readily in the context of other shared, compelling concerns (Brigstocke, 2013, p. 11).

Finally, organizing around the achievement of material change begins to change the way that people in a community think about themselves. It stimulates confidence and can kindle what Arjun Appadurai calls "the capacity to aspire". People in poverty, he explains, are often reduced by their poverty to a short-term view of things. Immediate survival decisions take priority, and they may have little experience with longer-term planning and the vision that this implies. People can be trapped within narrower ways of thinking, forced by their constraints "to subscribe to norms that further diminish their dignity, exacerbate their inequality, and deepen their lack of access to material goods and services" (Appadurai, 2004, p. 66). A little success can go a long way in terms of expanding this future-oriented "navigational capacity", which is closely tied to expectations for children, and to a willingness to reconsider old habits.

A good case in point for all of these rationales comes from the activities of a small women's savings group in Kwazulu-Natal, whose members belong to a federation of urban poor communities in South Africa. These federations use the organizational momentum of daily savings as one of several strategies in their larger effort to gain secure land, housing and basic services through negotiation with local government. The learning and energy from these savings groups becomes in effect the engine for more ambitious undertakings. Weekly savings group meetings can also serve as informal forums for discussing other local issues like waste management, community health or ration cards – all of which also involve coordination and negotiation with local government.

A woman from this particular group explained to me how the child protection angle had developed in their case. During their weekly meetings, they had started discussing their concerns about children and women in households where they knew there was a threat of abuse. The trust that had developed among these women over time, keeping savings records, making plans, negotiating with each other for loans and ensuring that these loans were repaid, made it possible to address these more sensitive issues. Gradually an informal surveillance system evolved, in which these women looked out for the welfare of neighbourhood children and women. The group went on to approach a child protection NGO in the city. They didn't want this organization to come work in their settlement – that, they felt, would have been intrusive and possibly futile. Instead, some of the women in the savings group asked to be trained to negotiate with parents in difficult situations. They also began volunteering in the NGO office, which started to provide a refuge for women and children when necessary.

The services provided by this child protection organization are not unusual; what *is* unusual here is that within this poor community, local women were driving the agenda and drawing on the NGO's services to further their own evolving vision of integrated local development. The women were working primarily towards secure housing, but they did not see that goal as incompatible with attention to the community's children. Both efforts required organization, attention and commitment, which followed naturally from their regular savings meetings.

Even if we acknowledge the potential synergies between protection and community-owned development, though, the appropriate role for the child protection world is another matter. Challenging though it is to protect children through targeted social interventions, acting on underlying issues is another order of business. Involvement in this range of concerns plainly goes well beyond the mandate of most child protection agencies and organizations, which have little connection with the actors and agencies responsible for housing, tenure, infra-structure, public space, transport and other aspects of physical development. We live in a sectoral world, and when it comes to taking action, it is seldom easy to go beyond the parameters of the conventional sectoral responses. But this is not only a matter of expanding the paradigm of child protection. It also means infiltrating the broader development agenda more successfully and not cordoning off the protection of children in ways that effectively remove responsibility from the far wider cast of actors that should be involved here. Placing child protection within this broader context makes children a primary focus of development.

What I am proposing here is not to throw away the child protection hammer, but to ensure that the nails are helping to hold up a real structure that can last for a while. The thrust is not so much on the programmatic responses that child-focused organizations or social service agencies can realistically undertake on their own, but on the efforts they might choose to coordinate with and support, the policies they might advocate for, the fellow travellers they might want to collaborate with.

With regard to those fellow travellers – it cannot be assumed that anything with a "community" label will fit the bill. Area-based community-driven development comes in many forms that can differ along a number of dimensions. This is very relevant to the potential success of child protection collaborations. Mansuri and Rao, in evaluating the success of over 500 community-based participatory initiatives, make an important distinction between "induced" and "organic" forms, noting that the induced, externally conceived versions of community-driven development are more likely to be short-term, project-oriented and externally funded (Mansuri and Rao, 2013). The induced and organic forms can certainly overlap in situations where the state opens up genuine spaces for long-term local involvement and decision-making. But in general, the induced forms are less likely to focus on a breadth of engagement, on the long-term incremental development of local capacity, or on the actual ownership on the part of communities. These more superficial project-oriented forms can be successful, say Mansuri and Rao, in identifying solutions that are better aligned with local needs, and they may result in more effective management of resources. But they tend to have little impact on social cohesion, which is arguably a critical outcome where child protection is an issue. It is not by chance that local ownership is considered critical in the evaluation of community-based child protection efforts.

The savings group in KwaZulu that I described above is an example of the more organic and locally owned form of community-based action. This savings group was part of one of the many community organizations that make up a federation of urban poor communities in South Africa and that collaborate to achieve a collective voice across cities. This federation, in turn, is part of an international social movement, a membership-based network of urban poor federations, called Slum/Shack Dwellers International. or SDI, which has spread over twenty years to more than thirty countries. In the discussion of practical responses in the next chapter, alongside other examples, I will draw repeatedly on the work of SDI and its affiliates because the efforts of this network are well documented, because I am familiar with them, and because their work embodies a long-term, integrated, community-driven approach to local development that is especially salient to the concerns of this book.

I will turn for the same reasons to the Baan Mankong programme in Thailand, a government-funded slum upgrading programme that is unusual in its facilitation of an entirely community-driven process. Communities first organize themselves to register as cooperatives and are then able to access loans, determine their priorities, negotiate tenure and manage their housing and settlement projects. Using a similar model, the Asian Coalition for Housing Rights (ACHR), another network of grassroots organizations and local NGOs, has supported slum upgrading in nineteen Asian countries. Like the federations that are members of SDI, they address land tenure, decent housing, basic infrastructure, community space, but through small grants or loans to savings groups to catalyse or support local organization and action. All are rooted in the context of strengthening social capital in communities. All bring community organizations together to engage with local government, and where possible to work with it. These models provide a valuable point of reference in thinking about an additional, alternative, bottom-up platform for child protection. The potential for transformation, both of the local environment and the community, is central to these efforts. The goal goes well beyond simply implementing a project to shifting the structures that cause the poverty and exclusion of these communities. These are the kinds of partners that could be invaluable allies for child protection.

Because this expanded model of protection through the collaborative mending of the physical environment is so moored in concepts of community and participation, and because these terms are so easily oversimplified and idealized, it seems important here to scrutinize them. The way they are understood affects the way they are employed. The word "community" is surrounded by a bit of a glow and can suggest an inclusive, supportive, conflict-free entity. It is widely recognized, however, that this romanticized vision tends to ignore the micro-politics within most poor communities, the realities of exclusion and the complex power relations that can complicate any community-driven process. Those involved in community planning processes are often the most vocal, the most affluent, the most powerful community residents. Community decisions can simply reinforce existing hierarchies, failing to take account of those who most need development to work on their side. Opportunism and self-interest are present in every community. This is not reason to jettison community-based efforts as a valid approach, though. "Community" is most likely to be a necessary basis for action in situations of inequity and powerlessness, where a collective voice is critical for people to be heard, and collective action is necessary for people to get what they need. In most settlements, there is no way families on their own can realistically address the material deprivations they experience. Accessing improved water supplies, adequate waste disposal, decent schools and legal tenure depends at the very least on some kind of collectively negotiated action.

But the danger of "elite capture" has to be acknowledged in order for the needs of the most marginalized to be addressed. The SDI and ACHR models described above have generally been able to apply the kinds of internal checks and balances that demand downward accountability from community leaders. And these models, unlike externally conceived, project-oriented "community-driven" initiatives, have a longer time horizon, which according to Mansuri and Rao, can "fundamentally improve the incentives of citizens to confront local elites and fight for their interests" (2013, p. 40). There is also the matter of money. Externally introduced programmes often involve the influx of more funds than an emerging group can handle well, and this can stimulate opportunism. Somsook Boonyabancha, the founder of ACHR, has a "theory of insufficiency", according to which the provision of a small amount of money, not enough for the task, unleashes people's creativity and resourcefulness, without providing reason for elite capture.

Participation, in theory an essential ingredient in the programming of many organizations and agencies and an integral component of rights-based approaches, can differ enormously in quality and intent. Too often, it is undertaken simply as a mechanism for delivering projects, or even as a project or deliverable in its own right – rather than as a genuine process of engagement by local residents, young or old, in identifying and acting on their own needs. Real participation can also not be confused with consultation or informational meetings – the smallest coins of the currency that passes for participation in many development initiatives. Genuine, inclusive participation is messy, and it can be inconvenient for organizations and government agencies. It takes time – being effective is not always about being efficient. It is often incompatible with pre-determined plans of action, log frame outputs or free standing projects that are isolated from the more general development priorities of a group of people. True participation requires a willingness to support a process rather than to push for pre-determined outcomes, and an acceptance that the development and nurturance of a collective voice around problems collectively experienced can lead in unanticipated directions.

Where children are concerned, the obstacles to the right to participate may be especially apparent. In situations of violence, it is common to consider children as passive victims and to focus on the damage to their developing minds and bodies rather than on their capacity to identify problems and help negotiate solutions. The more formal responses to violence seldom take place in collaboration with children. Natasha Blanchet-Cohen points out that genuine agency among children in this regard is not simply a matter of their right to participate, but a recognition of the fact that children's powerlessness is at the root of their vulnerability to violence (Blanchet-Cohen, 2009). Yet participatory projects often focus more on how children *feel* than what can be done about it – missing the all-important aspect of supporting their agency.

An informed concern with their physical surroundings comes very naturally to children and can, as noted, be a fine entry point to other more sensitive concerns. Although many fine participatory projects have focused on revealing children's experience of physical space and their assessment of local environments, those children are rarely brought into decision-making and planning for their housing and neighbourhoods. Girls may have a chance to identify the lack of streetlights as a problem, but it is far less common for them to be involved in addressing the problem or for their concerns to be drawn out and taken on seriously by others. Practical follow up to their concerns is complicated for all kinds of reasons. In the absence of concrete change, it becomes all too common in the assessment of participatory projects with children to point instead to the educational values of civic participation. But when children have become engaged out of a genuine interest in improving their surroundings, the substitution of educational value for material change can result more often in cynicism than in citizenship (Clements, 2005).

Among children's organizations, it is also fairly common to conduct participation exercises with children only. While children's perspectives on violence or the local environment is critical, these are family wide and community-wide concerns and should be addressed as such. Unless children's concerns and priorities are integrated into the more general priorities of a community, they can easily get lost. There is also the fact that involving infants and very young children is problematic – and so their concerns are often sidelined. Mothers and other caregivers are best placed to represent small children's needs and best interests and to help establish the conditions that support optimal care and security. Yet often they are the family members or community members least likely to have the time or opportunity for involvement in local affairs, unless some provision is made to accommodate their busy schedules.

This is all to say that while it is easy to recommend and advocate for participatory local responses to a concern with the local environment, and through it to the issues of violence and child protection, this is easier said than done. It takes patience, commitment, follow-through and an openness to supporting communities, in all their diversity and complexity, to clarify their own priorities for this to make a real difference. Deeper seated changes to social norms and practices, especially, involve gradual, negotiated change, and this is essential for child protection. Participation, as Brigstocke points out, is not always about consensus or rational agreement, nor is it a "banal aggregation of preferences". Rather, it's "the creation of new voices and provocations" (2013, p. 11). Certainly it goes far deeper than the simple introduction of external norms.

Sustained local responses to community development do not happen in a vacuum. They require strong partnerships with local government and also within local government. Place-based community-driven solutions are about more than social ties, inclusiveness, a subjective sense of belonging. No matter how creative particular community responses may be, they cannot go to scale without local government involvement, given the primary role of these authorities in providing for or facilitating the provision of land, housing, infrastructure, basic services and law enforcement. Upstream laws, policies and budgets also provide an essential framework, but they play out locally and are only as effective as local governance and commitment allow them to be. Part of this effort, then, has to involve a commitment to facilitating, supporting, enhancing that relationship.

The relationship between local government and engaged communities does not always evolve in the same way. Sometimes an external programme or a top-down response can stimulate these local relationships. In Zimbabwe, for instance, a UNICEF project in several small towns, supporting local government to improve water and sanitation systems, led to self-initiated efforts by town committees to deal with refuse collection and street cleaning. Between the sanitation upgrades and the waste management, the local environment was much improved and children were able to play safely outdoors in the more pleasant surroundings. Appreciation for these changes led to greater trust between communities and local government, and encouraged these communities to start approaching the town council to discuss other problems. This is not specifically child protection, but the links are clear.

Concerted efforts undertaken in partnership to ensure child protection can also end up pointing to the need for housing and better community development, and possibly to new allies in achieving these ends. In Tippecanoe County, Indiana, for instance, a Community Report Card was developed by a local child protection policy board. Members of this board included representatives from medical, mental health, education, justice, faith, law enforcement and social service agencies as well as people from local communities. This group concluded that addressing basic housing deficits in the county was central to alleviating the risk of child abuse. Whether or not there was follow-through in this situation was not documented – but even the recognition of the central role of housing by all these local actors was a critical step in moving towards more effective responses to child protection (Biggs-Read et al., 2008). Cross-cutting task forces are not unusual in concept – but gathering a committed group and galvanizing the political will to act on its findings is another matter. The complexities of functional partnerships are beyond the scope of this discussion, but it is important to point out that complex problems require joint efforts, and that these efforts can tackle the issues from multiple directions.

The next chapter describes some of these joint efforts. All relate in one way or another to local living conditions and to the potential for transformative change that attention to these local conditions can involve. There is no hard experimental evidence to support the child protection value of any of these responses. In fact, there is little evidence of any kind of child protection outcomes beyond anecdote and extrapolation. It seems inconsistent to be advocating for untested alternatives, given how critical I have been of the evidence supporting the more conventional responses to violence against children. But as in the case of cash transfers, this lack of evidence is not surprising. Physical environment responses are not undertaken with child protection in mind, and are unlikely to be evaluated on that basis. Nor is it clear that experimental evidence is the most informative way to assess complex situations. It can provide reliable answers only to simple questions, and one hopes at best that those answers also tell a larger story.

In defence of my unsubstantiated assumptions here, consider that much of the existing research on parenting programmes and related interventions looks only at the reduction of presumed risk factors, not reductions in the prevalence of violence. If that metric is acceptable, then there is a good basis for accepting increased family and community stability or cohesion as promising indicators – given that their absence so clearly presents a risk to children. Granted, the evidence on the effectiveness of community-driven development on these fronts is quite mixed. Mansuri and Rao conclude, based on their extensive review, that the potential of these approaches for enhancing social cohesion appears to be limited. But they also make it clear that the initiatives they reviewed were "induced" rather than "organic", mostly time-bound, project-oriented and externally conceived. These authors point to the longer time frame that is necessary for deeper social change, and to the greater motivation, innovation and commitment associated with the more organic modes.

Even in the absence of specific evidence on child protection outcomes, it seems reasonable to assume that a stronger, better provisioned community makes for a safer child. It is also worth considering that the absence of hard evidence might not be as critical where improvements in material conditions are an associated benefit – we have to acknowledge that this is a move in the right direction regardless. Children have a right to living conditions that support their health and full development. Decent housing, sanitation, common space and all the rest unquestionably serve that function. Whether or not they also have the capacity to shift social norms and change parental behaviour could be added to the lengthy child protection research to-do list.

## References

Al-Hassan, Suha and Jennifer Lansford (2011) Evaluation of the Better Parenting Programme in Jordan, *Early Child Development and Care* 181(5), 587–598

Appadurai, A (2004) The capacity to aspire: Culture and the terms of recognition, in V Rao and M Walton (eds) *Culture and public action*, Palo Alto, CA: Stanford University Press, pp. 59–84

Biggs-Read, Pam, Angela Smith Grossman, Loretta Rush and Steven R Wilson (2008) White paper: Understanding child abuse and neglect in Tippecanoe County. Available at http://ourkidstippecanoe.homestead.com/Child_Abuse_Neglect_White_Paper1.pdf

Blanchet-Cohen, Natasha (2009) Children, agency and violence, in and beyond the United Nations Study on Violence Against Children, Innocenti Working Paper 2009–2010. Available at www.unicef-irc.org/publications/564/

Brigstocke, Julian (2013) Democracy and the reinvention of authority, in Tehsen Noorani, Claire Blencowe and Julian Brigstocke (eds) *Problems of participation: Reflections on authority, democracy and the struggle for common life*, Lewes, UK: ARN Press

Chaffin, Josh and Cali Mortenson Ellis (2015) Outcomes for children from household economic strengthening interventions: A research synthesis, Child Protection in Crisis Learning Network and Women's Refugee Commission for Save the Children UK. Available at www.savethechildren.net/.../Final%20version%20Outcome%20for%20Children

Child, Jennifer Christine, Dipak Naker, Jennifer Horton, Eddy Joshua Walakira and Karen M Devries (2014) Responding to abuse: Children's experiences of child protection in a central district, Uganda, *Child Abuse and Neglect* 38(5), 809–972

Clements, Je'anna (2005) "How crazy can it be?' An assessment three years later of outcomes from a participatory project with children in Johannesburg, *Children, Youth and Environments* 15(2), 105–116

Cook, Sarah, Naomi Neijhoft, Tia Palermo and Amber Peterman (2016) Social protection and childhood violence: Expert roundtable, Innocenti Research Brief 2016–2011. Available at www.unicef-irc.org/publications/850/

Cooper, Elizabeth (2012) Following the law, but losing the spirit of child protection in Kenya, *Development in Practice* 22(4), 486–497

Desai, Charlene Coore, Jody-Ann Reece and Sydonnie Shakespeare-Pellington (2017) The prevention of violence in childhood through parenting programmes: A global review, *Psychology, Health and Medicine*, doi:10.1080/13548506.2016.1271952

Gardner, Frances (2017) Parenting interventions: How well do they transport from one country to another? Innocenti Research Brief 2017–2010. Available at www.unicef-irc. org/publications/886/

Henderson, Patricia (2006) South African AIDS orphans: Examining assumptions around vulnerability from the perspective of rural children and youth, *Childhood* 13, 303–327

Horn, Rebecca et al. (2013) Community-based child protection mechanisms amongst urban refugees in Kampala, Uganda: An ethnographic study, New York: Columbia University Mailman School of Public Health, Child Protection in Crisis Network for Research, Learning and Action

Huebner, G, N Boothby et al. (2016) The case for investing in young children globally, Discussion paper, Washington DC: National Academy of Medicine

Jaycox, Lisa H (2011) *Evaluation of safe start promising approaches: Assessing program outcomes*, RAND Infrastructure, Safety, and Environment, Santa Monica, CA: Rand Corporation

Knerr, W, F Gardner and L Cluver (2013) Improving positive parenting skills and reducing harsh and abusive parenting in low- and middle-income countries: A systematic review, *Prevention Science* 14(4), 352–363

Know Violence in Childhood (2017) *Ending violence in childhood: Global report*

Kostelny, K, M Wessells, J Chabeda-Barthe and K Ondoro (2013) *Learning about children in urban slums: a rapid ethnographic study in two urban slums in Mombasa of community-based child protection mechanisms and their linkage with the Kenyan national child protection system.* London: Interagency Learning Initiative on Community-Based Child Protection Mechanisms and Child Protection Systems

Kostelny, K, M Wessells and K Ondoro (2014) *Community-based child protection mechanisms in Kilifi, Kenya: A rapid ethnographic study in two rural sites*, London: Interagency Learning Initiative on Community-Based Child Protection Mechanisms and Child Protection Systems

Landers, C, C Da Silva e Paula and T Kilbane (2013) Preventing violence against young children, in P R Britto, P L Engle, and C M Super (eds) *Handbook of early childhood development research and its impact on global policy*, Oxford: Oxford University Press

Lundhal, Brad, Janelle Nimer and Bruce Parsons (2006) Preventing child abuse: A meta-analysis of parent training programs, *Research on Social Work Practice* 16(3), 251–262

Mansuri, Ghazala and Vijayendra Rao (2013) *Localizing development: Does participation work?* Washington DC: World Bank

Maternowska, Mary Catherine, Alina Potts and Deborah Fry (2016) The multi-country study on the drivers of violence affecting children: A cross-country snapshot of findings, Miscellania, Florence: UNICEF Office of Research, Innocenti

Mikton, Christopher and Alexander Butchart (2009) Child maltreatment prevention: A systematic review of reviews, *Bulletin of World Health Organization* 87, 353–361

Myers, William and Michael Bourdillon (2012) Introduction: Development, children, and protection, *Development in Practice* 22(4), 437–447

NCCPR (2011) *Child abuse and poverty*, National Coalition for Child Protection Reform, Issue Paper 6. Available at www.nccpr.org/reports/6Poverty.pdf

Palermo, Tia (2015) Measurement of interpersonal violence in national social cash transfer evaluations, Innocenti Research Brief 2015–2004. Available at www.unicef-irc.org/publications/790/

Pelton, Leroy (2015) The continuing role of material factors in child maltreatment and placement, *Child Abuse and Neglect* 41, 1–190

Shiva Kumar, A K, Vivien Stern, Ramya Subrahmanian, Lorraine Sherr, Patrick Burton, Nancy Guerra, Robert Muggah, Maureen Samms-Vaughan, Charlotte Watts and Soumya Kapoor Mehta (2016) Editorial: Ending violence in childhood: A global imperative, *Psychology, Health and Medicine* 22(S1), 1–16

Sweis, Rana F (2012) Jordan struggles to protect children, *New York Times*, 25 January 2012

UNICEF (2014) *Ending violence against children: Six strategies for action*, New York: United Nations Children's Fund (UNICEF)

USAID (2012) United States government action plan on children in adversity: A framework for international assistance: 2012–2017. Available at wwwchildreninadversity.gov/docs/default-source/default-document-library/apca.pdf?sfvrsn=2

Ward, Catherine, Matthew R Sanders, Frances Gardner, Christopher Mikton and Andrew Dawes (2016) Preventing child maltreatment in low- and middle-income countries, *Child Abuse and Neglect* 54, 97–107

Wessells, Michael G (2009) *What are we learning about protecting children in the community? An inter-agency review of the evidence on community-based child protection mechanisms in humanitarian and development settings*, Westport, CT: Save the Children

Wessells, Michael G (2015) Bottom-up approaches to strengthening child protection systems: Placing children, families, and communities at the center, *Child Abuse and Neglect* 43, 8–21

Wessells, Michael G, Neil Boothby et al. (2013) *A rapid ethnographic study of community-based child protection mechanisms in Somaliland and Puntland and their linkage with national child protection systems*, Columbia Group for Children in Adversity. Available at Final-ethnographic-report-Somaliland-and-Puntland.pdf

WHO (2014) *Global status report on violence prevention*, Geneva: WHO

WHO (2016) *INSPIRE: Seven strategies for ending violence against children*, Geneva: WHO

# 7

# RESPONSES THAT START FROM THE PHYSICAL ENVIRONMENT

This chapter is a brief account of some responses to space and place that might contribute to ensuring the protection of local children, or that could serve as entry points. Most of these examples are community-driven efforts, although not all. But even those initiated by organizations or government agencies tend to entail local involvement on some scale, and in many cases they become a galvanizing experience for furthering that involvement. These examples are not a set of recommendations, nor are they in any way comprehensive. They are best seen as a sampler that illustrates some of the different possibilities that are relevant to this book's approach to a complex issue – the important overlap between rights to provision and rights to protection. These examples, like the chapters that precede them, start with home, move on to neighbourhood and finally to the circumstances that face children and families displaced by various kinds of upheaval.

These efforts are heavily tilted towards Asia, and towards India in particular. This is not because there aren't good examples in other places as well. But the examples from Asia are often the best documented or, in the absence of formal documentation, those I am most familiar with.

## Housing security

Insecure tenure is a pressing concern for hundreds of millions of households worldwide. It undermines family stability, contributes to stress and perpetuates poverty. When it culminates in eviction, especially forced eviction, the impacts for young children and their families can be extreme. Some of the most successful efforts in resisting eviction, establishing secure tenure or negotiating relocation alternatives have come out of the work of various federations of the urban poor, many of which belong to SDI (Slum/Shack Dwellers International) and ACHR (Asian Coalition for Housing Rights).

While SDI's member federations differ in terms of both national and local realities, they share a set of proven flexible tools, developed over thirty years, that help them to build local capacity and to negotiate effectively with local government on the issue of tenure (along with access to services). The mapping and enumeration of settlements by their residents is an important first step that helps communities identify themselves, their neighbourhoods and their shared problems through the collection of detailed, up-to-date information on households and neighbourhoods. This is a collective ritual that goes far beyond local documentation and becomes a tool for group formation. The process, as Arjun Appadurai explains it, can "enable poor urban communities to mobilize knowledge about themselves in a manner that can resist eviction, exploitation and surveillance in favour of advancing their own rights, resources and claims" (2012, p. 641). Conflicting interests and power struggles within a community, for instance between tenants and structure owners, are dealt with through the numerous checks and balances within the process, and the involvement of all residents in confirming or contesting their neighbours' accounts and claims. When profiles of each slum settlement are produced by community groups and pooled across a city, this information on otherwise "invisible" unrecorded settlements provides the basis for negotiation with authorities around secure community tenure arrangements or appropriate relocation to secure land (Patel, Baptist and d'Cruz, 2012). This process has helped to address the stress of insecurity for hundreds of thousands of households at this point, establishing the basis for more stable families and communities and freeing energy and resources to move on to other concerns. The organization and collaboration involved in the process, at the same time, builds the kind of social capital and confidence in joint efforts that is fundamental to addressing these other concerns.

All these enumerations used to be managed by hand, with tape measures and ledgers and long lists, painstakingly cross-checked. The federations have been cautious about digitizing this process, wanting to be sure that even the least computer-literate people in a community are able to understand, scrutinize and contest the information that is collected. Increasingly, however, communities are becoming tech savvy, and young people inevitably take the lead in digitizing the process. In the railway slums in Khon Kaen in Thailand, for instance, one of ACHR's networked communities, active youth groups and children's groups were able to figure out how to use GPS apps on smart phones to map their settlements, number the houses and link the communities' survey data to GIS maps.

It is not always possible for a community to negotiate its way out of eviction. Resettlement by the state is often, although certainly not always, the next step. But even where resettlement is offered, it is not always on terms that avoid further destabilizing the lives of the people and communities affected. Here too, the federations of the urban poor have proven themselves capable of negotiating a far better transition to better housing on better terms than would have happened otherwise, and they have been able to make the resettlement and rebuilding process something that, to a greater or lesser extent, is managed by the communities in question

(Patel and Bartlett, 2009). In the best situations, they actually execute all the phases of the resettlement themselves.

Children have been deeply involved in such efforts as well. Sudeshna Chatterjee recounts five years' worth of efforts in Delhi by children, their households and a broad coalition of partners around the long, drawn-out process of forced eviction from their settlements along the Yamuna River. Although these efforts were not sufficient to halt the evictions or to counter all the difficult impacts for children and families, they did help to humanize the process of resettlement and gave many children the relief of doing something active in a context that would otherwise have framed them only as victims. Their efforts ultimately resulted in improved living conditions in the relocation areas. They also drew broad attention to the impacts of eviction and resettlement for children, leading to redefinitions of state responsibility on resettlement in India (Chatterjee, 2007). Chatterjee's account demonstrates the range of ways that child advocates and agencies can insert themselves into action around various aspects of eviction and resettlement, coordinating with other actors to realize a better outcome for and with children. One much needed contribution is more research and a better understanding of eviction and insecurity as it affects young children.

## Women's ownership of land and housing

A particular aspect of secure tenure is the way that it relates to women and their control over their lives. As outlined in earlier chapters, research from both the global north and south clarifies how domestic violence can precipitate homelessness and insecurity for women and children, and the extent to which secure tenure and property ownership by women can serve as a protective measure. But this kind of security is more often the exception than the rule.

Simply securing the legal right of women to be property owners is not sufficient, as research from Kenya and elsewhere makes clear (Gaafar, 2014). Nor is women's home-ownership something that can reasonably be tackled one household at a time where structural realities do not support it. SDI again provides a compelling model for the achievement of this kind of security in the context of low-income countries. The membership of most of SDI's city and national federations is made up primarily of women, who become members of local savings groups, as described in the previous chapter. The practice of daily savings is not just about saving money. Humble and low-profile though it is, saving becomes a galvanizing process that empowers women to work in groups, to federate with other similar groups, and to turn their individual need for housing into a collective solution.

In a jointly crafted working paper, women from these savings groups in six countries describe how leveraging their savings into a pooled resource changes their relationship with the traditional male leadership within communities and with the formal world of funding and credit. It can even transform the custom-bound relationships with their husbands. A woman in Uganda explained, "When I can't do any work at home, my husband helps and if I have to travel to Arua, he takes full responsibility for the children. This never happened before I was in the federation. Before, we were parallel. Now we work together. He has also changed you see" (d'Cruz et al., 2014, p. 40). Adding women's names to titles, once they are secured, or even putting them in the woman's name, is encouraged by the federations and has become the norm in most places where they operate. In the Kambi Moto settlement in Nairobi, community members decided that the names of every member of the family, including children, should be entered in ownership documents.

In many communities, children also contribute to the savings, knowing how much difference improved housing will make in their lives. One woman explained that her daughter had also become a federation member.

> She loved to watch me save the UGX100 (USD 0.4 cents) every day and wanted to follow my footsteps. I encouraged her to join because every woman should try to save some money whenever she can because relying on a man or on others all the time is not good for a woman, as we all know. Girls and women are very vulnerable, people take advantage of you if you do not have anything.
>
> *(p. 40)*

## Housing that works for families

> It takes no research to know that if children are removed from parents due to homelessness or inadequate housing causing endangerment to the children, then improvement of the housing or housing the homeless will eliminate such endangerment and may allow the children to remain with the parents. Such is the case with many of what we call concrete services, aimed at changing the environment, such as ensuring proper home heating, removing the dangers of ingestion of lead paint, or providing child care to parents who have no safe place to leave their children when necessary. Yet it is still not at all unusual for children to be placed in foster care because of a family's inadequate housing or outright homelessness, lack of adequate food and clothing, or inability to obtain day care, problems which child welfare agencies have been unable or unwilling to address.
>
> *(Pelton, 2014, p. 35)*

Pelton's concern was with the United States, where figures indicate that the average cost of placing children from a homeless family in foster care is over five times the average cost of a permanent housing subsidy for that family (National Alliance to End Homelessness, 2006). In most regions in the world, children are less likely to face forceful removal from their families, but the principle still holds – facilitating access to decent housing is fundamental to child protection.

Yet around the world the social housing responses that are intended to address the huge backlog of need are limited in scale, seldom affordable to the poorest and often fail to meet the actual requirements of households, whether in terms of location, space or provision. Units seldom accommodate extended families or make it possible to conduct the informal livelihoods that are often home-based. In many cases families may even have to turn down the housing they are offered, preferring to take their chances somewhere else.

There is extensive experience from the global south on effective approaches that *do* bridge the gap between household needs and available resources. The common thread in most of the successful initiatives is the close involvement of residents in decisions that affect the planning of their housing, and often the management of construction. In India, for instance, the Alliance (two federations and a support NGO that work together and are members of to SDI) has repeatedly negotiated effective responses, whether for affordable units in upgraded settlements or, when relocation cannot be avoided, for new settlements that are more carefully planned than the usual state-provided solutions (Patel and Bartlett, 2016). Some of these negotiations have involved resourceful responses to the problem of insufficient space – for instance, obtaining permission for higher ceiling heights and an added mezzanine level that provides additional separate sleeping space within the 150 square feet footprint that is officially allocated to each household. Another negotiation in the context of high rise housing was for wider hallways, making it possible for small children to play together outside their one-room apartments without having to go outside, several storeys down and too far away for mothers to supervise them. Yet another modification involved a joint decision to have shared toilets on each floor rather than sacrificing that much of each family's very small allocated living space. It has often required long years of sustained effort to negotiate workable solutions with the government, and especially to find ways to include the poorest households within these communities, who find it difficult to raise sufficient funds to pay their share of the costs.

Effective community decisions about housing design can also happen in the absence of the deeper level of organization that ideally equips communities to cope with all the challenges that inevitably present themselves. In some cases, the Alliance in India has had to seize opportunities for upgrading without there being time for the communities involved to go through the extended period of learning and organization that is ideal. This can result in a messier process, but communities learn as they go, and the outcomes are always preferable to the more top-down alternatives.

Even in the absence of the kind of long-term structure and process that the federations can provide, communities can negotiate better results if there is an organization or agency willing to accept the need for flexibility and patience. After the 2004 tsunami, for example, Save the Children made it possible for my colleagues and I to work closely with the small Tamil Nadu community of Cooks Nagar, where housing had been largely destroyed (Bartlett and Iltus, 2007). For the sake of efficiency, all replacement housing in the district was supposed to follow the pre-approved plan of the collective humanitarian response. We had permission, however, to work with the Cooks Nagar residents to make modifications to this basic plan, provided they did not end up adding to the planned costs.

There were two weeks of intensive daily discussions, first among separate groups within the community (women, men, older girls, older boys, younger children), and then with each group's representatives presenting their solutions to the entire community. This process led to a long list of options and trade-offs that family members could discuss and choose among, with the agreement of the construction company. For instance, rather than having a more expensive but durable tile roof on their small one-storey replacement house, many families decided to settle for a cheaper palm frond roof, accepting that it would need annual replacement, and to use the saved money to construct (on their own) an additional low-cost storey. Some decided to forego the planned indoor kitchen area in favour of extra living space – instead they constructed a traditional outdoor kitchen. Other families decided to leave out the window in one wall, using the saved money instead to put towards a lean-to room they would construct later on.

The small group discussions provided a good entry point for talking about more sensitive issues. There appears to be a natural synergy here, as mentioned in the last chapter. Talking about housing layout with other women, for instance, led women to discuss difficult family issues that might not otherwise have been aired. Debates about the practicality of the one-bedroom design planned by the aid agencies gradually turned into a discussion of the challenges of managing sexual dynamics and violations in housing that would need to accommodate extended families with no provision for privacy. The women said they had seldom, if ever, talked about these issues with one another, but once the concerns were raised, they quickly started discussing changes and improvements to the existing plan that they felt might alleviate the difficulties – the added storey just discussed, extra dividing walls to create more, smaller rooms, or an easily moveable curtain by the kitchen, allowing greater privacy for washing and dressing, especially for young girls who were uncomfortable washing outdoors. None of these changes were extraordinary – they fell well within the incremental strategies that households commonly use to develop their housing over time. The important thing was that the changes that were proposed and accepted ensured that this externally provided housing would come closer to meeting their actual needs, saving both time and money and providing them with some sense of control in the context of an otherwise top-down rebuilding process.

Other concerns were also raised by men and women, girls and boys. Indoor latrines, for instance, part of the house plan, were initially designed to be entered through an outside door. This was because a toilet in the home was still an unusual feature in this part of the world, and it was widely considered unhygienic and distasteful to have it open directly into the house. In the course of their group discussions, however, young girls acknowledged that they felt embarrassed and vulnerable being seen entering the toilet outside by non-family members. They said they would find it less threatening to have an inside door. Having discussed this among themselves, they felt more confident raising the issue at the larger community meeting, where it was finally resolved that this decision should be up to individual families. Debating practical, material needs in this way can become an entry point for reconsidering tacit norms and practices. Once this toilet issue had been broached, mothers and older women also began to consider the relief it would be to be able to use their latrines from inside the privacy of their homes and the practicality of being able to reach them quickly with very young children. People went on to discuss the fear small children felt about falling into the latrine openings, and they adopted the solution of metal handle bars anchored in the floor next to the squat plate. Very quickly, old people announced that they wanted handle bars as well to make it easier to get back up from squatting.

Several other design modifications were discussed for small children's safety and comfort, including windows in kitchens that allowed mothers to watch their children while they played outdoors, built-in shelves out of the reach of small children for storing medicines and pesticides, and wider steps leading out of the house where children could play and adults could sit – in many cases with a bamboo overhang for shade. Not only did this process allow for design options that the community found more practical, it also provided the novel experience of debating and deciding on these options together and discovering that every group in the community had something interesting to contribute. Especially gratifying was watching fathers' pride when their daughters presented their ideas, or the pleasure that children took in seeing their shy mothers stand up in front of the community to describe a novel solution.

## Neighbourhood space and amenities

### Common space close to home

The "eyes on the street" neighbourhoods that make children feel safe and welcome and that encourage the growth of social capital are the product of many large and small components acting together, not a matter of a some universal blueprint. There are a number of simple fixes, locally identifiable, that can help to sustain a stronger social fabric. The availability of pleasant local spaces, where both adults and children can escape from household tensions and where social ties can be supported and strengthened, can be addressed in piecemeal ways or planned into larger-scale slum upgrading or new construction.

Too often, common space is not something that is seriously considered a vital part of site planning, or it may be inserted by planners who have little insight into the way people actually use these spaces. Playgrounds for instance, when they even exist, are often placed on the far edge of settlements. Few young children ever have the chance to use them because people have too little time to take them there. In most places, people create their spaces and opportunities informally – a water point where women congregate to talk as they collect water, a tea shop where men meet at the end of the day, a small patch of vacant land where boys play cricket or football, the steps to a neighbourhood temple where small children chase each other up and down while their mothers do laundry nearby. These solutions do not need to take up much space, but in order to be respected and preserved, their value needs to be acknowledged.

Sometimes, especially in the course of local upgrading, these uses and the needs they represent must be actively identified and addressed – whether it is the need for a convenient place to wash clothes without provoking tensions with neighbours, or the desire of young girls to have spaces where they can sit together and talk without being harassed or viewed with disapproval, or a place for boys to play cricket without facing the anger of adults.

Space for children's play is a critically important ingredient of common neighbourhood space, and can be met in ways that really respond to expressed needs. It cannot be overstressed that young children prefer to play close to home, that their caregivers are happiest when they are near by, and that the elaborate provision of play equipment is unnecessary. The critical requirement is that children's play be valued enough to allow the opportunity for many small informal solutions. Whenever possible, the provision of safe space for this purpose immediately outside the home, or very close by, should be a priority in the planning and financing of housing for families with young children. Safe outdoor play space can be a critical source of relief from the stresses of crowded indoor time. It also provides the opportunity to experiment safely and gradually with autonomy, attachment and separation, with long-term benefits for both parents and children and the ways they relate to one another.

In Nairobi, the upgraded Kambi Moto settlement, designed and built in place over time by the community, had a layout carefully planned to accommodate large numbers of people in a small area, to protect children from the heavily trafficked road that bounded the area, and to provide a secure network of paved lanes and courtyards that allowed small children to play safely. Further away were larger open spaces where older children could play. Kambi Moto is just one representative community among many that have upgraded as part of the SDI-member federation there.

Some of the best neighbourhoods I have seen for young children have been upgraded slum settlements that benefited from the Baan Mankong programme in Thailand. These projects, as noted in the last chapter, were designed and managed by communities and supported by a country-wide government-funded programme. Lanes were widened and paved, drainage was improved and in most cases residents opted for two-storey row-houses built facing each other across the paved walkways. No cars or motorcycles were allowed to enter these lanes. Children played freely right outside their homes, and in one small settlement I visited a central playground had been built that all children could reach easily on their own.

In Cooks Nagar, an interesting measure was proposed by children, one that ran counter to traditional ways of handling the connection between home and neighbourhood. The tsunami had destroyed and damaged houses, but had also torn away the walls that traditionally enclosed the small yards and provided privacy for individual households. The original rebuilding plan for the larger district included the reconstruction of these walls. But in the months after the disaster, children living in temporary shacks or damaged houses had become accustomed to their new open neighbourhood. They were able to run freely from house to house and to play easily with each other and they asked at one community meeting that the walls not be replaced. At first they met with resistance. But then women began to talk about the new camaraderie they were experiencing. After finishing their housework, and before the men came home from work, they sat on their steps, relaxing and brushing their hair, watching the small children play and chatting from house to house. In the end, the community decided together to forego the walls and to use the saved funds to improve their common space. They also decided to keep and shape a large dead tree that had been uprooted by the tsunami because small children were enjoying climbing on it. Older girls also made their needs clear. They wanted places near home where they could socialize together – benches under trees, small nooks and corners – without being subject to gossip or disapproval.

Children's involvement in this settlement went well beyond advocating for a more open settlement. As construction began, eager for a role, they learned how to inspect deliveries of building materials, checking that everything on the list was there. They also checked for quality, testing bricks, for instance, by soaking a few in a pail of water to make sure they didn't start dissolving – this would indicate that they had been made of saline material and would not hold up. Children developed a relationship with the builders, making sure that they were alert to the different choices made by their households, and they also took on the responsibility for ensuring that concrete pads stayed damp and cured slowly for strength. In the evenings, it was common to see children all over the settlement sprinkling water together on newly poured slabs.

## Basic infrastructure and services

Provision of basic local infrastructure, while it initially seems remote from the issue of violence, is related to child protection in numerous ways, as has been detailed throughout this book. Decent levels of provision can help keep women from becoming so bone weary that they cannot avoid neglecting their small children. Adequate waste collection can help encourage the local stewardship of common space, rather than a weary abdication of control in a filthy settlement. Well-placed, well-maintained, well-lit toilets and water points can also ensure that every day routines do not become the occasion for tensions between neighbours, or for harassment and abuse.

In India, the Alliance from its early years has been involved in the construction and maintenance of community toilets. Although indoor toilets are clearly the more ideal solution, they are not feasible in many settlements because of space constraints. But the public toilet blocks built and managed by municipalities are generally notorious for their lack of maintenance, foul conditions and safety problems. The Alliance found that an important consideration in making their toilets safe, trouble-free zones was placing them in the centre of neighbourhoods rather than off at the periphery somewhere. The toilet blocks they build are properly lit and maintained, and include space where women can do laundry and an extra floor which can house a caretaker and provide space for local meetings or for a childcare centre. They have also made a point of including some toilets specifically for small children with smaller squat plates and handle bars. Members pay a small fee to keep the toilet blocks operating smoothly. These community toilets are often opened with a neighbourhood celebration – a so-called "toilet festival" – which involves flowers, invitations to local authorities and a ribbon cutting ceremony (Burra, Patel and Kerr, 2003). Making toilets an accepted and even celebrated centre of everyday life in this way, rather than dark dirty places to be avoided as much as possible, does a lot to keep this basic need from being linked to fear, violence, stigma and humiliation. Young girls in these communities can use a toilet without feeling abased by their own bodily functions. The toilets are a material response to an important protection concern, but also a symbolic change with even more profound implications.

## Places for community building

Social capital is widely recognized as an asset in managing local tensions and outbreaks of violence. Less often considered are the physical properties of a community that contribute to strong social ties. Gunnar Svendsen argues that face-to-face meetings in geographic space are what social capital is all about. Tensions between Hindus and Muslims in India, for instance, have been far more common in large cities where people live in segregated areas and have little contact with one another. In rural villages where daily contact is the norm, communal violence is less of an issue. But both physical proximity and conducive spaces are crucial to this. Svendsen asks, "Where do people really meet and get to know each other? Do some places stimulate formation of intra- and inter-group networks more than others?' (Svendsen, 2010, p. 60). He discusses specifically how large multi-functional meeting places within communities can counteract segregation between community factions. His examples are mostly from Scandinavia and the Netherlands, where arguably a historical ethos of democracy, equality, mutual trust and cooperation may contribute to the effectiveness of such meeting places.

But there are also documented experiences from the global south. SDI's member federations again provide good examples. A history of SPARC, the support NGO in the Indian Alliance, points to the importance of common meeting space as a catalyst for strong community networks. According to founder Sheela Patel, women in poverty know what changes they need. But "to develop the experience and skills to reflect together on their situation, they need a safe, local space where they can gather. Being marginalised means being cut off from networks and spaces of information and communication" (Patel and Bartlett, 2009, p. 5). The reason they took the name SPARC (the Society for the Promotion of Area Resource Centres) was that acquiring such a space, however humble, seemed like the first step. As these federations have spread in country after country, the identification or creation of such a space has remained a basic starting point for developing a community identity, along with the enumeration of households and mapping of the neighbourhood, and the establishment of savings groups.

Collete Daiute describes how the creation of community centres in the former Yugoslavia, often with international funding, has provided the setting for developing new ways of responding to the local scene in the aftermath of large-scale violence. These centres have allowed young people to meet and organize to mend the ruptures in their physical surroundings, rebuilding destroyed bridges, building day-care centres, in one case reclaiming a lake filled with trash from a nearby refugee camp (Daiute, 2011, p. 53).

In Cooks Nagar, once people had debated the kinds of changes they wanted to make to their house plans, they also began to think about their common space. Aside from the lanes that wound all through the settlement, and occasional spaces between house plots, there was just one larger plot of land, thick with weedy trees and tangled vines, that belonged to an absentee owner. This had never been a focus of attention before, but after all their discussions and community meetings – which had to be held outside the settlement to accommodate everyone – people started thinking about how much they needed a gathering space. They wanted space for weddings and other functions so they would not have to rent a place outside the community. They also wanted a place where children could go and do homework after school, because this was difficult in their crowded, noisy homes. Most of all, they wanted a place where groups could meet and where, when needed, the whole community could gather to discuss things. Excited by the prospect, they started to discuss a price they might jointly offer the absentee owner, and small groups could be seen sketching out their ideas all over the settlement. This development, not initially anticipated as part of the rebuilding process, seemed to be a natural way to channel the enthusiasm that had been kindled by the house-planning process and to provide a longer-term community focus.

## Vegetation and access to nature

The considerable body of work pointing to the restorative qualities of nature and the role of vegetation in minimizing stress makes it clear that the provision of trees and natural spaces must rank high in efforts to relieve the effects of violence for children and their families. Nancy Wells and Gary Evans note that even among rural children, more rather than less nature makes a difference, and the higher the level of stressful events, the stronger the effect of the natural surroundings (2003). Kuo and Sullivan, as noted, have amassed a good deal of systematic comparative evidence over many years on the positive influence of trees and other vegetation around inner-city housing blocks in Chicago. Their work has continued, and a 1996 summary of their findings holds true for their subsequent research as well.

> We are finding less violence in urban public housing where there are trees. Residents from buildings with trees report using more constructive, less violent ways of dealing with conflict in their homes. They report using reasoning more often in conflicts with their children, and they report significantly less use of severe violence. And in conflicts with their partners, they report less use of physical violence than do residents living in buildings without trees.
> *(Sullivan and Kuo, 1996, Technology bulletin (Urban & Community Forestry Assistance Program (U.S.)); 4. Forestry report R8-FR; 56. Available as reprint from http://www.rneighbors.org/?page_id=1422.)*

Kuo and her colleagues find that even a "low dose" of vegetation can have a restorative effect on mental energy. This work has resulted, among other things, in a transformation of much of the low-income public housing in Chicago, with a USD10 million tree-planting campaign.

No research that I know from the global south systematically compares social activity in settlements with and without trees. But qualitative evidence from Bangalore slums points to the heavy concentration of social activity under trees. People sell their wares here, women prepare food and wash clothes, children play and people gather in groups to converse. It is discouraging to learn, however, that forty-four representative Bangalore slums averaged only ten trees apiece – evidence more of the highly contested nature of slum space than of people's feelings about vegetation, given how frequently residents kept small potted plants instead (Gopal and Nagendra, 2014). There is also ample evidence of children's desire for natural surroundings, especially in the context of challenging urban environments. The international Growing up in Cities research found almost without exception that when children from low-income urban neighbourhoods documented their surroundings and talked about their priorities, they spoke repeatedly about trees and safe natural areas as a vital ingredient of a good place to live (Chawla, 2001). In Delhi, after a forced eviction, children were also insistent on the need for plants and trees in the barren site allocated for their resettlement (Chatterjee, 2007).

Given the indisputable benefits of vegetation, there are astonishingly few documented examples of the creation of green space in settlements that have lacked vegetation. There are more examples in post-disaster settings, as will be described in the next section. In dense urban settlements where space is heavily contested, trees and natural areas more often than not are considered an unnecessary luxury. But even in peripheral areas, there are not documented initiatives. It is far easier in fact to find examples of settlements that have been eradicated in order to make space for attractive parks for the rest of the city's residents than of low-income areas where vegetation was planted. There is an informal settlement in Lima, Peru, though, where residents decided that a green space should take priority over other potential investments, like a library or a health facility. With the support of visiting students, residents converted a barren hillside into a park with an irrigation system that recycled hand-washing water (Hodson, 2012).

Even in the absence of documented examples of tree-planting in stressful urban settlements, the qualitative evidence that is available on the priority that children give to natural spaces and vegetation should be sufficient to encourage this as a focus for child protection efforts as well as for more broad-based development and upgrading.

## The ripple effects for social cohesion

As noted in the previous chapter, there is little or no research that has focused specifically on the protective potential of these kinds of local improvements. But there is ample evidence of the more general boost for morale, mutual trust and the confidence to tackle difficult problems, especially where communities have jointly tackled all the challenges along the way.

In ACHR's documentation of the Baan Mankong settlements, for example, there are numerous comparisons of before and after that repeatedly realte the social well-being of the community with the material changes and the process these changes required.

> "We were a real slum before," said one resident. "There were drugs for sale, and lots of outside organizations did their drugs trading here. There were kids sniffing glue and paint thinner. There were lots of dark corners and plenty of vice. Back then, when the weekend came, most people would sit around and get drunk – that was the only way to relax. There was nothing else to do, no activities. And the worst thing was that the people here had no confidence in themselves, no idea that things could be different than this."
>
> *(ACHR, 2011)*

An assessment of the programme recorded a number of gains, over and above the improved physical conditions. Among them were tenure security and the formal address that accompanies it, which had helped people gain formal employment; easier access to credit; increased study time for children (an average of over three-and-a-half hours a week more than those in non-member households); and a 40 per cent increase in education expenditures (Bhatkal and Lucci, 2015).

For many of the SDI and AHCR-linked communities, the establishment of childcare centres has been a natural outgrowth of their joint work to improve their material environment. For young children in communities where people face difficult living conditions and the overburdened schedules that accompany them, the presence of a good early childhood programme can make a huge difference. This is not exactly a physical environment modification, but it is a valuable response to many problems within the physical environment, lessening the potential for neglect, for abusive behaviour by overstressed parents, and for the exploitation of older siblings who may be prevented from attending school because of the need for child-care. There is also evidence that those children who experience opportunities for early stimulation are less likely to become violent adults (Walker et al., 2011).

One of the more extensive considerations of the social, and arguably protective, ramifications is a 2011 account by Jack Makau, who works with SDI on documentation. He describes the loosely constituted youth version of the federation in Kenya that emerged around 2003 and its implications for younger children. The adult federation at that point consisted of savings groups in 250 Nairobi slums, a growing number of housing, water and sanitation projects, a zero-tolerance stance on forced eviction and a steady change in the nature of slum-government relations. Young people were viewed as a constant worry and nuisance, but basically as the problem of parents, teachers and police, and not the federation's concern. Then after the deaths in one month of three of the young people in a newly enumerated settlement – one by suicide, one from HIV-related disease and one from a violent altercation – people began to feel there was an important gap here, and one man took it on himself to become a federation resource for youth. An initial emphasis on football evolved into the older boys organizing themselves into groups around a variety of changing goals – access to football pitches, a beauty pageant, a slum newspaper, a neighbourhood waste collection businesses. Linking all these activities was a primary commitment on the part of all members to mentor three or four children between the ages of 4 and 12 – whether in football, dance, acrobatics or just homework. Mothers, says Makau, became the biggest supporters of the young people's movement (Makau, 2011). Makau points to an inherent challenge to the sustained viability of this kind of youth social movement. The young people grow up and move on – there are none of the long-term members that provide the staying power of the adult federations. Jane Weru, director of the Akiba Mashinani Trust that supports the federation, noted on losing yet another key youth mentor, "Maybe it's enough that we keep them off the streets in their formative years." But in 2008, they began to notice that the children who had originally been mentored by the older boys were stepping up to become mentors themselves (Makau, 2011, p. 206).

Also in the early 2000s, a parallel girls' organization emerged here, Miss Koch Kenya, responding to the fears of young girls about being out and about in their neighbourhoods. Starting with a handful of girls, it went on to become its own NGO with far-reaching connections and continued roots within the community, much of its work focused precisely on child protection in the most integrated sense. According to Emmie Erondanga,

> If the children are not performing well, we sit with the parents. Where is the problem? … Are the parents giving children time to play? Are they giving children time to study? Are they following them to school, to see if – just check, did she come to school, did he come to school? if not, where did they go? Why do we want to wait until we have a disaster and say, oh, my child was involved!? … And we need to parent them in a way that they have values and morals and they respect the communities they serve and they're coming from. Even the schools we take these kids to, we are in constant communication with the teachers – just to check and see, I hope they are not being recruited in something else.

Another parallel phenomenon emerged in Mumbai in the 1990s, this one a response to young boys on the street. The city's solution at that point was to round up these children and place them in detention centres – and the boys in turn would run away back to the street again. Many of the local federation leaders had themselves lived on the streets as children and recognized the need for a better response. Using a strategy that the federations used to build community networks, they invited boys from different locations in the city to a three-day event to share their stories and the challenges they faced. Their priorities, the boys decided, were protection from being rounded up by the police, and from sexual harassment when they slept on the streets. Mahila Milan, the women's network that was part of the Alliance, was already in dialogue with the police, and an informal arrangement was made – if children were picked up, they could instead be brought to any of the network's resource centres, and the women would take responsibility for them. Children were welcome at any time to spend nights at these resource centres and to get hot meals there. (The women responded to girls on the street as well, but in lesser numbers, and by taking them in and fostering them as family members.) The use of the resource centres evolved into the establishment of dedicated night shelters that offered a refuge but respected the boys' autonomy. Many of the women became "aunts" to the boys in their neighbourhoods, interceding for them with the police and encouraging the children to conduct themselves in ways that would not intimidate the larger community. Over the longer term, they functioned as family in helping to arrange their marriages and get a start in their adult lives. Many of these young people went on to become federation members themselves. The city adjusted its own responses, adopting this model of support in preference to the repressive "rehabilitation" responses that had been the norm, and over time the Alliance's involvement was no longer needed. More responsive, rights-based approaches are far more common now, but this early Mumbai response from local pavement communities to support and include these children on their own terms, rather than rejecting them, remains unusual.

Long-term collaborative community work on living conditions does not automatically spawn ancillary movements or services for the care and protection of children. The point is that the level of commitment and its longevity can provide fertile ground for the social development of a community, and for the emergence of activities specifically targeted at children's well-being – as in the case of the Kwazulu-Natal savings group described in the previous chapter.

## Responding to violence in school and on the way to school

Most responses within schools to violence, whether corporal punishment or sexual harassment and abuse, have focused on awareness raising, codes of conduct and mechanisms to ensure the detection and reporting of abuses. Some responses, however, have taken a more physical form. In West and Central Africa, documented initiatives have included the creation of clubs for girls, safe places where they can socialize, discuss the issues they face in school and build their joint capacity to deal with them. In Liberia support was also given to the establishment of safe houses that provide temporary shelter for girls who have been abused in school and who could not return to their communities and families. There is also the growing emphasis on separate latrines for girls, which can contribute to their willingness to attend school, and their families' willingness to allow their attendance (ActionAid et al., 2010). In villages in both Nepal and Afghanistan, faced with Maoist rebels in one case and the Taliban in the other, parents were also far more comfortable sending their children to school, and children were more willing to go, if there were boundary walls around the school. These walls offered no real protection, but the symbolic demarcation made the schools feel more secure, and the expense seemed well worth it to parent committees.

Many of the protection issues related to children's safe use of public space come to the fore around getting to school each day. One response has been the various "safe routes to school" initiatives that have developed in different countries, primarily in the global north. In most cases, programmes involve making streets safer for biking and walking, and training children to become more active, aware and competent in dealing with their surroundings. But there have also been efforts that involve much more local participation. In Buenos Aires, for instance, store-owners, neighbours and school staff were enlisted as volunteers to pay attention to children as they walked back and forth to school. Children were asked to use specific streets where merchants, neighbours and police were ready to watch out for them. If they had problems, children were free to come into any participating store that had placed a welcoming sign in its window, and to ask for help or call their parents or the police if needed. By 2004, when the report was written, there were eight of these "safe corridors" used every day by 28,000 students walking to fifty-nine city schools (Moore and Cosco, 2004).

In Chicago, where there were over 750 homicides in 2016 alone, the city's Safe Passage programme on the south and west sides has hired over a thousand community workers, many of them unemployed veterans, to stand within watching distance of each other on the walking routes to schools, wearing neon vests. Each school designs its own safety strategy to reflect local needs. Parents also volunteer and interested local businesses, as in Buenos Aires, place signs in their windows indicating that they are safe havens (CPS, 2016).

The very local nature of appropriate responses cannot be overstressed. During the work after the tsunami in Cooks Nagar, my colleagues and I were concerned about the unprotected access to the railroad tracks at one end of the settlement. We felt sure that residents should be encouraged to fence off the path to the tracks as they worked to repair the area after the tsunami's destruction. After a week in the settlement, we revised our hasty judgement. Only one train a day came down the track – slowly and with loud warnings whenever it approached a settlement. Local children used the tracks quite safely to get to school and back. It was a quiet route that allowed for conversation and play along the way, and it provided a shorter alternative to the very congested dangerous main road that they would otherwise have had to walk along. Here, the trick was not identifying a safe route to school, but ensuring that poorly informed consultants or over-vigilant authorities did not eliminate an existing solution.

Access to safe public transport for children is also critical. Few countries have a system of dedicated school buses, but concessions are available in many places that allow school children free transportation. This can carry its own hazards, however. According to Richard Mabala in Tanzania, when children pay just a fraction of the adult bus ticket price, drivers can be unwilling to take them on board, which can make them more vulnerable to harassment and abuse. The availability of special staff or volunteers to ride public transport during the hours before and after school could help to ensure that children travel safely. Transport for teachers can also be a help. In a remote and violent part of Afghanistan, when women teachers were provided with secure transport to schools from the towns where they lived, far more of them were willing to work in remote villages – and the enrolment of girls went up as a result (Bartlett, 2013).

## Crime prevention through environmental design and supportive policing

Crime prevention through environmental design (CPTED) has had its successes and failures, both pointing to the fundamental need for active community involvement in the management of such spaces. Although still primarily an approach in high-income countries, CPTED is also quite broadly used in the global south, where applications have been far more likely to stress the contribution of disparities in living conditions to the chain of causes of criminal activity and the need for community involvement in any responses. Caroline Moser, focusing on gender-based violence, described the specific case of Khayelitsha township in Cape Town, where the initial audit found a strong relationship between violent episodes and inadequate infrastructure, including distant latrines, unsafe transportation hubs, poor lighting. Responses were far-reaching and covered many of the solutions already discussed here, both physical and social. They also included the assignment of female police officers with training in domestic abuse counselling, and supervision for community toilets, for public transport and for schools so they could serve as recreational space after school hours (Moser, 2009).

The goal of reducing crime can be a strong incentive for local governments to get on board with funding and support, much of which is funnelled towards the improvement of the local environment through numerous small-scale interventions such as cleaning up dangerous open areas, creating clear activity zones, improving lighting, closing illegal liquor outlets and monitoring specific hot spots. In the experience of CPTED experts, the involvement of children is often fundamental to the success of the process – not only do they have an intimate knowledge of their own neighbourhoods, but their commitment also tends to interest and attract the adults in their communities (Stephens, Vargas and Kruger, 2004).

A South African manual on CPTED approaches stresses the importance of combining law enforcement, social prevention of crime and situational prevention through the modification of the environment, including such measures as community surveillance and monitoring of specific places, the provision of recreational spaces for young people and the modification of public space to reduce the opportunities for crime (Liebermann and Landman, 2000). This manual also emphasizes the need for community safety audits that take into account the full range of threats to safety in a neighbourhood. Domestic assault, for instance, receives as much attention here as muggings or property crime, and some of the interventions discussed include the creation of safe houses for women, and restrictions in the open hours of alcohol outlets.

Supportive community policing can be a major additional asset in any neighbourhood, yet those most in need of it are least likely to be well provided. In Mumbai and Pune, India, "police panchayats" are a solution that has evolved now over the course of ten years in a partnership between the police and the slum dwellers' federations (Roy, Jockin and Javed, 2004). The idea was developed by the police commissioner in Pune, who recognized that his police force lacked the staff and resources to patrol all the slums in the city, where most of the city's violence was occurring. Any solution to this issue had to take into account the inherently difficult relationship between these often illegal slum settlements and the police. The local police panchayats, which work out of a room in the neighbourhood, are made up of one police officer and ten locally selected residents, seven women and three men, who are authorized as police assistants and who serve as a liaison between local residents and the police. They patrol their neighbourhoods, staying alert to problems, becoming involved as needed, and only referring things on to the police when necessary. They also have daily meetings at their local centres to help resolve disputes. Women form the majority of each police panchayat since they spend more time at home and know what is going on in the neighbourhood. They are also in a better position to investigate any problem in depth. The implications for children are obvious, both with regard to family violence and to dangerous conditions within the larger community. With the active involvement of the police panchayat, the relationship between the police and the city's slum dwellers has been greatly improved. People are now reporting crimes and violent incidents to the police that would never have been reported before. The model has spread in India, where there are currently over 150 police panchayats, and it is starting to be adopted in other countries as well.

A similar response is the many women's police stations that have been established in Brazil, with the specific objective of addressing violence against women in a context where domestic violence is not taken very seriously by the judicial system. These police stations are staffed exclusively by women and they focus more on mediation between women and their partners than on judicial penalties (McIlwaine, 2013).

From the Bronx in New York comes a very different response – this one to repressive and often violent stop-and-frisk policing rather than to a lack of policing. The stop-and-frisk approach to preventing gun violence before it occurs has been credited by some with reducing the rate of violent crime in the city, but this analysis is contested, and the approach has been hugely controversial. The Morris Justice Project focused on a forty-block neighbourhood in the South Bronx, where stop-and-frisk activity had become so commonplace that it was almost accepted as the natural order of things. Young men and adolescent boys, mostly African American, found it impossible to move freely through their neighbourhood without the fear of aggressive encounters with the police, often accompanied by racial slurs. Several mothers from this neighbourhood, whose sons had been repeatedly stopped and harassed, started talking informally about this intrusive and intimidating police behaviour, documenting cases and keeping each other up to date on what was happening.

When two researchers from the City University of New York came to the neighbourhood, eager to collaborate with residents on local issues, the people who showed up were these mothers, along with some younger men and women, and they knew what they wanted to focus on. Together, they planned and carried out interviews, focus groups and a survey of 1,000 residents, selected to be as representative as possible. They also drew on NYPD (New York Police Department) data and mapped the department's activity and its results. Over 69 per cent of those surveyed had been stopped at some time in the past, many repeatedly. Over the course of the last year there had been almost 5,000 stop-and-frisk episodes in this forty-block area. As a result of these stops, only eight guns had been found – a 0.16 per cent "success" rate. Less than 10 per cent of the stops resulted in an arrest or a summons, most for very minor infringements. More than half the stops involved physical violence on the part of the police – clearly accounting for far more violence than the approach had actually prevented. The most significant outcome here of stop-and-frisk had been the transformation of this neighbourhood into a stage for the enactment of distrust, intimidation and anger, with ripple effects for all residents.

The data collected by the research team were made available to residents and police – most dramatically through the "illuminator event", during which the findings were projected onto the side of a large public housing building one evening in the form of a letter to the police department ("Dear NYPD"), and read aloud through a megaphone. The letter questioned the value of any approach that required 5,000 stops to secure eight weapons, and it asked that the police respect local residents and not treat them as strangers or as criminals. "This is our home," the letter repeated as a refrain (PSP, 2012).

Owning this information, sharing it and making it visible in the streets and on the walls of the neighbourhood was a galvanizing and celebratory experience, a way of re-appropriating neighbourhood space. Like the terrorization by the police, it has had ripple effects. A community safety workshop was planned subsequently, along with efforts to address local housing problems. The report that was produced was to be the first of several on local issues. T-shirts emblazoned with the findings of the study are very popular in the neighbourhood, as young people become billboards for their own information rather than for corporate advertising.

The project has also been part of a groundswell of resistance that found expression in an extended court trial of the NYPD's stop-and-frisk approach. The judge, clearly critical of a procedure that involved such a high error rate and that appeared to be driven by quotas and racial profiling, ruled against the city, claiming that police officers had been systematically stopping people without any legitimate reason for suspecting them of wrongdoing (Goldstein, 2013). The efforts rallied public outrage, and like the place-centred information-gathering of the federations of the urban poor, the process is stimulating the identity, the organization and the capacity of a community to have a voice and to make change for its young people.

## Reintegrating and reclaiming urban space

At issue here is not only the quality of local neighbourhood space, but the integration of local neighbourhoods into the life and fabric of the larger city. The evidence on the destructive impacts of segregated space within the urban landscape points to the need for the assertive control of public space by local municipalities in the face of growing privatization and enclosure. This is a daunting challenge, given the strength of this trend in cities around the world. Evidence has been emerging, however, on the positive impact of efforts to reintegrate and reclaim the urban fabric in places where social segregation is spatially expressed.

One such effort is the Summer Night Lights programme in Los Angeles (Lee, 2012). This strategy is at the heart of a larger city effort within communities with especially high rates of gang-related violence. Each summer from July to September, community leaders coordinate with law enforcement, gang intervention workers, community service providers, philanthropists and local residents to transform thirty-two city parks, usually dominated by gang activity, into community safe havens. Every evening the parks are open until midnight and there are family activities, late night sports and food for all. Everyone in the community is welcome, even gang members, but residents enforce strict standards for behaviour. The number of shots fired in these neighbourhoods over these summers has reportedly been reduced by 55 per cent.

A more far-reaching strategy in Medellín, Colombia, focused on projects to link some of the city's more marginalized communities to the rest of the city and to improve the amenities available within them. Part of this effort was a network of ambitious "library parks" built to embody the notion that in a new Medellín, violence could be addressed through knowledge and social inclusion. Much of the effort focused on physical projects involving access and public space, including improved lighting, pathways, bridges, stairs, cable cars and escalators climbing steep shanty town hills, parks and plazas, soccer fields – all things that draw people into common space. Community-based planning organizations were supported by the municipality to come up with smaller projects that complemented and expanded on the larger vision of integration, both connecting the city and enhancing the quality of life in poor communities (Sertich, 2010). The murder rate in 2012 was reported to be 15 per cent of what it was during the heyday of the violence (Kimmelman, 2012).

It might be difficult, of course, to determine whether these kinds of interventions had in fact been responsible for changes in rates of violence, since other efforts to counter violence were also happening city-wide. But by a happy coincidence, there was a large household survey in Medellín just prior to these interventions. This provided the baseline for a natural experiment, making it possible to compare the effects of these place-based interventions. Twenty-five project neighbourhoods were selected, and cluster analysis was used to select twenty-three matched comparison neighbourhoods that did not receive the interventions. The study found that between 2003 and 2008, the decline in the homicide rate in the intervention neighbourhoods was 66 per cent greater than in the comparison neighbourhoods, and that resident reports of violence dropped by 75 per cent more than in other neighbourhoods (Cerdá et al., 2012).

The Baan Mankong programme in Thailand, described earlier in the chapter, has also had the effect of mending the larger urban fabric through its many small-scale community-driven upgrading projects within local neighbourhoods. This demand-driven community-managed programme draws on government funding to make multiple local improvements tailored to each community's needs and priorities and in effect to integrate them into the framework of larger city development. According to Somsook Boonyabancha, who initiated the Baan Mankong programme, this liberates communities from the "vertical strings of patronage" which in many places are closely related to the kinds of coercion and control that can erupt into violence. Boonyabancha stresses that while physical upgrading is ostensibly the objective of the programme, it is actually the most superficial part of the process, simply the avenue through which people make larger and deeper changes in their collective capacity and their relationship to power structures within the city at large (Boonyabancha, 2005).

The choices made in the course of physical upgrading are critical in this regard, and in the context of urban reintegration, these choices can be telling. Almost a quarter of all the projects undertaken in the course of the Baan Mankong process have been the building or improvement of roads and pathways – and this in a setting where housing, toilets and water might well be considered the most important needs. Boonyabancha and colleagues speculate on why this might be the case, and they point to both the practical and symbolic importance of this choice:

> a road – even a very narrow one – provides a common open space in a crowded community, which can function as a playground, meeting place, market, workshop or festival venue. A block of toilets or a water supply system can certainly improve conditions, but a paved road has a greater symbolic power to change both internal and external perceptions of a community. A community with a proper road is part of the larger society. Most informal settlements are isolated, even when they are in the middle of a city. A paved road is a visible improvement and a potent symbol of connectedness, physically and symbolically linking the quasi-invisible community with the formal city.
>
> (Boonyabancha, Carcellar and Kerr, 2012, p. 442)

The symbolic and practical connectedness with the formal city has powerful implications for citizenship, pride and aspiration, transforming in the most material ways the marginalization that is so stressful to those who experience it.

## Protective environments in disaster and emergency

There is growing awareness of the impact of dysfunctional post-emergency environments for children, but there has been comparatively little research on measures to counter the problems. One notable exception has been documentation of the provision of "safe play areas" or "child-friendly spaces", especially for younger children, an effort in the turmoil of conflict, or within emergency camps and shelters, to provide some supervised place where children will be safe and where they can relieve their distress and anxiety through play with other children.

These spaces fill an important function, but they also present a dilemma in that they are a band-aid solution to a deeper set of problems. Although these play areas are designed to be temporary measures, the length of time that people end up spending in what are often abysmal physical conditions requires longer-term solutions to children's need for play. In this situation, attention to the more general safety and attractiveness of the local environment would surely be preferable, especially given that the purpose-built spaces are seldom accessible outside certain scheduled hours. But while the temporary measure is in place, there may be less incentive for residents to tackle the larger problem. Jason Hart suggests that in Palestine, important as the provision of "safe spaces" may be as a child protection measure within a dangerous environment, their very creation within the larger prison that is home to children could be viewed as an implicit acceptance of an intrinsically impossible situation (Hart, 2012). These are challenging issues for child protection agencies, which may have little scope for affecting the larger situation. As in so many other protection situations, however, whether a lack of tenure or unlit streets or unsafe transport, the critical issue is the focus and awareness that child protection agencies can bring to more general responses. Wherever possible, the creation of alternative special spaces for children is most effective within the context of support for larger measures to ensure pleasant surroundings for all residents.

An important contribution on this front was the preparation in 2012 of the *Minimum Standards for Child Protection in Humanitarian Action*, reviewed by over 400 people from agencies in forty countries, and tested in the field in a range of humanitarian contexts (CPWG, 2012). Following the structure of the well-known Sphere standards, each standard here is accompanied by key actions, indicators, targets and detailed guidance notes. Going beyond "child friendly spaces", the manual details issues around water and sanitation, shelter and camp management, making it clear that a range of deficiencies in these areas can put children at risk of physical and sexual violence. Guidance on water and sanitation, for instance, stresses the fact that provision must be adequate for health, but must also be situated and managed in ways that keep children and women safe; toilet blocks must be easily accessible, visible, well lit, lockable, separated by sex and designed to ensure privacy and dignity and to accommodate young children's needs. For very young children, it should be easy and safe for caregivers to dispose of faeces and launder diapers. Schedules for water distribution should be set up in consultation with girls and women, ensuring that they can reach their shelters while it is light outdoors. The manual also acknowledges the importance of secure shelter designed to flexibly accommodate household needs, including privacy. Special attention is given to the needs of children separated from family. Standards are not always reflected in practice, but this is an important step. If these same standards were met under "normal" non-emergency conditions, millions of children and women worldwide would be safer.

The importance of people's involvement in addressing their own environments becomes if anything more vital in these post-emergency settings than in any other. The chance to manage and improve their surroundings is a practical response to the demoralization of displaced people, for whom weeks, months and even years can drag by without any sense of progress or any opportunity to effect a change. My conversations with displaced people after the 2004 tsunami revealed very different states of mind on the part of those who were passive recipients of NGO services and those who were organizing themselves to work on local conditions. One emergency camp in Thailand stood out for its unusually pleasant surroundings and the level of positive energy on the part of residents. ACHR, the grassroots network in Asia, discussed above in the context of Bangkok slum upgrading, had been supporting its residents to take charge, negotiate with well-meaning providers, set priorities and determine the terms on which help would be delivered.

A more proactive, confident outlook makes it far more likely that social problems will also be more adequately dealt with, and that children will receive the care they need. For children, too, there is ample evidence of the psychologically protective impact of problem-solving, responsibility, active involvement in improving the post-disaster environment, and routines that provide predictable structure to the day (Boyden and Mann, 2005; Guyot, 2007). Among response organizations and agencies, however, in the pressure and rush to deal with chaotic post-emergency situations, the skills and resources of those affected are often bypassed, to the detriment of all. There are many specific responses, most of them outlined by the *Minimum Standards*, that can be relevant as part of joint planning and activity.

I have already discussed the protective value of vegetation, which takes on particular relevance in post-emergency situations, and has been more extensively documented in this context. Tidball and Krasny (2014) have compiled numerous examples of the value of natural spaces and the community-based stewardship of nature in post-catastrophe and post-conflict settings. They note the more than metaphoric connections between cultivating plants and cultivating community, and the transformative potential of the connection with nature. Chawla (2014), one of their contributors, points in particular to the healing potential of "greening" for children under the stress of extreme events.

In post-tsunami Tamil Nadu and Sri Lanka, I found that, while adults were understandably preoccupied by regaining livelihoods and permanent housing, children repeatedly raised concerns about the desolate, unshaded landscape left by the disaster and the need for trees, not only for their shade and beauty, but because many of the people they knew had relied on trees to save them from the wave. The children couldn't understand why rebuilding efforts included no attention to vegetation to break the long rows of identical small buildings on the ravaged land. Trees take a long time to grow, they reasoned; it made no sense to wait.

Vegetation was used to good effect with a very different emphasis in Nakuru, Kenya, where in the aftermath of intense, long-lasting post-election ethnic violence in 2008, tree-planting has been central to a peace initiative with children. Peace club members have been involved in establishing and maintaining tree nurseries and planting the trees as a practical and symbolic contribution to the restoration of the local environment. The initiative does not address the complex land distribution issues that contribute to the country's violence, but it is an opportunity for positive contact between children belonging to different ethnic groups and it uses care for the land as a way to repair the relationship with both the environment and other people (Zinck and Eyber, 2013). The authors of the report on this tree nursery initiative point to the influence of Wangari Maathai, the Kenyan environmental and political activist who founded the Green Belt Movement.

Rebuilding life after displacement calls for the same principles of local involvement, as described above in the context of post-tsunami efforts in the community of Cooks Nagar, where community members were able to shape generic rebuilding plans in ways that ensured that replacement housing actually met local needs. But community-based responses have to happen within the context of more general supports, and sometimes the urgency of post-disaster needs precludes the time for local participation. An impressive example on the part of UNICEF has been its role in restoring and expanding damaged and overstressed water and sanitation systems in many urban centres beset by conflict. In Yemen, for example, after the government collapsed in 2015, the rapid influx of IDPs into urban areas led to the near collapse of basic infrastructure, leaving millions in need of drinking water and at risk of cholera and other diseases. Other development partners had left the country and most skilled local government staff were also gone. This pushed UNICEF's emergency team towards a large-scale urban water and sanitation intervention for millions of residents, an effort that demanded a rapid learning curve. Water and sanitation becomes a clear protection priority in this emergency context, with an urgency that is far less evident when the lack of service provision is an everyday matter.

## Conclusion

Just a few pages ago, I discussed the road-paving projects that were so often a priority for communities taking part in Thailand's Baan Mankong programme. When taken at face value, road-paving seems a far-fetched response to the violence and neglect that distorts the lives of so many young children. There is no evidence that points to any social effects. Research investigating the impact of road-paving projects in Mexico, for instance, found an increase in household consumption, but pointed to no other social impact (Gonzalez-Navarro and Quintana-Domeque, 2010). But taken in context, the connections are compelling. I want to return to this counter-intuitive example in closing.

The communities in Thailand that choose to upgrade their neighbourhoods by first paving their roads are engaged in a profound process. They are working together, first of all, free from those "vertical strings of patronage" to identify their problems and prioritize solutions. In making collaborative decisions about practical ways to improve their shared surroundings, they are operating on multiple levels.

When they decide that road-paving is the action of choice, they are taking the practical and symbolic step of connecting themselves and their marginal settlements to the larger city – becoming citizens in effect. At the same time, they are working to improve a shared space that serves them in a multitude of ways. Streets, as Somsook Boonyabancha points out, allow for mobility but they are also a place to meet people, to talk, to play, to buy and sell, to see and be seen. The use of this shared asset, but even more important the negotiation, decision-making and planning that precede it, can feed the self-perpetuating project of community building, repairing the social fabric along with the physical terrain. This disposition towards involvement and stewardship is fundamental to the capacity to care as a community for the community's children. The fact that road-paving projects have not been found in more general research to affect rates of violence is a moot point here. Paved roads in the absence of that proactive local involvement may mean little or nothing to the community capacity for caring. What counts most here is the catalytic effect that the physical project can kindle, stimulating greater ownership and an enhanced sense of control.

Of course, road-paving does not have unique value here. It is an appealing example partly because it has so little obvious relevance to a concern with young children and violence. We could also be talking about sanitation or secure tenure or waste removal or space where boys can play cricket without riling tempers. All of these things, in their absence, become a shorthand for the systemic inequities that are so entwined with violence. Patterns of deprivation and exclusion, often officially sanctioned and supported, constitute a form of violence in and of themselves, but they also feed violence of the most direct and immediate kind. Changing these patterns takes political will at the highest level. But the inclusion in that process of those who have been excluded is also fundamental to the process of addressing inequity.

Let's start from the other end – from the child who is beaten or neglected, who watches her mother cringe at her father's voice, who sees her elder brother come home angry from a clash on the street. There is abundant evidence of the effect that violence, experienced or witnessed, can have on young children. It can break bodies and minds and exert an insidious influence even at a cellular level. The effects are immediate but can also linger, undermining health, trust and capability. This applies not only to physical violence, but also to psychological abuse and even to neglect. These forms of violence can also have a deep and durable impact.

We have become accustomed to thinking of violence as emerging from social circumstances. We recognize that abuse can travel through generations, and that men whose manhood is sabotaged by unemployment may be more prone to wife-beating. We acknowledge that adolescents who engage in gang violence may be responding with anger to their place in the scheme of things. Structural violence is more than an abstraction. Going beyond the social ecology of violence to consider the material and spatial context is revealing in this respect. It does not simply add another facet to our understanding of violence. It provides a link between the metaphor of structural violence and the stark reality of intimate personal harm.

Insecure tenure, crowded housing, wretched provision for basic needs, walls and barbed wire segregating the rich from the poor – the violence inherent in these things becomes apparent in the violence that they spawn. Housing, neighbourhood space and territorial boundaries are the warp in the social fabric. The relations of power that are the context for violence within households, within communities and the wider society are often expressed through control over space and the material conditions of life.

Stress plays a fundamental mediating role in this relationship. Noise, crowding, dilapidation and insecurity contribute to stress in a myriad of ways. Standing in line to use a dark, foul smelling, overflowing public toilet is taxing all by itself. When the fear of rape, or even the anxiety about being late for work, are added to the indignity of these sub-human conditions, the stress is amplified. Long-term or repeated stress means constant wear and tear on the human system, undermining physical and mental health, increasing both aggression and vulnerability. An accumulation of stressful physical conditions can fan frustration and violence. Violence in turn shapes children's experience of the material world, diminishing their lives and opportunities, stunting their potential.

Going beyond a social perspective on violence makes it possible to consider alternatives that may help to shift the intricate pattern of circumstances in play. Considering material and spatial realities encourages a more rooted approach to child protection. It brings into sharper focus the fact that parenting education or awareness campaigns are necessarily partial approaches, exposed for their thinness by the continued absence of roots, the lack of a place where, in Mindy Fullilove's terms, true dwelling is possible.

It is of course naïve to see paved roads or streetlights, toilets, trees or property titles for women as panaceas when they are just isolated phenomena. They can for sure have a direct impact on the lives of families and children, lowering stress, increasing a sense of control over life, in some cases reducing opportunities for predatory behaviour. But in the absence of broader equity and local involvement, their impact is superficial. The deeper difference lies in the transactions that these efforts can jump-start. They can generate a transformative process that goes much deeper than most child protection interventions. The important thing is for communities to become creative, confident, problem-solving social structures that can continue identifying their problems, wrestling with them and developing solutions long after their roads are paved, their drains are installed and their housing is built.

A year after I spent time in the tsunami-ravaged settlement of Cooks Nagar, where people took over the planning of their reconstruction, I returned to see what was happening there. Mahalaxmi, a grandmother who had been very active in the whole process, was one of the people who was eager to show off her new house and the rapidly re-greening surroundings.

"Things are so different here now," she said while we drank tea on her steps. "In the past we didn't really relate to people outside our own family. This has really changed. Through this planning process we really started talking to each other and getting to know everyone. There's a lot of discussion now about everything. Now we frequently convene meetings on our own. When we have the community centre, it will happen even more because there will be a real place for gathering. There are still people in this community who are worse off – widows, people who are more vulnerable in different ways. We can't help them financially, but we are all much more concerned about each other now and can at least offer our friendship and support. And we're much more aware about what our children need and what they can do. Planning with our children has brought us all closer together. I'm ready to go show other communities how to work this way."

## References

ACHR (2011) Baan Mankong community upgrading programme of the Community Organisation Development Institute (CODI), Thailand: Case study of upgrading of communities along Klong Bang Bua, Bangkok. Available at http://mhupa-ray.gov.in/wp-content/uploads/2011/11/Anju%20Docs/111128%20Baan%20Mankong%20Klong%20Bang%20Bua%20Case%20Study.pdf

ActionAid, Plan, Save the Children, UNICEF (2010) Too often in silence. Addressing violence: Selected initiatives from West and Central Africa. Available at www.unicef.org/wcaro/VAC_Report_Directory.pdf

Appadurai, Arjun (2012) Why enumeration counts, *Environment and Urbanization* 24(2), 639–641

Bartlett, Sheridan (2013) Girls' Education Support Programme (GESP), Afghanistan, Aga Khan Foundation, unpublished document

Bartlett, Sheridan and Selim Iltus (2007) Making space for children: Planning for post-disaster reconstruction with children and their families, Save the Children UK and Save the Children Sweden. Available at http://cergnyc.org/files/2011/09/Making-space-full-version-11.pdf

Bhatkal, Tanvi and Paula Lucci (2015) Community-driven development in the slums: Thailand's experience, ODI. Available at www.developmentprogress.org/sites/developmentprogress.org/files/case-study-summary/thailand_summary_final.pdf

Boonyabancha, Somsook (2005) Baan Mankong: Going to scale with "slum" and squatter upgrading in Thailand, *Environment and Urbanization* 17(1), 21–46

Boonyabancha, Somsook, Fr. Norberto Carcellar and Thomas Kerr (2012) How poor communities are paving their own pathways to freedom, *Environment and Urbanization* 24(2), 441–463

Boyden, Jo and Gillian Mann (2005) Children's risk, resilience, and coping in extreme situations, in Michael Ungar (ed.) *Handbook for working with children and youth: Pathways to resilience across cultures and contexts*, London: Sage Publications, pp. 3–27

Burra, Sundar, Sheela Patel and Thomas Kerr (2003) Community-designed, built and managed toilet blocks in Indian cities, *Environment and Urbanization* 15(2), 11–33

Cerdá, Magdalena, Jeffrey D Morenoff, Ben B Hansen, Kimberly J T Hicks, Luis F Duque, Alexandra Restrepo and Ana V Diez-Roux (2012) Reducing violence by transforming neighborhoods: A natural experiment in Medellín, Colombia, *American Journal of Epidemiology* 175(10), 1045–1053

Chatterjee, Sudeshna (2007) Children's role in humanizing forced evictions and resettlements in Delhi, *Children, Youth and Environments* 17(1), 198–221

Chawla, Louise (ed.) (2001) *Growing up in an urbanizing world*, London: Earthscan/UNESCO

Chawla, Louise (2014) Children's engagement in the natural world as a ground for healing, in M Krasny and K Tidball (eds) *Greening in the red zone*, Dordrecht: Springer, pp. 111–124

CPS (Chicago Public Schools) (2016) Safe passage routes – Chicago public schools. Available at cps.edu/Pages/safepassage.aspx

CPWG (2012) Minimum standards for child protection in humanitarian action, Child Protection Working Group. Available at www.unicef.org/iran/Minimum_standards_for_child_protection_in_humanitarian_action.pdf

Daiute, Colette (2011) *Human development and political violence*, Cambridge: Cambridge University Press

d'Cruz, Celine, Elizabeth Amakali, Peter Chege, Viviane Kandundu, Edith Mbanga, Anna Muller, Selma Namwandi, Niloke Niingungo, Shellie Price, Albertina Shenyange, Hendrina Shuunyuni and Susan Waniru (2014) *Community savings: A basic building block in the work of urban poor federations*, IIED Working Paper, London: IIED

Gaafar, Reem (2014) *Women's land and property rights in Kenya*, Landesa: Center for Women's Land Rights

Goldstein, Joseph (2013) Judge rejects New York's stop-and-frisk policy, *New York Times*, 12 August 2013. Available at www.nytimes.com/2013/08/13/nyregion/stop-and-frisk-practice-violated-rights-judge-rules.html

Gonzalez-Navarro, M and C Quintana-Domeque (2010) *Roads to development: Experimental evidence from urban road pavement*, Social Science Research Network Working Paper. Available at https://papers.ssrn.com/sol3/papers2.cfm?abstract_id=1558631

Gopal, Divya and Harini Nagendra (2014) Vegetation in Bangalore's slums: Boosting livelihoods, well-being and social capital, *Sustainability* 6, 2459–2473

Guyot, Julie (2007) Participation: Children and youth in protracted refugee situations, *Children, Youth and Environments* 17(3), 159–178

Hart, Jason (2012) The spatialisation of child protection: Notes from the occupied Palestinian territory, *Development in Practice* 22(4), 473–485

Hodson, Jeff (2012) A Peruvian slum gets a massive green makeover, UW Today, Washinton.edu. Available at www.washington.edu/news/2012/02/13/a-peruvian-slum-gets-a-massive-green-makeover-with-slide-show

Kimmelman, Michael (2012) A city rises along with its hopes, *New York Times*, 18 May

Lee, Susan (2012) "A lethal absence of hope": Making communities safer in Los Angeles, *Early Childhood Matters* 119, 44–47

Liebermann, Susan and Karina Landman (2000) *Making South Africa safe: A manual for community-based crime prevention*, Pretoria: CSIR

Makau, Jack (2011) "Like we don't have enough on our hands already!": The story of the Kenyan slum youth federation, *Environment and Urbanization* 23(1), 203–206

McIlwaine, Cathy (2013) Urbanization and gender-based violence in the global south, *Environment and Urbanization* 25(1), 65–79

Moore, Robin and Nilda Cosco (2004) Children's rights and urban development in Buenos Aires, Save the Children Sweden, unpublished document

Moser, Caroline (2009) Safety, gender mainstreaming and gender-based programmes, in Ana Falu (ed.) *Women in the city: On violence and rights*, Santiago de Chile: Women and Habitat Network of Latin America, pp. 77–99

National Alliance to End Homelessness (2006) *Promising strategies to end family homelessness*, Washington, DC: NAEH

Patel, Sheela and Sheridan Bartlett (2009) Reflections on innovation, assessment, and social change: A SPARC case study, *Development in Practice* 19(1), 3–15

Patel, Sheela and Sheridan Bartlett (2016) "We beat the path by walking" Part II: Three construction projects that advanced the learning and credibility of the Indian Alliance, *Environment and Urbanization* 28(2), 495–515

Patel, Sheela, Carrie Baptist and Celine d'Cruz (2012) Knowledge is power – informal communities assert their right to the city through SDI and community-led enumerations, *Environment and Urbanization* 24(1), 13–26

Pelton, Leroy (2014) The continuing role of material factors in child maltreatment and placement, *Child Abuse and Neglect* 41, 30–39

PSP Public Science Project (2012) Morris Justice Project. Available at http://morrisjusticep roject.tumblr.com/post/44314811477/video-documenting-dear-nypd-night-in-the-morris

Roy, A N, A Jockin and Ahmad Javed (2004) Community police stations in Mumbai's slums, *Environment and Urbanization* 16, 135–138

Sertich, Adriana Navarro (2010) Medellin: Social urbanism. Available at http://favelissues. com/2010/02/01/medellin-%E2%80%9Csocial-urbanism%E2%80%9D/

Stephens, Robert, Macarena Rau Vargas and Tinus Kruger (2004) Public participation in developing countries, Proceedings of the 9 Annual International CPTED Conference 13–16 September 2004

Sullivan, W C and F E Kuo (1996) Do trees strengthen urban communities, reduce domestic violence? University of Illinois at Urbana-Champaign: Human Environment Research Laboratory Department of Natural Resources and Environmental Sciences. Available at www.aces.edu/urban/metronews/vol1no4/forestry.html

Svendsen, Gunnar Lind Haase (2010) Socio-spatial planning in the creation of bridging social capital: The importance of multifunctional centers for intergroup networks and integration, *International Journal of Social Inquiry* 3(2), 45–73

Tidball, K G and M E Krasny (eds) (2014) *Greening in the red zone: Disaster, resilience and community greening*, Dordrecht: Springer

Walker, Susan P, Susan M Chang, Marcos Vera-Hernández and Sally Grantham-McGregor (2011) Early childhood stimulation benefits adult competence and reduces violent behavior, *Pediatrics* 127, 849

Wells, Nancy and Gary Evans (2003) Nearby nature: A buffer of life stress among rural children, *Environment and Behavior* 35(3), 311–330

Zinck, Emily and Carola Eyber (2013) Environmental education to promote peace and cooperation: A case study of tree nurseries in Nakuru, Kenya, *Children, Youth and Environments* 23(1), 198–210

# INDEX